Ioanna Kuçuradi

Human Rights: Concepts and Problems

Philosophy in International Context
Philosophie im internationalen Kontext

edited by/herausgegeben von

Hans Lenk

in connection with:
Ioanna Kuçuradi, Matthias Maring, Herta Nagl-Docekal,
Gregor S. Paul, Hans Poser, William Sweet, Tran Van Doan

Volume/Band 7

LIT

Ioanna Kuçuradi

HUMAN RIGHTS: CONCEPTS AND PROBLEMS

LIT

This book is printed on acid-free paper.

Bibliographic information published by the Deutsche Nationalbibliothek
The Deutsche Nationalbibliothek lists this publication in the Deutsche Nationalbibliografie; detailed bibliographic data are available in the Internet at http://dnb.d-nb.de.

ISBN 978-3-643-90308-2

A catalogue record for this book is available from the British Library

Klosbachstr. 107
CH-8032 Zürich
Tel. +41 (0) 44-251 75 05
Fax +41 (0) 44-251 75 06
E-Mail: zuerich@lit-verlag.ch
http://www.lit-verlag.ch

LIT VERLAG Dr. W. Hopf
Berlin 2013
Fresnostr. 2
D-48159 Münster
Tel. +49 (0) 2 51-62 03 20
Fax +49 (0) 2 51-23 19 72
E-Mail: lit@lit-verlag.de
http://www.lit-verlag.de

Distribution:
In Germany: LIT Verlag Fresnostr. 2, D-48159 Münster
Tel. +49 (0) 2 51-620 32 22, Fax +49 (0) 2 51-922 60 99, E-mail: vertrieb@lit-verlag.de

In Austria: Medienlogistik Pichler-ÖBZ, e-mail: mlo@medien-logistik.at
In Switzerland: B + M Buch- und Medienvertrieb, e-mail: order@buch-medien.ch
In the UK: Global Book Marketing, e-mail: mo@centralbooks.com
In North America: International Specialized Book Services, e-mail: orders@isbs.com
e-books are available at www.litwebshop.de

Philosophy in International Context
Editorial

Hans Lenk
(Honorary President of the International Institute of Philosophy)

At the beginning of the 21st Century, in our epoch of globalization, almost all the parts and regions of the world more frequently interact, if not grow together, at least economically speaking and via electronic information exchange, leading to worldwide virtual ubiquity engendered and in fact transmitted by the electronic media seemingly as fast as light travels. Whether or not this sort of economic and informational globalization may and will lead to a cosmopolitan orientation, if not unity, of the different parts and regions or even nations of the world, seems to be and remains an extremely problematic prospect. Although the world has grown much more interconnected and interactive in terms of economics, information interchange and air-traffic, the different cultural orientations and heritages in dealing with and interpreting cultural and social traditions, if not even the meaning of lives, in the most colourful symbolisations still remain. They even seem to stick out in rather visible or noticeable relief and display the characteristics of different interpretations of rather diverse walks of life, although an overall tendency towards a uniformity of day to day behaviour as regards consumption, goods, markets and popular culture transported by movies, songs, fashion, sports, etc., is obvious. Though there is, at a surface assessment, such a unity or, rather, parallelism of cultural features, no real cosmopolitan understanding on the side of populations and peoples, including most individuals themselves, has generally thus far followed suit. Most of the inhabitants of most countries and regions of the world still are immersed in their specific cultural and traditional orientation as well as language and interpretation patterns, despite these overriding trends in economics and information exchange. Real cosmopolitanism did not yet succeed very widely.

The German physicist, writer and popular philosopher Lichtenberg once wrote that he who only knows chemistry would not ever really know it (i.e., from an in-depth perspective). One may transfer and generalize that to the understanding of one's own culture: he who knows but his own culture, does not even understand it in a deeper sense. Culture seems to be like the waters of the ocean for fish; as long as they are living and swimming exclusively therein, they would not notice, see and understand the ocean world.

Instead, in order to catch up with the overall reigning trends of worldwide exchanges and interactions as well as the ever-growing interconnections between different parts and perspectives of the world we should foster and develop further the intercultural discourse from an open-minded cosmopolitan perspective.

We have the UN Declaration of Human Rights of 1948, signalling a big step forward, despite some differences in interpretation. We have UNESCO for education and understanding of and between different cultures as well as for science and humanitarian philosophy. UNESCO, interestingly enough, recently set up and acknowledged an official "Intersectoral Strategy for Philosophy" as the route and kernel of UNESCO's humanitarian and non-partisan perspective, reaching beyond traditional particular religions and ideologies. What would UNESCO be without such an overriding and generalizing philosophical stance? However, the relevant sort of philosophy has to be a truly international and intercultural one – not just the particular philosophy of one region or tradition like ancient Greek or Chinese or Indian philosophy, to name but the ancient climaxes of philosophical thinking, having occurred roughly parallel in time within the different regions of the world. Philosophy for this task and in this interpretation has to become truly intercultural and international, even inter-traditional, in order to really cope with the necessities and objectives of the mentioned transcultural and intercultural discourse. Philosophy thus has to generalize and abstract from particular perspectives of specific traditions, partisan ideologies and limitations of orientations to gather the really worldwide humanity-oriented perspective of an encompassing character. Traditionally, philosophy, by ascending to theoretical and interpretative meta-levels or formal rules of argumentation and methodologies, as, e.g., in logics, did arrive at such an abstract level transcending cultural differences – but at the cost of abstraction and formalisation, if not a too general degree of universalisation in order to really capture the humanitarian content that the founders of the UN and UNESCO initiatives had in mind. Worldwide humanitarian ethics and philosophical general orientation beyond the specific vicissitudes and partial perspectives of particular religions would have to be broached to serve the truly encompassing all-human and humanitarian objectives in charge. The worldwide organizations of philosophy like the International Federation of Philosophical Societies (FISP) and the world academy of philosophers (the Institut international de philosophie, IIP) do indeed try on a worldwide basis to work for these general aims of cosmopolitan humanity and intellectual humanitarianism, characterized by intercultural respect and tolerance. (They do it by staging World Congresses [FISP], international workshops [IIP Entretiens] and through a manifold of series of respective publications of truly intercultural and international provenance.) Philosophy in general – and what is occasionally called Western philosophy in particular – has to open itself up for the really intercultural perspectives, the legacy and assets of different approaches to the overall human and grand philosophical themes and to truly devote itself to comparative international philosophical analyses and viewpoints. Language and cultural barriers should not explicitly prevail in our intercultural age, though the colourful cultural diversity may obtain certainly should remain, also in the future. We have to place philosophy in a truly intercultural and international context by trying, without ignoring one's own traditional orientations, to really go international and intercultural, by reaching out for all-human humanitarianism and cosmopolitanism. The human traces are to be found everywhere; we should respect them and dig them out as well as really disseminate them.

The idea of the series *"Philosophy in International Context"* is, amongst others, to enhance the intercultural understanding of truly humanitarian philosophical perspectives as well as to foster the intercultural orientation and exchange of ideas and knowledge of the existing traditions amongst philosophers themselves – notably on a practice-oriented and pragmatic route.

Philosophical and practical Problems of *Human Rights* certainly figure at center stage of the series "Philosophy in International Context".

PREFACE

Hans LENK
(Honorary President of the International Institute of Philosophy)

It is a special privilege and pleasure herewith to publish Prof. Kuçuradi's collection of studies, essays and lectures on human rights, since this is not only a special topic of hers fitting into the overall concept of the present philosophical series "Philosophy in International Context". The privilege is also very much due to the fact that Prof. Dr. phil. Dr. h.c. Dr. h.c. Ioanna Kuçuradi is one of the most outstanding philosophers in the world: she has been the first and, until now, only woman to be the President of the international world society of philosophy, the FISP (Fédération internationale des sociétés de philosophie), obtaining the highest post in the organized community of philosophers in the world. (Before, she had served as Secretary General of FISP for ten years.) Indeed, she is also an outstanding member of the International Institute of Philosophy (IIP), which is, so to speak, the world academy of philosophers. She has achieved many honors and distinctions like the UNESCO Aristotle Medal, the Goethe-medal, the Great Cross of Merits of the Federal Republic of Germany, among other international awards and prizes for peace and democracy, and, e.g., the "Council of Secular Humanism's Planetary Humanist Philosopher's Award" leading up to the topic of her life's work, namely human rights, humanitarian and humanistic perspectives on which the present volume is focused.

Indeed, she also was the founding director of the Centre for Research and Application of the Philosophy of Human Rights at Hacettepe University/Ankara as well as now at Maltepe University/Istanbul and has been the holder of a UNESCO chair on Philosophy and Human Rights (since 1998) – being a founding member of the Human Rights Foundation of Turkey, and of the national Advisory Council for Human Rights, and member of the International Commission against the Death Penalty, and of the Experts Committee for Human Rights, National Commission for UNESCO of Turkey – amongst many other scientific and professional distinctions.

Her scholarly work also centered on and led to an overriding focus around human rights and values. She started from studies on Scheler and Nietzsche as well as Schopenhauer regarding their perceptions of man, only to concentrate on *Problems and Values* (1971, 3 editions) and *Ethics* (1977, 6 editions). She analysed arts from a philosophical point of view, publishing a collection of papers about problems of our time in order to focus on the very important topic of human rights from the perspective of value analysis, philosophical humanism and ethical analysis from the standpoint of practical ethics in a pragmatic version dealing with really concrete problems including social, political and legal ones in a realistic setting. She also translated several ethical works by Kant and undertook various comparisons, e.g., Kant's "Categorical Imperative" with the "Golden Rule", as well as the concepts of human dignity and human rights, etc.

She contributed effectively in the Turkish and international scene for teaching philosophy in any educational setting, from school to university level and post-graduate programmes promoting the International Philosophy Olympiads. Thereby, she organised and led as a chairperson the World Congress of Philosophy in Istanbul (2003) under the topic "Philosophy Facing World Problems", a very fine and excellent congress among diverse intellectual cultures in the old city of Istanbul where since many ages representatives of cultures of every kind, of every religion, philosophy, and tradition used to argue and mingle with each other – certainly a milestone for intercultural and international approaches, communications and debates of philosophers and members of the humanities and other cultural disciplines.

In all her activities she always invoked the humanist and humanitarian point of view, the protection and accentuation of human rights from a prominent ethical, to note, beyond the legal, perspective, including a practical as well as theoretical evaluation from an overriding deeply philosophical stance. Already in one of her earlier papers, "From Revolt to Philosophy", she explicitly combined human ethics with human rights stressing: "If the 'value' or 'dignity of Man' means 'Man's special place in the universe', that which constitutes this place is certain human potentialities and their actualised outcome in history. Thus the protection of human potentialities in individuals constitutes a seemingly adequate criterion for the determination of the basic rights of the individual, i.e., human rights".

This certainly was a long-standing and developing topic of her work through the decades in which she time and again took up not only political and legal, but anthropological, moral and value problems of the genuine philosophy and anthropology of human dignity and human rights from different perspectives, always taking into consideration the practical contexts, outcomes and impacts of these rather basic philosophical factors and approaches.

Thus, it is to be considered a climax and sort of logical consequence that she put together many of the essays, lectures and philosophical addresses to theorists as well as practitioners under the present topic of *Human Rights – Concepts and Problems*, turning out to be somewhat like her life's summary of her philosophical enthusiasm and educational devotion and motivation.

The highlight of her "Lebenswerk" might be certainly called an outstanding example of practical or concrete humanity deeply rooted in philosophy and education: When I tried to trace the humanitarian tradition from Mencius to Albert Schweitzer by putting forth and using the Latin slogan: *'In dubio pro humanitate concreta sive practica'*, I realized this would also hold for Ioanna Kuçuradi's outstanding theoretical and practical work as well as for her life: not only "*in dubio* 'always' for practical humanity", but from a deeply philosophical, anthropological as well as ethical vantage point.

FOREWORD

The present volume consists of a part of the papers on human rights, which I wrote since 1980. These papers focus on the concept of human rights and on problems related to concepts of various human rights, as well as on concepts related to them – such as human dignity, laïcité, tolerance. They attempt to clarify them and subsequently to draw attention to what can be seen, and foreseen, when we look at the events on the ground of clarified concepts.

Most of the papers are texts of lectures delivered in different conferences, on different occasions. This is the reason why there is a repetition of certain parts in some of them. These repetitions constitute the framework of the new point made in each paper and make possible to connect papers written in different times.

I wish to cordially thank Prof. Hans Lenk for including this volume in his series and to express my sincere gratitude to Zeynep Ispir Toprak, Catherine Champniers and Grace Frank who helped me in making ready for print these papers – something that, due to the hectic tempo of my life, I had postponed for many years.

Istanbul, January 2013 — Ioanna KUÇURADI

TABLE OF CONTENTS

Instead of Introduction[*]

Almost thirty-two years ago at the time that this paper was drafted and now sixty-five years, it was officially declared that "all human beings are [...] equal in dignity and rights" and almost all the nations of our world approved this statement, as well as the twenty-nine articles on "human rights" that were considered to be its extension. Where are we standing now?

Whether human rights have, indeed, been less violated or more protected – that is respected or fulfilled – in the countries, whose governments have approved the *Universal Declaration of Human Rights*, is a question to which no one could give a justifiable answer. Yet, reports on violations of human rights and, consequently, disputes about these rights did increase in the course of the last decades. Human rights are the most exploited weapon, when parties want to attack each other in international fora. Everyone is ready to accuse the other of violations, but very eager to disguise his own violations, and what is more – and strange enough – in the name of other "human rights". This hypocritical attitude is so widespread that many people – people of good will, no doubt – are inclined to think that any discussion on human rights has no significance any more, that any endeavour in this direction is condemned to boil down to mere words.

This fact, I think, not only shows the importance which the thorny question of the protection of human rights bears for our world, but also calls our attention to some deadlocks which humanity today is led into with respect to this question.

Where are these deadlocks to be found? To put it in a general way, I would say, that what has led to these deadlocks is the lack of a clear and justifiable insight into the essential relationship between human rights and value questions: into the fundamental relationship between human rights and the knowledge of the value of the human being – or of the content of his "dignity", if you like. And to specify, I would mention three main points, related to each other, around which, I think, we may sum up, if not only but at least, the theoretical source of the difficulties we come across with regard to the protection of human rights: 1) Conceptual confusions, e.g., the confusion of opinions about the criterion of a right being a "human" right, and consequently, the perplexity in which we are left with respect to the content of this concept, as well as with respect to the content of various individual rights, a result of which is the uncertainty about the implications of these contents. 2) Confusion of principles, e.g., the confusion of principles to be adopted and of ways to be followed for the protection of human rights today, especially at the international level. Such a confusion is sometimes the outcome of not evaluating

---

[*] Inaugural speech of the International Seminar on "Philosophical Foundation of Human Rights", held on June 9-13, 1980, at Hacettepe University, Ankara.

the prevailing principles and ways by taking into consideration at the same time both the content of "human dignity" and the existing conditions, and sometimes the outcome of the lack of a world-embracing reflection bold enough to give officially an answer beyond political interests, to the question "how can human rights be better safeguarded under the prevailing conditions?" 3) Deficiency in evaluation, e.g., the deficiency of most decision-makers in evaluating a given case of violation – or claim of violation – of human rights with respect to human value and not with respect to interests, as a result of the lack of an early systematic training in acquiring an eye able to discern the exact point where the dignity of the human being is at stake in a given case, this dignity which these decision-makers also share.

Such appear – at least to me – to be the main theoretical deadlocks and their reasons; deadlocks in which today as humanity we find ourselves, in spite of all declarations, covenants, commissions, committees, courts, etc., with which we have supplied ourselves in connection with human rights.

Put forth in that way, the reasons of these deadlocks are obviously closely related to philosophy and philosophical education.

What we expect from this Seminar and what we also expect from the following selection of papers is to start an international discussion with regard the concept of human rights; a discussion aiming to clarify which rights (or kind of rights) are "human" rights and which are not. Our expectation may, at first glance, seem too theoretical, when people are killed, tortured, subjected to any kind of inhuman treatment, to arbitrary arrest in different parts of our world. But we should not forget that the concept of human rights we have – as individuals and decision-makers – is the main determinant of the theoretical and practical conclusions we arrive at, with regard to questions of human rights; we must not forget that the concept of human rights we have can be the only counterweight in favour of the protection of human rights against interests and passions in action. If we know – if each one of us knows – what are the rights we call human rights, we may arrive at a clearer insight into the implications of their essence; and if we have a clearer insight into these implications, we can hope to reach more responsible conclusions with regard to disputable points in connection with human rights and with regard to questions about their protection.

If we know what human rights demand, as well as why and from whom they demand it, we shall also know why they have to be protected at every moment by everybody for every body. If we know that, we shall also know why we should not be so eager to attack others for the violations they perpetrate and to disguise our own violations. If we know that, we shall also know why these inalienable rights of every individual, being themselves ends, have to be made the basis of every social and political decision.

If we know what human rights demand, we can find a firm basis in order to determine the content of individual rights.

If we know what human rights demand and why they demand it, we can, perhaps, obtain a criterion to use in questions of restriction of rights. Perhaps we can decide more easily which of the rights of the individual may be restricted and which must not be, and deduce some principles in restricting the former, so that these restrictions may, in fact, protect human rights.

If we know what human rights demand, we can become more certain in determining the duties of the individuals and of the states in protecting them; we can leave less room open for evasions.

If we know why human rights demand what they demand, i.e., if we become aware of their foundation, we can give to human rights their proper place – or philosophy her due place – in our educational programmes, in mass-media, etc.

If we know which rights of the individual are h u m a n rights, we can perhaps realize better w h i c h r i g h t s can be protected and have to be protected by international organizations, in cases where they are not protected or are violated by their natural protector – i.e., the State. And when we realize that, we can find the way to protect human rights, all nations coming t o g e t h e r, as "humanity", overcoming the theoretical obstacles we encounter today; to give an example: the principle of non-interference in the internal affairs of a state.

*

The most important issue in international relations today, is considered to be world peace. But where human rights are violated, there peace cannot dwell; where human rights are not fulfilled, there peace can only be superficial. In most endeavours to protect world peace (in the endeavours for the so-called *détente* for example) the link between the protection of peace and the protection of human rights seems to have grown dim in the minds of the decision-makers. It escapes attention that respect for and fulfilment of human rights constitute the foundation of permanent peace, as well as of all constructive international relations. Something else also escapes attention: the fact that the protection of world peace is a p o l i t i c a l question, while the protection of human rights at the international level is not, though it may be (partly) so at the national level. Thus questions of protection of human rights are considered and treated as political questions, where the input and output of interests play the decisive role. This is the source of the main obstacles encountered with regard to the protection of human rights through international organizations.

Thus, in the last quarter of the 20th Century, humanity aware of her right, but unable to protect human rights, stands as a helpless witness of human rights violated in different parts of our world, by states and terrorists, in the name of other "rights".

Thirty years of experience have shown that the official representative of today's humanity, the United Nations, w i t h i t s p r e s e n t s t r u c t u r e , can do very little in coping with problems which mankind faces today with regard to the fulfilment of human rights; and almost nothing against actual violations. We observe also that the United Nations is conscious of its weakness, as well as we observe endeavours to identify this weakness, but then, only in connection with the former point. The Twenty-five Experts Report is an example of these endeavours. But we know of no official efforts with respect to the second point. Though the demand to protect individuals as human beings – not as citizens – is addressed now to the UN, some of its members stand and look perplexed at some other members, who deal with human rights as with political questions.

What we need now in this respect, is to develop a world project, which will put forth the ways through which humanity as a whole will become able to protect human rights everywhere in the world; a project which will make possible for humanity – as a whole – to interfere where the development of the potentialities of the human being is impeded in our world. This has to be a project based on the justifiable assumption, that the protection of human rights at the international level is not a political question, but an ethical one; a project which will also pave the way for the international order demanded for everyone in the art. 28 of the *Universal Declaration*.

Since the most comprehensive organization that we possess, as humanity, is the United Nations, and being aware that the implementation of such a project, once developed, presupposes political decisions, I think that the place where such a project has to be developed is the United Nations.

And taking into consideration the present structure of the UN and the composition of its various organs, I think that this place in the UN could be UNESCO, whose special task is to promote some of the principal activities which constitute the value or dignity of the human being: education, science and culture – UNESCO in which and through which also philosophy can pay its tribute to today's humanity.

Couldn't UNESCO take the initiative?

PHILOSOPHY AND HUMAN RIGHTS*

If you were asked to enumerate dangerous things, would you, for instance, mention among them, concepts?

Concepts are not innocent of what is happening in our world.

We are responsible of their becoming dangerous, as well as of their implications.

Concepts become dangerous, when their content, though obscure, is taken for granted. I am afraid, human rights have already become a dangerous concept. Philosophy has to take them up anew and scrutinize them.

Here I shall confine myself to saying a few words on the concept of fundamental or inalienable human rights and their foundation, i.e., "the dignity" or "value" of the human being, through which all human beings are declared to be equal. This, I hope, can also shed some light on the reason why inalienable human rights, being themselves ends, have to be made the basis of every social and political decision, and w h y t h e y h a v e to be protected at every moment by everybody for everybody. Some other implications may also follow.

*

Human rights express some necessities, related to each human being. These necessities appear as demands to recognize and observe the value of the human being, i.e., they appear as demands to protect individuals for the sole reason that they are human beings.

By the term 'the value of the human being' I mean the special place this being occupies among other living beings. What provides this special place to him is the entirety of his characteristics, his potentialities which distinguish him from other living beings. They appear as activities proper to the human being and as products of these activities. These are properties i n a d d i t i o n to those which he possesses in common with other living beings. These properties or potentialities and nothing else, constitute "the value of the human being", or his dignity.

Thus to protect these ontical properties of the human being in individuals, i.e., to develop his potentialities in individuals, becomes the cause of mankind and is also the task of each individual. On the other hand, this protection of the potentialities of the human being b e c o m e s t h e r i g h t of every individual belonging to the species called human: the possibility to develop these potentialities must be secured a l s o f o r h i m o r h e r.

---

* Paper presented at the international seminar on "Philosophical Foundations of Human Rights", held on June 9-13, 1980, at Hacettepe University, Ankara and published in the *Proceedings*.

These demands to protect in individuals the potentialities proper to the human being only constitute the inalienable human rights, rights which humanity took consciousness of and put forth, stumbling, in the long run of the history of ideas. To ask for the protection of these potentialities for each individual is but asking for the safeguard of our place in the universe; it is the will to protect our own value. This amounts to protect individuals for the sole reason that they are human beings.

For this reason, when a human right is at stake, it makes no difference *who* the person in question is, it makes no difference even if he himself has violated the human rights of others. That he is a human being, makes him or her the holder of the right that human rights be protected *also for him*. What makes each individual human right a *right*, i.e., the necessity either not to be violated or to be fulfilled for every human being, finds its foundation in the knowledge of the potentialities of the human being. So long as we do not intend to *wipe out* ourselves – the human race – from the earth, we have no other choice than trying to protect these rights of ours in individuals, aware that no action is indifferent to human dignity; and by virtue of the right we gain in doing so, to demand at the top of our voice – from the states, from today's humanity – the protection of these rights for everyone.

*

Now, which are these rights, that are called 'human rights'? When we take a look at their names and the existing classifications, things appear quite confused. In various international documents and in various constitutions we find as categories of the fundamental human rights the rights of the person and social-economic-cultural-civil-political rights, and under these categories various rights and freedoms, some different and some in common.

Reading these documents, some questions arise concerning the fundamentality of some rights. At the same time, some demands, which could be considered as fundamental rights, are not found in these documents.

What could be used as a criterion in revising our lists of human rights and also for determining "new" rights, a criterion which would not leave too much ground for dispute concerning the fundamentality of some rights?

The systematic knowledge of the potentialities of the human being, acquired by means of the achievements of the humankind *and* a clear knowledge of the conditions securing the ground for the actualization of these potentialities, affords us the criterion: a criterion to distinguish the fundamental rights from the non-fundamental ones, which altogether form an indivisible whole, but because of their different connections with human potentialities have, I think, different implications. This knowledge backed and justified by its counterpart, i.e., by observations showing how these potentialities are blunted today, not only affords us the criterion to distinguish which kind of demands are and can be fundamental rights and which not, but also opens for us a way to become more and more aware of the implications of the essence of the fundamental rights.

To give but a few examples, I would mention that this criterion helps us to answer disputable questions about restriction of rights; it blocks the ways of evasion while determining the duties of the states in the protection of rights; it makes us see which rights can and have to be protected today through international institutions and mechanisms, in such a way as to prevent claims of clashing with other rights.

*

Human rights are rights of the individual. Now, when we look at the rights of the individual using the criterion proposed, we notice that, though with respect to *each* individual they are interrelated and form an indivisible whole, *as demands*, they show some remarkable differences: a part of these demands is connected directly with human potentialities, another with the preconditions necessary for their development, *in general*, while another part of them is connected with *certain (changing) conditions*. Personally I am inclined to restrict the term 'human rights' to the first two kinds of demands and to include in the concept of human rights the interdictory demands concerning the security of the individual and/or the so-called "fundamental freedoms", as well as the demands related to the preconditions for the protection of human potentialities *in general* (rights such as the right to a standard of living adequate for one's health, the right to education, the right to work, etc.).

The demands of the first kind are directly connected with the exercise of human potentialities. What they demand is that individuals be not hindered while exercising activities proper to the human being only. They demand the protection of rights which cannot be *given* (by a state), but can only be respected (or violated) in individuals by individuals (Government officers are individuals, too).

So, the respect for these rights appears first of all as an ethical question. The role of the State with regard to these rights is – or is expected to be – to prevent violations and in cases of violations to re-establish balances. Since we can speak of protection of these rights only when there are *attempts to violate* them, from the point of view of the State to protect these rights would mean to place them under the guarantee of Law, i.e., to try to prevent, by laws, the violation of these rights, and in cases of violations to intervene through its various organs.[1] Rights such as – to use the conventional wording – liberty and security of the person and its implications (: no one shall be held in slavery or servitude; no one shall be subjected to torture or to cruel, inhuman or degrading treatment or punishment; no one shall be subjected to arbitrary arrest) and freedoms, such as of thought, opinion, expression, and peaceful association fall under this category of rights, which are demands, demanding from everybody to

---

[1] Saying that, of course, I don't forget the innumerable cases in which State organs violate these rights, thus undermining the very foundations of the State in question and bringing today's humanity face to face with one of its greatest dilemmas.

do no harm to the value of the human being. It is the human being calling out: *noli me tangere*!

The so-called "fundamental freedoms" are the legal guarantees of these rights of the individual; they are there in order to guarantee that "nobody" touch an individual for any reason, while this individual is engaged in actualizing a human potentiality. Put in a legally valid document they guarantee the possibility to be demanded of everybody, but n o t the respect of these rights.

These rights constitute one part of the human rights in which a l l *h u - m a n b e i n g s* a r e e q u a l. Where these rights are respected, there the related freedoms e x i s t: people "enjoy" these freedoms. Where they are not, there prevails insecurity – or anarchy and terror. And where they are violated by State organs, there reigns oppression. Viewing just once the news on television is sufficient to get an idea of what is going on: though everybody officially declares that all human beings are equal in dignity, insecurity and oppression prevail in a large part of our world, almost, perhaps, everywhere.

*

There is also another group of rights in which all human beings are equal, fundamental rights that b e l o n g to each individual, as human individual, i.e., which are not given, but neither can be respected nor violated. They are demands related to the preconditions affording each individual t h e p o s s i - b i l i t y to develop his human potentialities. Rights such as the right to a standard of living adequate for one's health, the right to education, etc. The difficulty with such rights is that their fulfilment is dependent on rights of another kind, that they can be protected only indirectly, through other rights g i v e n to individuals by the State – through social, economic, (and some) political rights – and through public institutions and organization founded, not always but mostly, by political decisions.

In opposition to the first group of human rights, the protection of these (also human) rights does not depend directly on individuals, but on the social arrangements made and the political decisions taken in a country, not to forget: by individuals. They can be protected, i.e., fulfilled for the individuals in a country, only through g i v e n rights, the limits of which may be drawn in different proportions according to the existing conditions in each country. What makes the limits drawn to these rights protect or not protect the human rights of which they are the means, depends on whether these limits are drawn with respect of the equality of all c i t i z e n s in a country. For, these are rights in which a l l *c i t i z e n s* a r e e q u a l, in spite of the fact that they are means to protect rights in which all h u m a n b e i n g s are equal.

These social and economic rights cannot be "protected" but only given – or "taken" as many people like to say. Where such given rights are equally shared by all the citizens concerned, some human rights are protected, where they are not, the preconditions necessary for the actualization of human potentialities are missing. To speak of the protection of such a right is meaningful only in connection with individuals (or groups of individuals) and would mean to make it a l s o for them possible to take their portions as citizens from a given right, which will make it also for them possible to develop their potentialities as human beings.

This chain-dependence of the rights of individuals is a dependence from the perspective of the individual, but not a d e p e n d e n c e of demands among themselves. So, the protection of no human right or group of human rights can be postponed in favour of another right or group of rights i n a c o u n t r y, since we are not creating the world right at this moment! To claim the opposite is a deception, springing from the lack of a clear conception either of what human rights are or of the content of an individual right. As a result we observe restrictions of human rights, which cannot be restricted without doing harm to their essence (even if many restrictions claim the contrary); and often we observe no restriction in "rights" of individuals, in economic rights for example, rights which, essentially, are nothing but the drawing of certain limits.

Now, when we conceive of human rights as the demands to protect human potentialities in individuals – i.e., as practical principles demanding that no human being be, directly or indirectly, h i n d e r e d in developing his human potentialities (not hindered only in t h i s and nothing else) – any argument in favour of the restriction of human rights, a n d a l s o any argument in favour of not restricting social and economic rights according to the existing conditions on the basis of the principle of equality of the citizens, amounts to closing one's eyes in front of individuals or classes, each running after its own interests and clashing with the other; it amounts today to close one's eyes in front of exploitation and terrorism. Any argument against restriction in the long run, cannot but turn out to be a demand of non-restriction of interests; it means forgetting that human beings have also some properties in common with other living beings.

So the first prerequisite for the promotion of human rights seems – at least to me – a clear conception of the essence of human rights and of the content of each individual right, clear enough to allow us to see its full implications. And this expects from us much work and organized work. A second prerequisite is sufficient courage to declare each one of us as human – to declare ourselves human to ourselves – which amounts to bear and carry out the responsibilities which such a declaration involves for us as individuals and as humanity. Thus the question of the protection of human rights appears as a *philosophical, ethical* and *political* question. It is *philosophical*, for we badly need a clarification of the concepts of human rights, which will enable us to arrive at more certain conclusions about their implications. It is *ethical*, for in everyday life, i n d i v i d u a l s are those who respect or violate these rights; i n d i v i d u a l s are those who contribute to their protection by their votes or by their decisions while carrying out their public functions. It is also *political*, for it is the task of each state to provide the conditions which directly or indirectly make possible for all its citizens to develop their human potentialities and live "far from fear and want". But states also – whatever we may be inclined to say in connection with that – are governed by individuals. So we see that the protection of human rights as an ethical and political question is also related to philosophy, to philosophical education. For one of the main functions of the latter, is to train people as early as possible in acquiring an eye able to discern where human dignity is at stake.

*

The protection of human rights depends on individuals and on states. But today what do most of the states do? If we give an ear to various reports – of the United Nations, of Amnesty International and some other world organizations – we are forced to confess that very many states not only do not protect enough human rights, but also often violate them through their organs, either within their own boundaries or in their relations with other states. This fact is well known. As humanity we get sufficient information; for nobody tries to disguise violations that others perpetrate. But as humanity what do we do? What can we do?

The conception of human rights proposed here has also an implication connected with this question: when human potentialities are at stake, i.e., when human rights are violated by their natural protector, to protect these rights becomes the right of humanity – of humanity as a whole, but not of any part of it, as it is sometimes claimed.

This right today puts us as humanity in front of some complex legal and political problems, for we have forgotten the truth, that among human rights –: among demands to recognize and observe the value of the human being – no conflict can arise, but only among interests. To the demand that humanity protects human rights is opposed the demand of non-interference in the domestic affairs of states. But with regard to human rights, is it clear which questions are "domestic affairs" and which are not? The classification of rights made above, gives us a clue as to the answer to this question as well.

The problems we, as humanity, face today with regard to particular instances of violations of human rights, make necessary to revise and elucidate all our concepts and principles in connection with human rights. This will enable us not only to revise misleading interpretations of political principles, in which governments take refuge in order to avoid being accused either of violations or of indifference at the fulfilment of human rights; but also to shape new concepts and deduce new principles in politics, for the protection of human rights.

To do this is Philosophy's job, as well as it is Philosophy's job to fight against the exploitation of dangerous concepts.

PHILOSOPHY AND SOCIAL INJUSTICE*

My dear colleague and friend Prof. Odera Oruka asked me to speak at this Conference on "Philosophy and Social Injustice", mark you, not on "Philosophy and Social Justice". This was a gratifying request, because it not only gave me an opportunity to shed a stronger light – I hope – on the ambiguous and controversial concept of social justice, but also because it made me test, from a different point of view, my concept and classification of the so-called "human rights", both of which are at variance with those I meet and with those presupposed by the various documents regarding human rights and which involve different implications as well. I am thankful to him.

For this request made me start from the analysis of the concept of social injustice, which is not a principle as its opposite, but a state of things appearing under different guises, and thus supplies us with a firmer basis in determining our concepts and leads to some concrete practical conclusions for today.

*

What is this state of things we call social injustice? And how does it appear today?

When in a country, a part of the citizens lives in air-conditioned villas or flats while another part of the citizens lives in caves or mud-brick houses, there prevails social injustice. Wherever some children are taken to school in Cadillacs, while some other children of the same age have to carry loads in order to earn their living, there prevails social injustice. Where some women can afford to buy at once three fur coats – because they like them equally and cannot decide for one against the other – while some others, in order to survive, consent to be sold, there again we meet social injustice. These are snapshots from Third World countries.

And if in some countries biologically or physiologically maimed children are made to survive, through all means imaginable, while in other countries hundreds of children may die from measles owing to lack of medical care; if in some countries, late in the afternoon, pet-dogs are taken around in baby-carriages for a stroll, while in some other countries some children have to go through the garbage looking for something to eat, that means that social injustice prevails in our world.

---

* Paper presented in the Second Afro-Asian Philosophy Conference, held on October 30-November 3, 1981, in Nairobi, and published in H. Odera Oruka and D. A. Masolo (eds), *Philosophy and Cultures. Proceedings of Second Afro-Asian Philosophy Conference*. Nairobi, 1983, pp. 63-71.

So, the question of social injustice must be treated as a state of things we meet today at two different levels, that is at the national level and the global one, and then, in their relation to each other.

Here I'll confine my examination to social injustice at the national level, in its relation to basic rights, focusing my attention on the "developing" or Third World countries. For, social injustice puts on different faces in the so-called "developed" and "developing" countries, and the omission of such a distinction can easily lead us to erroneous conclusions.

*

According to the most easily accepted opinion, social injustice is nothing but the result of monstrous inequalities in the distribution of income in a country. Yet though important, this is only one aspect of the phenomenon, and its absence from the picture does not signify the absence of social injustice.

When we consider the question in its relation to human rights, social injustice appears as a problem related to all basic rights which can be protected only indirectly.

In order to make explicit this connection, allow me to say first a few words about my classification of the rights of the individual, because of its implications with regard to our topic.

The so-called 'human rights', i.e., rights in which "all human beings are equal", rights which they possess only because they are human beings, constitute a part of the rights of the individual, i.e., his basic rights. A part of these basic rights are demands for the direct protection of the human potentialities in individuals: demands that "nobody" touch an individual for any reason, while this individual is engaged in actualizing a human potentiality. All interdictory demands concerning the security of the individual and/or the so-called fundamental freedoms belong to this category of basic rights. The other part is that of demands related to the general preconditions necessary to afford each individual the possibility to develop his human potentialities. Rights such as the right to subsistence, the right to a standard of living adequate for one's health, the right to education, the right to work, etc., belong to this category. These are also rights which individuals possess for the sole reason that they are human beings, i.e., they are basic rights of the individual or human rights. But they differ from the rights of the first category in that they can be protected only indirectly, through other rights given to individuals by their state – by means of social, economic and some political rights – and through public institutions and organizations founded, not always but mostly, by political decisions.

These given rights, i.e., the social and economic rights, are rights of the individual, but not basic rights, i.e., they are not rights in which all human beings are equal. They are limits drawn by the states to the individuals in a country, they delineate some areas within which individuals may act as they like and they demand that no citizen transgress these limits. These are rights the limits of which are, and must be, drawn today differently in different countries, but they are rights in which all (concerned) citizens in each country are equal. The determination of the lowest payment or of the minimum number of years of work required for retirement is drawing the limits of such rights.

Now, the way the limits of these given rights are drawn in a country determines whether they may protect or not protect, or even hinder the protection of, the basic rights to which they are related.

Thus social injustice appears as a question related to the connection between these two kinds of rights of the individual, the given rights and the indirectly protected basic rights; and it is a state of things having to do (a) with what these given rights are, i.e., why and how the existing social and economic relations are arranged in a definite country and also with the way they are operated; consequently (b) with the establishment or non-establishment and the functioning of some institutions and organizations in the existing conditions.

*

So, the question of social injustice in its relation to basic rights, at the national level, can be treated from two different perspectives: that of the individual and that of the State. The former affords us the possibility of grasping what kind of a state of things social injustice is, the latter to understand how it originates today in many Third World countries.

So far as the individual is concerned, social injustice is not a state of things in which basic rights are not at all protected; it is the situation in which such rights are not protected for all individuals concerned, in a country: a state of things in which the possibilities of protection of the rights in which all human beings are equal, but which can be protected only indirectly, are not equally afforded – that is afforded at the same degree – to all citizens. From this point of view social injustice appears as an ethical question.

As far as the State is concerned, social injustice appears as a political fact, i.e., a fact related to the arrangement of social relations in the broad sense – the way they are established and the way they function –; in other words a fact related to the rights given or not given and the possibilities afforded to the citizens by the State. Where governments do not fulfil the two main *raisons d'être* of the State, there we find the two main causes of social injustice in many of the Third World countries.

Social injustice arises first of all when governments, while drawing the limits of social, economic and some of the political rights, do not take into consideration the connection existing between this kind of rights and the indirectly protected basic rights; when, during this drawing of limits, factors other than the demand to protect the respective basic rights interfere – ignorance above all, and interests: personal, group and class interests, etc. Or, when laws determining the establishment and operation of social and economic relations, for example, tax-laws, the civil code and other acts and laws of narrower scope are enacted without taking into account the intimate connection existing between this kind of rights and the indirectly protected basic rights, i.e., are drawn without taking into account their principal implications under the existing conditions.

This lack of connection between these two kinds of rights of the individual appears sometimes as enacting laws giving some "rights" or possibilities, which hinder the fulfilment of the basic rights of many citizens in the existing conditions. It often appears as not abrogating laws which impair such rights, or as not enacting some other laws which could indirectly protect them in the existing conditions, that is laws which would make possible the enforcement of other laws protecting them.

Such are cases in which governments cannot or do not fulfil one of the main *raisons d'être* of the State, its duty of arranging the relations among the citizens, cases in which governments cannot or do not keep a part of the citizens from exploiting other citizens – and the State as well – and consequently cases in which they cannot or do not prevent a part of the citizens from securing for themselves certain privileges while protecting mostly their personal interests, or, sometimes, their basic rights, at the expense of the basic rights of many other citizens and to an extent surpassing the measure that the country's conditions may allow. Where the State does not indirectly prevent – by appropriate laws, etc., some of its citizens from exploiting some others, there emerges social injustice.[1] In these cases it is the way of arranging social relations that causes the emergence of social injustice.

From the point of view of the State, another cause of social injustice in Third World countries is something that the governments do not or cannot do: to "distribute" equally among the citizens the p r i v a t i o n s a n d p e n u r i e s. (Forgive my wording which may sound a bit strange.) This is a fact we observe especially in countries in which the resources available to the State are limited: though laws demanding the protection of the indirectly protected rights are in fact enacted, the non-existence of some other laws and the lack of a satisfactory number of institutions necessary for the implementation and operation of the former in the existing conditions, makes it unthinkable for the State to afford the possibilities of equal protection of these rights for all citizens. Thus some such basic rights of some citizens are "protected" more than the means available to that state allow, while rights of many others are not protected at all. Some citizens, for example, buy three pots at once of an imported beauty-cream, while others cannot find on the market a medicine for heart, or if they find it, cannot buy it because it is too expensive for them.

It is usually claimed that social injustice is the result of the unequal distribution of what "exists". Yet, in those countries on which our attention is focused, either the State cannot dispose of what "exists", or, what is at its disposal is not enough for the fulfilment, even to a minimum extent, of the rights of all its citizens at any one moment. Thus, from the point of view of the State today,

---

[1] The fact that a lot of low-income people in Third World Countries prefer to work for a less satisfactory pay than what their labour justifies in a State job, is, I think, typical.

social injustice appears also not because of the unequal distribution of what "exists", but because of the unequal "distribution" of the p e n u r i e s. For, as I have already said, social injustice at the national level, has almost nothing to do with the degree of protection of the indirectly protected rights – i.e., with the dimensions of the limits of the given rights which protect their relative basic ones – but with a failure to afford the possibilities of equal protection of these rights for all citizens, whatever the degree of this equal protection may be. In a country where, by the equal "distribution of penuries", these rights of all citizens would be protected equally, even though at a low degree, there would be no question of social injustice at the national level; there we would raise only the problem of global social injustice.

In many Third World countries today, social injustice exists because governments do not distribute unequally what is at the disposal of the State, that is distribute in such a way that the basic rights of all citizens are equally fulfilled.

This means that social injustice emerges also when governments do not fulfil another *raison d'être* of the State, i.e., when in public administration they do not use what belongs to the public, so that the needs relative to the basic rights of all citizens may be fulfilled equally, when they do not establish the institutions and organizations necessary to fulfil this aim in the existing conditions.

What most governments do is well known. In 1977, Cyrus R. Vance, the State Secretary of the U.S., in a speech on the U.S. policy on human rights, put forth this point: Besides the right to security "[...] there is the right to the fulfilment of such vital needs as food, shelter, health care, and education. We recognize that the fulfilment of this right will depend, in part, upon the stage of a nation's economic development. But we also know that this right can be violated by a Government's action or inaction – for example, through corrupt official processes which divert resources to an elite at the expense of the needy, or through indifference to the plight of the poor."[2]

Thus considered from both perspectives, social injustice at the national level in many Third World countries today, is the state of things in which the rights given and the possibilities afforded to individuals by the State – the social (including the so-called cultural), economic and some of the political rights – either do not protect equally or hinder the equal protection of the indirectly protected rights of all the citizens.

This is a state of things which, considered in the light of the value of knowledge achieved in our age, is unbearable to those who are conscious of being human.

I am sure that you have not missed to notice two knots which the above formulation of social injustice carries in it. The first one concerns what I call here "indirectly protected rights". In official "human rights" documents, five or six of them appear under the heading of economic, social, or cultural rights,

---

[2] From Henry Shue's *Basic Rights*. Princeton University Press, 1980, p. 5.

considered as species of human rights. Yet, to mix up the rights in which all human beings are equal and which they possess for the sole reason that they are human beings – rights which should be considered violated when not fulfilled – with rights in which all citizens are expected to be equal (i.e., social and economic rights given to the citizens in a country, rights which are nothing but limits drawn); and also to include among them the so-called cultural rights, a part of which are not rights of the individuals but rights of groups or "peoples", creates considerable problems with regard to the protection of these basic rights and gives governments the possibility to escape, i.e., to defend their failure to fulfil these rights equally for all citizens.

For example, one negative implication of such a confusion of rights, closely connected with our topic, is the way that many governments today interpret articles to be found in certain international documents and constitutions, such as the following: "The State shall carry out its duties to attain the social and economic goals proclaimed in this section, only insofar as the economic development and its financial resources permit".[3] Such articles, concerning the duties of the State, duties which have to be carried out by governments, are often not interpreted in relation to the degree of fulfilling the basic rights in question, but are used in order to defend the strikingly unequal fulfilment of these rights. And this makes it possible to present – on purpose or owing to ignorance – social injustice only as an economical problem, and consequently as a state of things inevitable for poor countries. Still, social injustice is also a problem of "rich" countries. Who could claim that there is no social injustice in some countries of the Middle East, which occupy the top part on lists with regard to *per capita* income in the world today?

The second knot calling attention in the formulation of social injustice I made above has to do with the causes of this injustice, especially with the question why governments do not carry out the duties of the State. This latter question gets usually an ideological answer. I'll not try to give here a short-cut reply to this question.

*

Starting from the above formulation of social injustice as a state of things, we can now define the principle of social justice, as the demand that the State – i.e., each government that comes to power – must afford uninterruptedly the possibilities of protecting equally the basic rights of all its citizens, their rights which constitute the general preconditions of developing, as individuals, their human potentialities and which can be protected only indirectly.

[3] This is art. 53 of the Constitution of the Republic of Turkey.

*

What are, now, the implications of having put forth, as I have done, social injustice? And what can philosophy and philosophers contribute to the fight against social injustice? What can we do, and how?

The first and, perhaps, most important implication is that social injustice at the national level can today be abolished immediately, that is, without waiting that poor countries become prosperous. Yet, philosophers know better than everybody else what the relation between the possible and the real is! The possible, as long as no one undertakes it, can never become real.

I am convinced that there are some theoretical and practical endeavours philosophers can make, so that this possibility may become a reality.

Something they can do at the theoretical level is to throw a strong light on this possibility. In order to be able to do this, it is necessary to show, in general and in each individual case, the role that the rights given by the State play with regard to the protection of the indirectly protected basic rights, in other words, to put the finger exactly on the point where social injustice appears. This presupposes a different classification of rights and the exclusion of social and economic rights – i.e., the rights in which all citizens in a country are equal – from "human" or basic rights – i.e., the rights in which all human beings are equal. This means that it is necessary to make clear the concept of human rights, basing ourselves not on Western morals, but on the knowledge of Man's potentialities, and to found human rights on this knowledge and nothing else.

For the so-called human rights appear as a kind of demands, i.e., they express some necessities to be fulfilled. But what kind of demands are they?

Especially after the Second World War, the United Nations and other international organizations tried to fix in Charters, Declarations, Covenants, etc., and fixed – i.e., codified – indeed, a considerable part of such demands, also including a few which are no "human" rights. These are valuable documents, no doubt. Yet, when we look at these documents, we observe that what is codified there – sometimes in great disorder – appears often as a reaction against what had happened before (for example "the scourge of war, which [...] has brought untold sorrow to mankind", "the barbarous acts which have outraged the conscience of mankind", etc.) and which the makers of these documents do not want to happen again. We also observe that their wording bears deep traces of Western morals.

For these and such reasons, I suppose, and also in the face of innumerable violations of, and broad indifference in fulfilling, "human" rights, these necessities remain in the eyes of very many people, even in the Western World, abstract-romantic demands, not convincing at all. While many others, outside the Western World, propose a "cultural approach" to human rights.

This "cultural approach", which constitutes today an important theme of theoretical discussion concerning human righs at the international level, seems to me as an endeavour to correct an error by committing another error.

All these happen because it is not clear enough what such d e m a n d s are, i.e., what as a whole is demanded, and because this lack of clarity leaves room to consider social and economic rights as "human rights". This also makes many people consider the necessities which human rights express as "hypothetical imperatives" in Kant's terms.

According to the *Universal Declaration of Human Rights* "the advent of a world in which human beings shall enjoy freedom of speech and belief and freedom from fear and want has been proclaimed as the highest aspiration of common people". But how can we persuade those who do not feel any such aspiration? The leaders who give the order to launch an atomic or nuclear bomb, the politicians who "through corrupt official processes direct resources to an elite at the expense of the needy" in Cyrus Vance's words? How can we persuade so many others, who do not think that human rights have to be protected for everybody, even for those who have violated or failed to fulfil such rights, e.g., the terrorist who, at the rejection of his demands, shoots his hostages, or those decision-makers who, at the expense of a hostage's life, reject such demands, with reasons widely approved? So long as the prevailing concept and classification of human rights is valid, we shall not be able to provide a firm basis upon which to rest the necessity that the rights in which all human beings are equal be protected for everybody by the State and by everybody.[4]

It is the job of Philosophy to revise the prevailing concept of human rights and their classification, as well as to show their "categorical" necessity. And only such research, I think, may furnish the ground for a promising education of human rights. So, this distinction between the rights in which all human beings are equal and those in which all citizens in a country are equal seems very important.

Keeping in mind this distinction and taking into account the existing conditions in each country and in the world today, we have also to revise the international documents relative to human rights, and our Constitutions and laws in force as well. Such a work may supply us with a starting point to deduce and propose new principles, to conceive new institutions and to find out new ways for the abolition of social injustice. Such an endeavour may help governments, sincere in their aspiration, to abolish social injustice in their countries; to those who are not sincere, it may be a call to honesty, a call to which it would not be so easy to turn a deaf ear.

*

Another cause of social injustice at the national level and one which aggravates it, seems to be the conception of "the State" prevailing today, a conception shared both by those who rule and those who oppose them.

---

[4] Of course, I don't forget that to show this necessity is not enough to prevent violations or to guarantee the fulfilment of basic rights, as it is not enough to persuade somebody to admit that something should not be done, in order to stop him from doing it.

Very many people today think of the State as an entity, no matter whether they consider it from a positive or a negative perspective; that is, they think of the State as an entity to be protected (by those who rule), or an entity used for pressure (upon the ruled). Used in connection with domestic affairs, expressions such as "to protect the State", "to demolish the State", "to abolish the State", etc., are not comprehensible, unless we assume the above-mentioned conception of the State.

But, as far as domestic affairs are concerned, why should we not be able to think of the State as a body of organs, established according to principles deduced from the existing conditions – "the needs" – in order to make possible, for a nation, the equal protection of the rights of all its members, of those rights which all human beings equally possess; in other words, in view of arranging the relations among the citizens and of administrating the public so that the basic rights of all citizens may be protected and equally fulfilled? Why not think of it as a body of such organs, some of which are to be renewed in the course of time, some others abolished to make room for new ones?

Owing to the failure to establish the connections among the *res publica,* the State and politics, governments, while taking decisions or enacting laws, often do not keep in view the indirectly protected rights. Though the demands concerning basic rights are to be found in most Constitutions, who would claim that when governments "give" social and economic "rights", or when they defend old or new institutions, they do in fact take into account the intimate connection existing between these two kinds of rights and the inevitable – positive or negative – implications that the given rights have for the protection of the indirectly protected basic rights? Thus, politics appears as an arena where opposing interests – of the rulers and of the ruled – fight each other "unto death", and the belief that this is the "nature" of politics takes root even more strongly.

So, in the fight to abolish social injustice at the national level, something that philosophy could do, is, to revise the prevailing conception of State, to put forth its implications and to show why this conception has to be changed today.

Something else that philosophy could do for the abolition of social injustice at the national level is related to the concept of "development". For those who want to fight against social injustice in the so-called "developing" countries, there is something to learn from the "developed" countries, something in connection with my claim that social injustice at the national level can be abolished right away in Third World countries, on condition that they are sincerely determined to abolish it. "Developed" countries today have become conscious, at least at the intellectual level, of an impasse they actually are at: the impasse to which the principle of "the bigger the better" had led them – a principle which determined their national policies during the past few decades.

To get out of this impasse, a new concept of development is proposed. The general theme of the Third Conference of European Ministers Responsible for Cultural Affairs, held in Luxembourg, May 1981, was formulated as "The Role of Cultural Aims in Social and Economic Development" and the choice of the theme justified as follows: "There seems to be [...] general consensus on the need to give national social and economic policies this 'cultural dimension', which may be defined as the sum of efforts to go beyond material improvement of human life and enable men and women to achieve moral, intellectual, artistic and emotional fulfilment. In making 'the role of cultural aims in social and economic development' the theme of the Luxembourg conference, the Ministers wanted to foster the emergence of a new concept of social 'development', not solely determined by economic and quantitative considerations, but also by the desire for a qualitatively better life embracing cultural values."[5]

Third World countries do not face such a problem for the moment. Yet, the social injustice prevailing there is ascribed to their being "undeveloped", and all efforts of national policies are oriented towards the increase of the *per capita* income. Still, we observe that the increase of the *per capita* income in these countries, in fact, does not help to reduce – let alone abolish – social injustice. Now, what the "developing" countries can learn from the experience of the "developed" ones, is, to make the necessary changes in the hierarchy of aims of their national policies, namely to put the aim of abolishing social injustice – i.e., to afford the possibility of equal protection of the basic rights of all their citizens – before the aim of economic development, that is, to invert the order that is now assumed to exist between them.

Philosophers in each country can contribute a lot to this inversion of aims, as well as to the changing of the prevailing conception of the State and to making the actual protection of basic rights the actual aim of the national policies of their countries; to contribute not only by theoretical endeavours, but – whenever this is possible – also by practical ones: they can, by their treatment of individual cases, give examples of the advantages, and consequently of the necessity, of a co-operation between politics and philosophy, for the protection and fulfilment of basic rights.

Something else that the teacher-philosophers can do, for the abolition of social injustice, is to extend the teaching of, and training in, human rights, wherever this has already begun; and where it has not yet started, to explore possibilities to start this training, by giving, within the framework of philosophy-teaching, the topic of human rights a place proportionate to its significance and by trying to introduce the philosophical teaching of human rights in the programmes of other disciplines connected with Man, and of vocational training.

Such endeavours are, I think, only a part of what we can do as philosophers for the abolition of social injustice at the national level.

So long as social injustice is not abolished at the national level, the efforts to blunt – I dare not say abolish – global social injustice, seem to be condemned to remain ineffective to a great extent. Those who make efforts today for the creation of a new global economic order should not fail to realize that interna-

[5] See *The Role of Cultural Aims in Social and Economic Development*, Council of Europe, Four Studies. Strasbourg, 1981.

tional co-operation for the abolition of social injustice in the world cannot abolish social injustice in a country, unless its government is sincerely determined to doing so. They should not fail to see that international co-operation can influence the degree of protection of the indirectly protected basic rights, but cannot guarantee their equal protection; they should not forget Cyrus Vance's words.

Still, the problem of global social injustice is quite different from that of social injustice at the national level. Global injustice is connected with the rights of the peoples and not solely with their economic rights.

In conclusion, I would like to emphasize the following: in the efforts to abolish social injustice – whether at the national level or the global one – the co-operation between politics and philosophy is a *sine qua non.* And even if international efforts cannot abolish social injustice at the national level, they can reinforce the impact of the efforts shown at the national level to make value knowledge influential in public life.

For this reason, international and especially regional co-operation between philosophers seems very important in order that philosophy may fulfil its vocation in today's world.

This is also the reason why our conference, the first meeting of which was realized through Prof. Mourad Wahba's initiative and which we wish to continue, is very important. It is important for each one of us with regard to the efforts we make in our countries and it is also important for what we could do – for what we could try to do, if we want to – by certain attempts as the *Afro-Asian Philosophy Conference.*

Even if our countries cannot compete with "developed" countries in economic questions, I believe that we can, indeed, contribute perhaps more than the "developed" countries to the emergence of a more humanized world: to add to the treatment of political questions of our world the value dimension, may result in an important contribution to our epoch, that our co-operation will have made possible.

JUSTICE: SOCIAL AND GLOBAL[*]

The aspiration to justice is a perennial aspiration of humankind and the question of what justice is, appears as a perennial question of philosophy. Yet the latter question becomes more important the more the population increases on our globe. It has become more urgent too, since we witness also an increase in the number of those who don't aspire at, but w a n t justice, and in their despair of "having" it, they take up arms by which they annihilate people at random and themselves as well: an increase in terrorism marks the past few decades, yet decades in which the main items on the agenda of the "international community" have been the question of peace and development – economic, social and cultural.

What do people aspire at or want? In other words: what is justice?

For twenty-five centuries different answers were, and are still, given to this question – a fact which perplexes most of us. Is any attempt to answer this question bound to be only one among many possible?

Maybe. Yet, in spite of the impression which the history of philosophy creates, if we still wish to try to give a c o g n i t i v e l y j u s t i f i a b l e answer to the question of what justice is, or to evaluate the existing answers from the viewpoint of such a justifiability, w h e r e shall we look at?

The latter is an epistemological question which, if not scrutinized, I think, is impossible to answer and consequently to find appropriate ways to fight against social and global injustice which appear in different historical conditions under different guises, given that we do sincerely care for reducing social and global injustice in our world.

*

ON JUSTICE IN GENERAL

What is justice? Something we learn from Plato in this respect, even if we have certain objections to his relative general view, is that justice is an i d e a .

By 'idea' *I* mean a special kind of thought: a conception of the human mind, which, in distinction from 'knowledge' – each piece of which is related to an object independent from itself – engenders its object; and which, in distinction from 'belief' – which also creates its object – is not bound to those who "have" it. Ideas are brought to history, where they remain effective for a while or for good, i.e., they are added to the historical being.

---

[*] This paper was published in Finnish: "Yhteiskunnallinen ja globaali oikeudenmukaisuus", *Niin & Näin*, Filosofinen aikakauslehti, Syshy 3/98, Tampere, 1998, pp. 58-64, and in Chinese, in World Philosophy 2010/2, *Logos*, Chinese Academy of Social Sciences (CSSCI), 2010, pp. 144-154.

This specificity of ideas seems to be the cause of their obscurity, and consequently of the variety of definitions given of them. Yet this specificity makes it possible for philosophy to objectify them, i.e., to make them the object of philosophical inquiry and evaluation, the first step of which is to conceptualize them.

Yet how? Where shall we look at, in our attempt to answer the question of what justice is, provided that we do not intend to add a new "theory" to the already existing ones, which usually deal with what we ought to do in general, so that justice will prevail?

A first clue in this quest of our object of knowledge may be found by following the way Aristotle usually uses in starting an inquiry, and this is the lingual context, his λέγεται ...: what or whom people call this or that, i.e., what people try to express when they call something or somebody this or that. Thus with respect to justice I'll ask: what do people try to express, or, what do they mean, when they ask for justice?

The first thing we can notice is that when laymen do so in general, they express a vague aspiration; while in a special case they try to express a demand: they mean that something should be fulfilled for themselves or for somebody else, something – whatever it may be in every individual case – that they have not just at this moment, but they think, rightly or wrongly, belongs to them; they mean that they are deprived of something which should be restored to them: they mean something due to them.

And this reminds us, in fact, of one of Plato's definitions of justice: "Τὰ ὀφειλόμενα ἑκάστῳ ἀποδιδόναι".[1]

Yet how do we know that somebody has not something and consequently on which ground do we claim – rightly or wrongly – that one should have it?

The answers given to this question in individual cases seem to afford another clue for philosophical inquiry in its endeavour to determine its object, in view of putting forth what the ὀφειλόμενα to human beings as human beings are, and why they are ὀφειλόμενα, i.e., to justify the "should" that the term 'ὀφειλόμενα' implies.

How is it possible to know what someone has not? For when we speak of something that we claim somebody is deprived of, we mean an absence of that thing. How do we know others' or our have-nots?

In order to see how we do this, we may follow our eyes when we claim that somebody is deprived of something. If we follow our look in such individual cases, we see that we look at two different objects which we compare in the light of a middle term: at those things which someone has at a given moment, and at those different things which someone else has at that same moment,

[1] *Πολιτεία*, 335e, "to give each one that what is due to him", but without meaning what follows.

which we compare from the viewpoint of something w e v a l u e, something which one of them is in possession of, and makes, in our eyes, his conditions "better", i.e., the amount of his possibilities greater than those of the other who is not in possession of this special something, but which we think, rightly or wrongly, should belong to him, or, to him too. This is the something we think he is deprived of, the lack of which deprives him of some possibilities the former has, owing to this something.

This comparison of two facts in the light of something w e value – or this triple relationship we establish in everyday life – appears to be the source wherefrom we deduce our claim that something is due to someone, or, it is the ground on which we base such a claim.

*

This simple observation affords a starting point for philosophical inquiry, enabling us to come to grips with the idea of justice: by showing us the way in which we determine the ὀφειλόμενον in a given case, it teaches us where we can look at, in order to become able to conceptualize the idea of justice in a cognitively accountable way: and this is i n j u s t i c e, which is a state of affairs, a fact, and not an idea as justice is. Injustice is the p l a c e where we find the ὀφειλόμενα to human beings as such; or, if we wish to call t h e s e ὀφειλόμενα by their modern name, it is the source wherefrom we deduce the principles we call basic human rights.

This means that we have to change our initial question in order to become able to answer it, and to ask first what injustice is.

*

Injustice, in general, has to do with violation or disregard of rights.

There are different kinds of rights, which have varying implications in different actual situations, since there are various ways of violating and disregarding them. This means that there are different kinds of injustice too.

Though such violations and disregard appear under innumerable facets, yet in every age we observe some p a t t e r n s of violations and disregard, patterns which change in history. This means that we have to uncover these patterns in every age.

In connection with the individual, injustice appears as a certain way of treating individuals, a treatment which, directly or indirectly, violates or hinders the fulfilment of, one or some of their rights.

In connection with the State, injustice appears t o d a y as the state of affairs, in which a state itself – through its own organs – either violates, or does not carry out in the existing conditions the implications of, the basic rights o f a part of its citizens, or it does not interfere effectively – through its appropriate organs – with such violation and disregard.[2]

Global injustice also appears as a state of affairs, in which basic and other rights of the individuals of a group, or of the majority in a country, are violated or disregarded in favour of the interests of other groups or countries. This is, at present, the most characteristic mark of interstate or international relations in our world.

Thus put, injustice, in general, would denote the state of affairs in which the existing conditions are unfavourable to, or hinder individuals or groups from, exercising their human rights – conditions created directly or indirectly, by other individuals or groups, either at the national or international levels.

But how can we judge that certain existing conditions are unfavourable in this respect? Or: how do we get the knowledge of basic rights?

By a similar comparison I mentioned before: the comparison of the conditions in which at a given historical moment some human beings are, with the different conditions in which some other human beings are at the same historical moment, i.e., with the conditions of the human being or of humanity in this age, in the light of the knowledge of the value of certain human potentialities: those potentialities which made Edison discover the uses of electricity, Marie Sklodowska Curie discover radium, Saint-Exupéry write *The Little Prince* and many others achieve what they have indeed achieved, the blessings of which only some of us enjoy. This is the knowledge of what a human being can become and of the significance, for humanity, of the achievements of those who have actualized such potentialities. Made under the light of this knowledge, such a comparison affords us an hypothetical or conditional knowledge: the knowledge of one or some conditions, in which it is normally impossible for a human being to actualize such human potentialities.

It is from this knowledge that we deduce, as a conclusion, the opposite conditions, as conditions necessary for the actualization of such human potentialities.

Thus the starting point in such a deduction appears to be our knowledge of human potentialities and their value. The knowledge of these potentialities we get from philosophical anthropology, while that of their value from the evaluation of human achievements in history.

What we do during this complex knowing activity is the following: a) keeping in mind the knowledge I just mentioned, we look at humanity at a given historical moment and we see the stage of actualization of such potentialities the human being, as a species, has reached at that historical moment: we see the achievements of humanity as a whole, or where the human being is at that historical moment. This affords us the third term, or the basis of our com-

[2] "The rule of law" and "social state" are terms designating demands against injustice in this connection.

parison.[3] b) Through this knowledge we look at different human groups living at that moment: then we see groups in which individuals actualize such potentialities to a higher degree, compared with the degree to which in some other groups individuals actualize them: there are human groups, the members of which contribute more than the individuals of other groups do, to the welfare of humanity. c) In our endeavour to explain such a fact, we connect these different contributions to the different conditions in which these human groups are: in this comparative connection certain existing conditions appear to be unfavourable for, or hindering, the actualization of such human potentialities. d) It is from this comparison that we conclude that the "opposite" of those unfavourable existing conditions – or some conditions existing in other groups – are the necessary conditions or the preconditions for actualizing such human potentialities. In other words, this comparison is the source wherefrom we deduce the demands we call today human rights.

Thus, human rights or such principles or demands we deduce from the state of affairs we call injustice, secure for us the ground to step on for the conceptualization of the idea of justice.

For 'injustice' and 'justice', though they are used as opposite terms, denote two relative yet not opposite concepts: the former denotes a state of affairs, i.e, a fact, the latter an idea, i.e., a conception of the human mind and not any state of affairs.

In view of the state of affairs denoted by 'injustice' under its various facets today, the idea of justice could be formulated or given such a content as: the demand that the basic rights of the individual – whatever they may be – should be protected and fulfilled, and their various implications in the existing conditions at a given moment – group rights included – should be found and carried out in every country and at the global level.

Thus justice appears to be a meta-principle: the demand that the norms determining the arrangement of social relations and political action, be deduced, at every historical moment, considering the existing conditions in the light of the knowledge of human rights.

And if we wish to have a formulation of 'justice' which would sound – but only sound – more general, i.e., a formulation without the term 'human rights' which may sound to many as vague as 'justice' does, we may formulate justice as: the demand of the permanent creation of conditions affording individuals the possibility to actualize, in the existing conditions of the historical moment at which they live, their human potentialities, as well as certain of the potentialities of the human being – those I mentioned before.

Thus justice appears to demand the permanent creation of different and changing conditions favourable to, or not hindering the devel-

---

[3] Apart of which any other third term, let us say "national income", is and will probably always be misleading.

opment of, human beings and of the human species, or in today's terminology, the protection of human rights in the different and changing conditions of any country and the world. For human rights express the general conditions under which individuals – we think – could and might actualize their human potentialities, i.e., may, as human beings, get as well as give the ὀφειλόμενα to every human being.

What justice demands is not the effectiveness of some special, "material" principles, as the theories of justice usually think and try to put forth,[4] but t h e w i l l to fulfil permanently a chain of conditions leading to orders – different and changing orders but – of a special character: orders determined by historical –: changing – norms and consequently laws, deduced at a given historical moment from the knowledge of the unchanging general preconditions of the actualization of human potentialities which make up what we call human dignity, i.e., from the knowledge of human rights.

Thus the concept of justice considered in its connection with human rights, appears to be a principle of v o l i t i o n – to use Kant's terminology – while human rights appear to be principles of a c t i o n for the treatment of individuals, as well as principles for the deduction of law in general and of historical norms guiding the decisions taken in the arrangement of social relations and political action.

This is probably the reason why justice seems to many to be only a "lofty idea", an empty word, not worthwhile to dwell on. This is probably the reason why, when its connection with human rights is overlooked, justice seems to many to be something "relative". And this is probably the reason why theories try to put forth "principles of justice".

Yet justice seems to have no special principles. It only points at t h e s p e c i f i c i t y of the principles – whatever they may be – which, if, as implications of the basic rights at a given moment, they determine social, legal and political decisions and actions, human beings could exercise their rights, i.e., actualize their human potentialities and might promote humankind.

ON SOCIAL JUSTICE

In our attempts to conceptualize what we call social justice, we can now follow the same way we used in connection with justice in general and ask: what is this state of affairs we call social injustice? And how does it appear today?

When in a country, a part of the citizens live in air-conditioned villas or flats while another part of the citizens lives in caves or mud-brick houses, there prevails social injustice. Wherever some children are taken to school in Cadillacs, while some other children of the same age have to carry loads in order to earn their living, there prevails social injustice. Where some women can afford to buy at once three fur coats – because they like them equally and cannot de-

[4] For example the two principles of justice, which Rawls has put forward.

cide for one against the other – while some others, in order to survive, consent to be sold, there again we meet social injustice. These are snapshots from so-called developing countries.

And if in some countries biologically or physiologically maimed children are made to survive through all means imaginable, while in other countries hundreds of children may die from measles owing to lack of medical care; if in some countries, late in the afternoon, pet-dogs are taken around in baby-carriages for a stroll, while in some other countries some children have to go through the garbage looking for something to eat, that means that social injustice prevails in our world.

So, the question of social injustice must be treated as a state of affairs we meet today at two different levels, that is at the national and the global levels, and then, in their relation to each other.

*

According to the most easily accepted opinion, social injustice is nothing but the result of monstrous inequalities in the distribution of income in a country. Yet though important, this is only o n e aspect of the phenomenon.

When we consider the question in connection with human rights, social injustice appears as a problem related to all basic rights which can be protected only indirectly.

In order to make explicit this connection, allow me to say first a few words about my classification of the rights of the individual, because of its implications with regard to our topic.

The so-called 'human rights', i.e., rights in which "all human beings are equal", rights which they possess only because they are human beings, constitute a part of the rights of the individual, i.e., the basic rights. A part of these basic rights are demands for the direct protection of certain human potentialities in individuals: demands that "nobody" touch an individual for any reason, while this individual is engaged in actualizing such a human potentiality.[5] The other part is that of demands related to the general preconditions necessary to afford each individual the possibility to develop his or her potentialities. Rights such as the right to a standard of living adequate for one's health, the right to education, the right to work, etc., belong to this category. These are also rights which individuals possess for the sole reason that they are human beings, i.e., they are basic rights of the individual or human rights. But they differ from the rights of the first category in that they can be protected only indirectly, through other rights g i v e n to individuals by the State – by means of social and economic rights – and through public institutions founded, not always but mostly, by political decisions.

[5] All interdictory demands concerning the security of the individual and/or the so-called fundamental freedoms belong to this category of basic rights.

These given rights, i.e., the social and economic rights, are rights of the individual, but not basic rights, i.e., they are not rights in which all human beings are equal. They are limits drawn by the State to the individuals in a country, they delineate some areas within which the citizens of a given country may act as they like and they demand that no citizen transgress these limits. These are rights the limits of which are, and must be drown today differently in different countries, but they are rights in which all (concerned) citizens in each country are equal.[6]

Now, the way the limits of these rights are drawn in a country, determines whether they may protect or not protect, or even hinder the protection of, the basic rights to which they are related.

Thus social injustice appears as a question related to the connection between these two kinds of rights of the individual, the given rights and the indirectly protected basic rights; and it is a state of affairs having to do (a) with what these given rights are, i.e., with how social and economic relations are arranged by Law in a given country and also with the way the relevant laws are operated; consequently (b) with the establishment or non-establishment and the functioning of some public institutions in the existing conditions.

*

So, the question of social injustice in its relation to basic rights, at the national level, can be treated from two different perspectives: that of the individual and that of the State. The former affords us the possibility of grasping what kind of a state of affairs social injustice is, the latter to understand how it originates today in many non-affluent or developing countries.

So far as the individual is concerned, social injustice is not a state of affairs in which basic rights are not at all protected; it is the situation in which such rights are not protected *for all* individuals concerned, in a country: a state of affairs in which the possibilities of protection of the rights in which all human beings are equal, but which can be protected only indirectly, are not equally afforded – that is afforded *at the same degree* – to all citizens. From this point of view social injustice appears as an ethical question.

As far as the State is concerned, social injustice appears as a political fact, i.e., a fact related to the arrangement of social relations in the broad sense, the way they are established and the way they function; in other words a fact related to the rights given or not given and the possibilities afforded to the citizens by the State.

Social injustice arises first of all when governments, while drawing the limits of social and economic rights, do not take into consideration the connection existing between this kind of rights and the indirectly protected basic rights; when, during this drawing of limits, factors other than the demand to protect the

[6] The determination of the lowest payment, or of the minimum number of years of work required for retirement are such rights.

respective basic rights interfere – ignorance above all, and interests: personal, group and class interests, etc. Or, when laws determining the establishment and operation of social and economic relations, for example tax-laws, the civil code and other acts or laws of narrower scope, are enacted without taking into account the intimate connection existing between this kind of rights and the indirectly protected basic rights, i.e., are drawn without taking into account their foreseeable implications for these rights under the existing conditions of a country.

This lack of connection between these two kinds of rights of the individual appears sometimes as enacting laws giving some "rights" or possibilities to a part of the citizens, which hinder the fulfilment of the basic rights of the majority of the citizens in the existing conditions. Or often it appears as not abrogating laws which impair such rights, or as not enacting some other laws which could indirectly protect them in the existing conditions, that is laws which would make possible the enforcement of other laws protecting them.

Such are cases in which governments cannot or do not fulfil one of the main *raisons d'être* of the State, its duty of arranging the relations among the citizens, cases in which governments cannot or do not keep a part of the citizens from exploiting other citizens – and the State as well – and consequently cases in which they cannot or do not prevent a part of the citizens from securing for themselves certain privileges while protecting mostly their personal interests, or, sometimes, their basic rights at the expense of basic rights of many other citizens and to an extent surpassing the measure that the country's conditions may allow. Where the State does not indirectly prevent, by appropriate laws, etc., some of its citizens from exploiting some others, there emerges social injustice.[7] In these cases it is the way of arranging social relations that causes the emergence of social injustice.

From the point of view of the State, another cause of social injustice in developing countries is something that the governments do not or cannot do: to "distribute" p r i v a t i o n s equally among the citizens. This is a fact we observe especially in countries in which the resources available to the State are limited: though laws aiming to protect the indirectly protected rights are in fact enacted, the non-existence of some other laws and the lack of a satisfactory number of institutions necessary for the operation of the former in the existing conditions make it unthinkable for the State to afford the possibilities of equal protection of these rights for all citizens. Thus certain basic rights of some citi-

[7] The fact that a lot of low-income people in developing countries prefer to work for a less satisfactory pay than what their labour justifies as government officers is, I think, typical.

zens are "protected" more than the means available to a state allow, while rights of many others are not protected at all.[8]

It is usually claimed that social injustice is the result of the unequal distribution of what "exists". Yet, in those countries on which our attention is focused, either the State cannot dispose of what "exists", or, what is at its disposal is not enough for the fulfilment, even to a minimum extent, of the basic rights of all its citizens at any one moment. Thus, from the point of view of the State today, social injustice appears also not because of the unequal distribution of what "exists", but because of the unequal "distribution" of p r i v a t i o n s. For, as I have already said, social injustice at the national level has almost nothing to do with the degree of protection of the indirectly protected rights – i.e., with the dimensions of the limits of the given rights which protect their relative basic ones –, but with a failure to afford the possibilities of equal protection of these rights for all citizens, whatever the degree of this equal protection may be.

In many developing countries today social injustice exists because governments do not distribute u n e q u a l l y, in favour of the needy, what is at the disposal of the State, that is they do not distribute it in such a way that the basic rights of all citizens are equally protected.

This means that social injustice emerges also when governments do not fulfil another *raison d'être* of the State, i.e., when in public administration they do not use what belongs to the public, so that the needs relative to the basic rights of all citizens may be fulfilled equally, when they do not establish the institutions necessary to fulfil this aim in the existing conditions.

Thus, considered from both perspectives, social injustice at the national level in many developing countries today, is the state of affairs in which the rights given and the possibilities afforded to individuals by the State – the social (including the so-called cultural) and economic rights – either do not protect equally or hinder the equal protection of the indirectly protected basic rights of all the citizens. In a country where, by the equal "distribution of privations", these rights of all citizens would be protected equally, even though at a low degree, there would be no question of social injustice at the national level; there we would raise only the problem of global injustice.

Starting from the above considerations we can now formulate the principle of social justice as the demand that the State, i.e., each government that comes to power, must afford uninterruptedly the possibilities of protecting e q u a l l y the indirectly protected rights of all the citizens, e.g., their rights to food, health, education, etc., rights which constitute the general preconditions for the development of certain human potentialities and which can be protected only indirectly. This means that laws regulating social and economic issues

[8] Some citizens, for example, can afford to buy three pots at once of an imported beauty-cream, while others cannot find on the market a medicine for heart, or if they find it, cannot buy it because it is too expensive for them.

should be drafted by taking into account their foreseeable implications for the human rights of all the citizens in the existing conditions of a country.

GLOBAL INJUSTICE AND THE QUESTION OF GOALS

Fifty-six years ago "the people of the United Nations determined [...] to promote social progress and better standards of life in larger freedom, and for those ends [...] to employ international machinery for the promotion of the economic and social advancement of all peoples, had resolved to combine [their] efforts to accomplish these aims".[9] To this ends they put "development" as the main objective of national and international policies.

Yet in a UNESCO document written in 1982, i.e., 36 years later, we read the following:[10] "In the Third World, vast populations frequently enjoy none of the benefits of the progress and towns and cities – in many cases and at least as regards certain categories – are like islands of modernity cut off from the hinterland". "In 1979 four industrialized countries alone accounted for just over half of the world gross product, and in 1980, whereas the average per capita product in the industrialized market economy countries amounted to 10.660 dollars, in the so-called low-income countries it came to only 250 dollars – or forty-two times less." "Broadly calculated 1.300 million people are without access to drinking water."

All these striking figures witness to the fact that developmental policies not only deepened social injustice, but global injustice as well.

The situation in 1995 does not seem better. In the document of the Copenhagen World Summit for Social Development we read exactly the same sentences: "a) within many societies, both in developed and developing countries, the gap between the rich and poor has increased. Further, and despite the fact that some developing countries are growing rapidly, the gap between developed and many developing countries, particularly the least developed countries, has widened; b) more than one billion people in the world live in abject poverty, most of whom go hungry every day. A large proportion, the majority of whom are women, have very limited access to income, resources, education, health care and nutrition, particularly in Africa and the least developed countries."[11]

I shall not dwell here on how the gap between developed and developing countries has widened.[12] I shall confine myself only to observing that put together all these and many other official statements witness to the fact that "development", which was introduced and adopted as the most appropriate and

---

[9] From the Charter of the United Nations.

[10] Draft Medium-Term Plan 1984-89, par. 19.

[11] Draft Declaration of the Copenhagen Summit, par. 16a and b.

[12] See my "Les droits de l'homme et la Décennie du développement culturel", in *Birleşmiş Milletler Türk Derneği 1988 Yıllığı*. Ankara, 1990, pp. 25-30; or "The Idea of Development. Its Past and its Present", in *The Idea of Development. Between its Past and its Future*. Ankara, 1993, pp. 3-17. In the present volume pp. 75-83.

promising way, i.e., as *the* way anticipated and followed up, in view to abolish social and global injustice and to get rid of poverty; in other words "development" as main objective of national policies based on "foreign aid" or "development aid" made by rich countries to the poor ones, has created results contradicting the expectations of its introducers. While it afforded a few people the possibility of living on "islands of modernity", together with the rapid increase of population in these countries, it did increase the number of those who are deprived of the means to answer even their most basic needs.

What can we learn from this fact?

FREE MARKET AND HUMAN RIGHTS

At present among the promoted ways out of the current stalemate of poverty, which are expected to lead to social development, we see free market economy – "the new economic order", "privatization", "globalization", etc. Especially after the dissolution of the Soviet Union the new trend in this respect is the fashionable linking of human rights, democracy and free market. This triadic motto has become very popular all over the world.

Yet, their linking appears rather to be a result of linking value judgements than to express a factual or conceptual (necessary) connection among them, a linking which, if taken for granted, as it is done now, might among others, intensify even more social and global injustice and the already existing sharp economic disparities within and among countries, as well as create new disparities and disillusions in countries "on the way to demarxisation" as they are called.

It is not difficult to foresee it, provided that we are sufficiently aware that social injustice is a state of affairs which emerges when social and economic rights are given, i.e., laws delineating *the limits* of social and economic rights are enacted (and often quite "democratically", through parliamentary decisions), without taking into consideration the implications they bear, *at that moment*, for the indirectly protected basic rights of the individual (for the right to health, to education, etc.) in the existing conditions of a given country; in other words, aware that social injustice is a state of affairs emerging when determinants *other than* the demands that the basic rights express, determine the delineation of the limits of social and economic rights in a country.

Let me give here only one theoretical reason of this claim of mine:

The demand of free market, in principle, amounts, simply put, to the demand that governments do not interfere in the economic activities of individuals, that governments leave them alone in this respect. In this case the order of socio-economic relations, i.e., their establishment and change, will follow a spontaneous open process. In this process individuals would not only better protect their interests, but they would also have to protect the interests of other individuals.

The linkage of free market with human rights betrays an intention to protect economic "freedom" as a basic right and to protect it in the way that *only one kind of basic rights*, which I call directly protected rights (e.g., the so-called freedom of thought, freedom of opinion, etc.), can be protected.

This seems to be due a) *to lack of distinction between different kinds of rights of the individual*, between basic human rights and non-basic social and economic rights, and b) *to a confusion of the ways of protecting two different kinds of basic rights of the individual*. The way to protect, for example, the so-called "right to freedom of opinion and expression" is assumed to be also the way to protect what is assumed to be an individual's "economic freedom" in a broad sense.

Yet, the two kinds of human rights presuppose different ways of protection. To protect the first kind of rights would mean to put them under the guarantee of Law: to put under the guarantee of Law that nobody (State organs included) will hinder an individual *while* this individual is actualising a given human potentiality, i.e., "nobody" will give damage to his or her other rights, and if there are any attempts to do it, this individual would be protected by the appropriate State organs.

Yet the protection of the second kind of basic rights (of the rights to health, education, etc.) depends on public institutions and on other given rights, the social and economic rights, which, as I said earlier, are *limits drawn* by Law, within which any concerned citizen is free to move. It depends on *how* the limits of social and economic rights are drawn, by taking or not taking into consideration their foreseeable implications for the human rights of all the citizens in the existing conditions of the given country. And all such social and economic rights, both protecting and not protecting basic rights, are given by laws, i.e., by parliamentary "democratic" decisions.

Thus "freedom" with regard to economic rights (or economic freedom) would mean *the absence of limits in the economic activities of the individual*, which would be in contradiction with the very nature of such rights: *their being limits* set thereto – be they in accordance or not with human rights. It would mean the absence of limits in the economic activities of the individual, whatever their products, or their results, might be.

In connection with our problem, it would amount to demanding that "nobody" interfere with individuals, not only while they are engaged in actualising special human potentialities, i.e., while they exercise their basic rights of the first kind, but also while they act to protect their own interests, which not only clash inevitably with the interests of other individuals, but in many cases also with their human rights.

Consequently, the demand that the "free" market now brings in the case of non-affluent-developing countries would amount not only to discarding governments, which mostly delineate the limits of economic rights according to private or group interests; but also to discarding *the possibility of* making basic rights determinant in the establishment and changing of economic relations within and among countries.

Thus, a misconception of freedoms seems to be at the root of considering the free market as a way out from the current stalemate of poverty, because the free market may function in the economic relations among countries which are, more or less, on the same level of economic development, but constitutes a trap in the economic relations between developed and developing countries.

HUMAN RIGHTS AS A GLOBAL GOAL

These considerations, and others not mentioned here, lead us to anticipate a different possible way out of the present stalemate. This way out would be to put as the main objective of national and international policies, in the place of 'development' – whatever its epithets might be[13] – the protection of clearly conceived and differentiated basic human rights, which express demands for the treatment of human beings and are a special kind of practical principles or norms for the establishment of social relations and the deduction of Law.

To what such a change of objectives or goal would amount?

At the national level it would amount to abolishing social injustice in many countries immediately, that is to securing, by appropriate legislation, the possibility that the indirectly protected basic rights of all the citizens of a country (their rights to a minimum standard of living, to health, to education, etc.) be protected in the same degree, whatever this degree might be. This in turn would amount to enforcing laws concerning social and economic issues, i.e., laws delineating the limits of economic and social rights, by taking into consideration their foreseeable implications for the basic rights of all citizens in the existing conditions of the given country.

I am well aware of the difficulties involved in such a legislation, to be made by "democratic" parliamentary decisions: for example the difficulty to formulate such laws and, if formulated, to pass them through parliaments where the interplay of small interests play a decisive role. Though this is difficult, it is not impossible, on the condition that those who possess sufficient knowledge for this and the sincere will to do so, are also able to find the appropriate strategy in each country.

The abolishment of social injustice, in order to be followed by an increased protection of the basic rights of all citizens in non-affluent countries, makes necessary the support of the affluent ones, still not in the way it is done up to now and is done at present.

At present, to use Katarina Tomaševski's formulation,

---

[13] See my "Philosophy Questioning Cultural Development", in *Philosophy and Cultural Development*. Ankara, 1993, pp. 9-17.

> free trade, which even in theory conflicts with human rights obligations of governments, is combined with free elections to form human rights conditionality:
>
> The recent spread of aid conditionalities to 'democracy' and 'human rights' at the level of rhetoric is in practice often reduced to the former, and 'democracy' is further reduced to multi-party elections. Contrary to what the public in donor countries may believe, this is not necessarily good for human rights. The reasons can be summarised as follows:
>
> * At the level of rhetoric donors are using 'democracy' and 'human rights' interchangeably, while in practice concentrating on support for multi-party elections. This may well result in the replacement of human rights by 'democracy' and the loss of donor interest in human rights once elected governments are in place.
>
> * 'Democracy' (both in rhetoric and in practice) has been confined to electoralism where countries are labelled 'democratic' as soon as elections have taken place. The fact that democracy takes centuries to develop (to which donors can testify themselves) is forgotten.
>
> * It is assumed that such instant 'democracies' can and will guarantee human rights and fundamental freedoms. Both history and the multitude of current examples prove this assumption to be erroneous.[14]

The conditions of extending aid to non-affluent countries are at present "progress in democratization" and privatization, which latter is a direct implication of free market economy. "The two main trends in the current aid policy concerning the social sector" observes Tomaševski "are the decrease in investment into social services and the advocacy of privatization." Still privatization is based on the criterion of efficiency, as exemplified by the World Bank: "The administrative capabilities of all governments, not least those in developing countries, are severely strained by the weight of their numerous activities. The question I wish to pose [says G. Roth, in *The Private Provision of Public Services in Developing Countries*, Oxford, 1988, p. 5] is whether economic development could be accelerated by moving to the private sector those responsibilities, that would be handled more efficiently there".[15] Thus development aid, i.e., the loans given according to these criteria to many developing countries, suffices only to pay the interests of their debts to the developed countries.

In the face of those and similar facts, the need to change the main goal and the objectives of national and international policies, becomes, I think, obvious. And this new goal should be the protection of human rights.

To set as the global goal the protection of basic human rights would amount to becoming aware – among other things – of the trap hidden in the current unconditional promotion of the "free market" and to transform "devel-

[14] Katarina Tomaševski, *Development Aid and Human Rights Revisited.* Pinter Publishers, London and New York, 1993, p. 15.

[15] *Ibid.*

opment aid" to grants, given with the view to increase the degree of protection of certain basic rights (of nutrition, health, education, etc.) to countries which take the necessary steps to abolish social injustice and which remain truthful to the universality of human rights, e.g., countries which increase the number of schools in which children are given the possibility to develop each his or her own human capacities, and do not increase the number of schools in which any cultural or other brainwashing is done.

Development and arms race have marked the second half of the Twentieth Century. Let us try to do more than we think we can, so that the Twenty-first Century be marked by a "race" in the protection and for the protection of our few basic human rights.

The State, the States and Human Rights*

The Problem

When our world was divided in two blocs, their representatives in international fora use to oppose human rights to peace and *vice versa*. At that time whoever in a Third World country spoke of peace was considered to be a communist, as the citizens of a socialist country, who dared to speak of human rights were considered to be enemies of the regime.

Another issue of dispute between the two blocs was the priority given to the two kinds of human rights: the Western Bloc was giving priority to so-called liberties, the Eastern Bloc to so-called social and economic rights. The simultaneous enforcement of two *Covenants* – on *Civil and Political Rights* and on *Economic, Social and Cultural Rights*, whose certain parts are totally identical – is probably the result of this dispute.

There was nevertheless something that both blocs agreed upon: this was development, understood as economic development, i.e., as increase of industrial production and national income, which the countries belonging to both parties had put as the main objective of their national policies and which led these two blocs to a deadly competition or race to which they subordinated everything else.

After the dissolution of the Soviet Union and the Eastern Bloc, the new trend which spread all over the world is the fashionable linking of human rights, democracy or democratization and the free market, the latter based on privatization and aiming at the globalization of the market economy. For this aim t h e State has to be "minimized" in various States, the advocates of free market economy say.

So far as I can see, this unscrutinized demand, advocating the minimization of the State is based on a given conception of t h e State – a conception of the State, which strangely enough lies also behind the Marxist claim of the necessity "to abolish the State", as well as behind the attempts of those who deify the State and try to "protect" it against a part of the citizens who are assumed to constitute a danger for t h e State. This is the conception of the State as an entity in itself, the Entity-State, as I call it.

---

* This paper was published in *Enlightenment and Human Rights*, ed. by Mona Abusenna. Cairo, 1998, pp. 1-21; its German version "Der Staat, die Staaten und die Menschenrechte", in *Synthesis Philosophica*, vol. 13, fasc. 2. Zagreb, 1998, pp. 471-485; and in Gregor Paul, Thomas Göller, Hans Lenk und Guido Rappe (eds), *Humanität, Interkulturalität und Menschenrechte*. Peter Lang, 2011, pp. 374-394 and its Chinese version in *Logos*, World Philosophy 2010/2, Chinese Academy of Social Sciences (CSSCI), pp. 135-145.

For this reason it is worthwhile to raise once again the question "what is *the* State?", which Marxists wished to abolish and nowadays the advocates of the free market, privatization and its globalization wish to minimize.

To tackle this question, the first conceptual distinction we have to make is between *the* State and the state*s*.

THE STATE AND THE STATES

Stat*es* are legal-political units of sovereignty with reference to other similar political units. When we speak of the Republic of Turkey, the Republic of France, the Republic of Benin, etc., we mean such political units. Such a political unit is established now, only when a considerable number of other such existing political units recognizes it legally as an independent political unit, whatever its constitution or regime might be. As examples we can think, on the one hand, of the establishment of many African states in the seventies and of the Central Asian Republics, which have become independent states after the dissolution of the Soviet Union. They are historical, juridical persons: they are established by a group, at a given historical moment, they continue to exist or come to an end in different ways, at another historical moment, after some years, decades, or centuries. As recent examples we can think of the German Democratic Republic, of the Union of Soviet Socialist Republics and of Czechoslovakia.

The State, on the other hand, is a human institution, consisting in the *legal* arrangement of social relations within a group. It expresses a voluntary interference in and codification of the establishment of social relations or role relations, which are established by themselves, i.e., in a natural way. When we speak of *the* State, we mean *not* a political unit with reference to other political units, but a given arrangement of domestic affairs in such a unit. Epithets such as socialist, democratic, Islamic, etc., which we see qualifying some stat*es*, express the specificity of the arrangement of social relations or of *the* State in a given historical state, i.e., the specificity of the norms determining this arrangement.

Thus we see that when a group gains its political independence from another group, i.e., when a new state is created, the first thing that people, in the present world, do, is to draw up a constitution: they *constitute the* State, their State. We also see radical changes of structures, or of "constitutions", in one and the same state as a political unit. Bloodless revolutions and the changes we see in the Eastern European countries and which are reflected in the dropping from their names the word "socialist", can be considered as such examples.

Now, the conception of the State underlying this inner structure or constitution of a state as a political unit, i.e., the assumptions concerning the goals of *the* State constituted within a state, constitutes the difference of State-*types*, which is a more fundamental difference than that of regimes. What we call 'State under the rule of law' *(état de droit)* or 'social State' express such a difference.

The point to which I wish to draw your attention here is the question of what makes the State in a state to be – or not to be – under the rule of law or a social state, or both of them, i.e., the relationship between the conception of the State and the determinants of the legal arrangements of social relations in a given state. Here, so far as I can see, we find a crucial point which needs scrutiny, both in theory and practice.

What are these determinants? Or: what determines the forming of legal instruments or positive law in general? In other words: wherefrom legal norms are deduced?

THE GOALS OF THE STATE

Considered as a human achievement or human institution, i.e., considered together with its "what for?", law appears to express the wish not only to create an order in human societies, but also an order of a special quality; it appears to express the concern not to lose sight of certain ethical principles in the arrangement – the establishment and administration – of social relations; i.e., it appears to express the will to interfere and arrange social relations in accordance with the idea of justice and not according to other determinants.

Still, when we look at legal instruments – including constitutions, i.e., at how the State is constituted in a given state – we see, in general, only a faint reflection of this concern; we even see, in many among them, arrangements reflecting conceptions which can hardly be reconciled with the idea of justice. In most of these arrangements, made at different levels, it is only expected that regulations and statutes be in accordance with laws, laws with constitutions, etc.; but little attention is paid to the specificity of the norms on which these constitutions are based.

On the other hand, especially after the Second World War, we observe that the idea that (positive) law should be deduced from ethical principles gained ground in public opinion all over the world and on the focus of the relevant debate we find the concepts of the State under the rule of law and of the social State. Recently we even observe an increase in the intention and attempts to deduce legal norms from the principles of human rights.

Still, when we read various constitutions keeping in mind this point, we are faced with the following strange fact: in many constitutions we find, indeed, articles or sentences expressing such ethical principles – or to use the term of our day, we find articles concerning human rights –; but we also find, next to them, norms contradicting human rights, i.e., norms which – as we can easily see, provided that we possess sufficiently clear knowledge of what human rights demand – make *a priori* impossible the determination or functioning of these ethical principles. In other words: we see the juxtaposition of incompatible norms.

Thus, in spite of the introduction of the principles of human rights in the constitutions, the conception of the State as an entity in itself continues to prevail – as an entity which threatens its subjects (and consequently has to be abolished, as certain Marxist used to claim), or an entity which interferes and limits the freedoms of the people (and consequently has to be "minimized", as the advocates of privatization and the "free" market claim now), or even an entity which is expected to protect its subjects and tell them what they should do. Democracy, which is so much promoted at present, cannot be the form of government of the entity State.

There are certain objective and subjective conditions to fulfil, so that democracy can be a form of government "of the people, by the people, for the people".

Such a main objective condition is a conception of the State as a human legal institution, whose *raison d'être* is to protect the citizens against each other and to administrate what is public according to the demands of justice – i.e., the conception of the State as a body of organs established (constituted) in order to make law determinant in the historical reality: in order a) to transform social relations – rights-duties or role relations – established in this or that manner into relation based on justice, i.e., to establish these relations or to transform them on the basis of human rights and b) to administrate public affairs in accordance with the implications of human rights in those historical, given-particular conditions.

The expressions 'State under the rule of law' and 'social State' intend to express such a conception of the State, but, I am afraid, they don't sufficiently manage to do so, since we see many discrepancies between human rights and positive law. We have to explain the origin of these discrepancies. And this seems to be at present legislation – "democratic" legislation – without keeping in mind the goals of the State.

The goals of the State as a human legal institution are not a kind of thing which can be decided democratically, but a kind of thing to become aware of. Democracy can function only in a state whose citizens are aware of the fact that the State (the body of organs and institutions that constitute the State) exists in order to introduce justice in the establishment of social relations – in positive law – in other words, in order to protect equally the human rights of the citizens.

Such a State can have two main functions: to protect the citizens against the citizens, i.e., to arrange the relations among the citizens taking into account the demands of human rights, and to administrate public affairs in a civic society, so as to secure for all the citizens the possibility of answering equally their needs related to basic rights.

Democracy, as a form of government, seems to be related with the second main function of the State, i.e., with the administration of public affairs.

Thus democracy could be the form a government, in which decisions concerning the administration of public affairs are taken by the participation of all concerned citizens – still of citizens who are aware of the truth that the State exists for the equal protection of the basic rights of all citizens. Thus 'democratization' would mean the process leading to the increase in the number of such citizens.

Objects of democratic decisions can be only the ways to be followed, in the given real-historical conditions, so that human rights can be protected in those conditions. In other words: What citizens have to look for and decide about – to use Aristotle's words – deliberatively and critically concerning a public issue, is what should be done in the existing conditions of their country, so that the human rights of all the citizens can be protected in t h o s e conditions.

Thus an objective condition of democracy appears to be putting consciously as main objective of national policies the protection of human rights, which in turn presupposes the conception of the State based on human rights and n o t of the State "respectful to human rights", as many people of good will at present think.

In order that democracy can function in a given state, a first unanimity – like that of Rousseau's social contract – concerning putting the protection of human rights as the main objective of national policies is necessary.

At the turn of the century there is at least a verbal unanimity concerning the necessity to protect human rights. But we are not sufficiently aware that human rights, in order to be protected, should constitute the main objective of all policies. And we are not sufficiently aware of the kind of issues which can be and of those which cannot be objects of democratic decision – we are not sufficiently aware that democracy is not a goal or objective, but a form of government concerning what is public in a state, as we are not sufficiently aware that positive law at all levels has to be deduced from human rights, perhaps because we are not sufficiently aware of what human rights a r e and how they differ from other rights of the individual, i.e., we are not sufficiently aware of what kind of norms they are.

This is probably the main reason why we promote the free market economy (privatization of everything and globalization) and advocate the minimization of the State; and also promote the equal respect of all cultures – i.e., we promote these very little noticed traps for human rights.

We have to scrutinize these ideals of our times, which we expect to help us overcome poverty, social injustice and other global problems we are faced with. To do this, we need, first of all clear knowledge of what human rights are.

THE CONCEPT OF HUMAN RIGHTS AND THEIR KINDS

What are human rights? This simple question is crucial, because its answer also constitutes the c r i t e r i o n used, or to be used, in order to distinguish a human right from other rights and to tackle all other issues related to the theory and implementation of human rights.

What we call 'human rights' is first of all a n i d e a, a conception of the human mind: the conception that human beings, b e c a u s e they are h u m a n beings – i.e., because they belong to a species, which, due to its specificities, has produced the bread we eat, has discovered the electricity we use every moment, has written *The Little Prince* which some of us read, has brought the idea of equity (ἐπιείκεια), the institution of *ombudsman,* which some countries established, etc., i.e., because it has achieved all these – should be treated in a special way, in a way that makes possible for a human being to actualize such potentialities of the human being. It should be treated in this special way, because in life, human beings deprive other human beings of this possibility.

This is what art. 1 of the *Universal Declaration of Human Rights* intends to express, by stating that "all human beings are born free and equal in dignity and rights. They are endowed with reason and conscience and should act towards one another in a spirit of brotherhood".[1] This is, if I am not mistaken, the only article which words the conception of human rights underlying the main international human rights instruments.

Human beings should be treated by, and treat, other human beings in a special way, in a spirit of brotherhood, still not as Cain and Abel treated each other. But how?

The subsequent 28 articles of the *Declaration* are an attempt to answer this how. And the two *International Covenants* and other similar international instruments are attempts – or intend – to put forward the conditions of the possibility of such a treatment, i.e., to put forward norms – basic "universal" norms – to be made effective in the arrangement of social relations: in legislation at various levels and in the administration of public affairs, so that individuals have the possibility to actualize – each one as much as he or she can – the potentialities of the human being, I just mentioned.

What we call human rights are first of all ethical norms for the treatment of individuals, not only in the passive but also in the active sense. They are an attempt to introduce ethical concerns in social organization, in law and politics.

Human rights are rights of the individual. Now, when we look at the rights of the individual using the criterion proposed, we notice that, though they are interrelated and form an indivisible whole, as demands, they show some remarkable differences: a part of these demands is connected directly with human potentialities, another with the preconditions necessary for their development in general, while another part of them is connected with certain (changing) conditions. Personally I restrict the term 'human rights' to the first two kinds of demands and I include in the concept of human rights the interdictory demands concerning the security of the individual and/or the so-called "fundamental freedoms", as well as the demands related to the preconditions for the protection of human potentialities in general (rights such as the right to food, the right to health, the right to education, etc.)

The demands of the first kind are directly connected with the exercise of human potentialities. What they demand is that individuals be not hindered while exercising activities proper to the human being only. They demand the

---

[1] Emphasis added.

protection of rights which cannot be *given* (by the State), but can only be *respected* (or violated) in individuals by individuals.[2]

So, the respect for these rights appears first of all as an ethical question. The role of the State with regard to these rights is – or is expected to be – to prevent violations and in cases of violations to re-establish balances. Since we can speak of protection of these rights only when there are *attempts to violate* them, from the point of view of the State to protect these rights would mean to place them under the guarantee of Law, i.e., to try to prevent, by laws, the violation of these rights, and in cases of violations to intervene through its various organs.[3] Rights such as – to use the conventional wording – the liberty and security of the person and its implications (: no one shall be held in slavery or servitude; no one shall be subjected to torture or to cruel, inhuman or degrading treatment or punishment; no one shall be subjected to arbitrary arrest) and freedoms, such as of thought, opinion and their expression, fall under this category of rights, which are demands, demanding from everybody to do no harm to the value of the human being.

The so-called "fundamental freedoms" are the legal guarantees of these rights of the individual; they are there in order to guarantee that "nobody" touch an individual for any reason, while this individual is engaged in actualizing a human potentiality. Put in a legally valid document they guarantee the possibility to be demanded of everybody, but *not* the respect of these rights.

These rights constitute one part of the human rights in which *all human beings are equal*. Where these rights are protected, there the related freedoms *exist*: people "enjoy" these freedoms. Where they are not, there prevails insecurity – or anarchy and terror. And where they are violated by State organs, there reigns oppression. Viewing just once the news on television is sufficient to get an idea of what is going on: though everybody officially declares that all human beings are equal in dignity, insecurity and oppression prevail in a large part of our world, almost, perhaps, everywhere.

There is also another group of rights in which all human beings are equal, fundamental rights that *belong* to each individual, as *human* individual, i.e., which are not "given" by the State, but can be protected only indirectly. They are demands related to the preconditions affording each individual *the possibility* to develop his/her human potentialities, e.g., the right to food, the right to health, the right to education, etc. The difficulty with such rights is that their fulfilment is dependent on rights of another kind, on other rights *given* to individuals by the State – through social and economic rights – and through public institutions and organizations founded, not always but mostly, by political decisions.

---

[2] Government officers, too, are individuals.

[3] Saying this, of course, I don't forget the innumerable cases in which State organs violate these rights, thus undermining the very foundation of the State in question.

In opposition to the first group of human rights, the protection of these (also human) rights, does not depend d i r e c t l y on individuals, but on the social arrangements made and the political decisions taken in a country, not to forget: by individuals. They can be protected, i.e., fulfilled for the individuals in a country, only through public institutions and through g i v e n rights, the limits of which may be drawn differently according to the existing conditions in each country. What makes the limits drawn to these rights protect or not protect the human rights of which they are the means, depends on whether these limits are drawn with respect of the equality of all c i t i z e n s in a country. For, these are rights in which a l l *c i t i z e n s* a r e e q u a l, in spite of the fact that they are means to protect rights in which all h u m a n b e i n g s are equal.

IMPLICATIONS

Seen in the light of this knowledge of human rights the fashionable linking of human rights with the free market appears rather to be a result of linking value judgements than to express a factual or conceptual connection among them – a linking which, if taken for granted, as it is done now, might intensify even more social and global injustice and the already existing sharp economic disparities within and among countries, as well as create new disparities and disillusions in ex-socialist countries.

If we are sufficiently aware of what the state of affairs at present is and how it emerged, it is not very difficult to foresee it. Let me give you one main reason for this claim of mine: Social injustice is a problem related to the connection of social and economic rights with basic (human) rights. It is a state of affairs in which the possibilities of protection of one kind of basic rights, of the "indirectly protected basic rights" of the individual, such as the right to education, the right to physical and mental health, the right to a minimum standard of living, etc. – to use this time the conventional wording of these rights – are not e q u a l l y secured for all citizens in a country, i.e., the possibilities of fulfilling these rights are not afforded them in t h e s a m e d e g r e e, whatever this degree might be.

It is a state of affairs which appears when social and economic rights are given – i.e., laws delineating t h e l i m i t s of social and economic rights are enacted (and often quite "democratically", through parliamentary decisions) – without taking into consideration the implications they bear, a t t h a t m o m e n t, for the indirectly protected rights of the individual (for the right to food, to health, to education, etc.), in the existing conditions of a given country. In other words, it is a state of affairs emerging when determinants o t h e r t h a n the demands that human rights express, determine the delineation of the limits of social and economic rights in a country.

Thus economic disparities within non-affluent countries are the outcome of enacting laws, or of not abrogating laws, giving certain "rights", i.e., possibilities, used only by a few citizens, which have implications hindering the fulfilment of the basic rights of the majority of the citizens in the existing conditions of the given country. As a result, a few citizens may secure for themselves certain privileges while protecting their personal or group interests at the expense of the basic rights of the majority of the citizens, or sometimes even while protecting their basic rights to an extent surpassing the measure that the country's conditions allow. These are cases, in which governments cannot, or do not, keep a part of the citizens from exploiting other citizens and the State as well.

It is usually claimed that social injustice is the result of unequal distribution of what "exists". Yet in many developing countries, either the State cannot dispose of what exists, or, what is at its disposal is not enough for the fulfilment, *even to a minimum degree*, of certain of the basic rights of all citizens at that moment. Social injustice appears not only because of the unequal distribution of what exists, but also because of the unequal distribution of deprivations. Thus I dare say that social injustice has little to do with the degree of protection of the indirectly protected basic rights; it has rather to do with the failure to afford the *possibilities of equal protection* of these rights for all citizens, whatever the degree of this equal protection may be.

In a country where, by the equal distribution of deprivations, these rights of all citizens would be protected equally, even though to a low degree, there would be no question of social injustice at the national level; there, we are faced with the question of global injustice.

*

Global injustice and mainly economic disparities among countries have also to do with the way of putting in order economic relations among countries.

A global fact of the present time is that in a few countries of the world, the indirectly protected rights of the majority of the citizens are "protected" much more than human dignity requires, while in most countries of the world these rights of the majority of the citizens are protected very little or not at all.

A way to help developing countries to develop was economic aid, which developed-affluent countries extended to poor ones as an "aid" in the form of technical assistance and loans.

Still it appeared that most of the affluent countries, which extended this "aid", usually were not willing to make the least sacrifice in "protecting" to the maximum their interests, and that their "aid" consisted of loans with high rates of interest, given usually in view of their economic *and* political interests. Some economic projects elaborated with a more humane concern – like that of the North-South dialogue – did not reach their aim, and even deepened the already existing social and economic disparities, because they were probably elaborated without evaluating the social and intellectual conditions in these countries. As a result, domestic economic arrangements were made, without keeping an eye on human rights.

I am afraid that an unconditional promotion of the free market in poor and non-affluent countries, as well as in ex-socialist countries, if considered to be *the* solution to the economic problems they face, would lead to similar results for human rights in these countries; and on top of it, the free market coupled with the (well-minded, but not sufficiently scrutinized) demand to "respect all cultures" (*ergo* fundamentalism included), i.e., with a demand implying the "respect" also of cultures possessing basic elements contradicting human rights, could lead step by step to a new communalism and a new Middle Ages.

Thus it appears that any solution deemed to be a way out of the current stalemate of poverty, which is not put in connection with, and is not evaluated at least from the viewpoint of its predictable implications for, the protection of the different kinds of basic rights in the existing conditions of a country at *this* moment, and at the global level, would probably make the existing situation more and more chaotic in non-affluent countries.

Let me put it quite sharply: not only do I not see any conceptual or factual connection among human rights and the free market, but I also see a potential new impasse in the expectation that the free market (based on privatization, etc.) will lead to a better protection of human rights in most non-affluent countries.

The demand of the free market, in principle, amounts, simply put, to the demand that governments do not interfere in the economic activities of individuals, that governments leave them alone in this respect. In this case, it is claimed, the order of socio-economic relations, i.e., their establishment and change, will follow a spontaneous open process. In this process individuals would not only better protect their interests, but they would also have to protect the interests of other individuals.

The linkage of the free market with human rights betrays an intention to protect economic "freedom" as a basic right and to protect it in the way that *only one kind of basic rights*, which I call directly protected rights (e.g., the so-called freedom of thought, freedom of opinion, etc.), can be protected.

This seems to be due a) *to lack of distinction between different kinds of rights of the individual*, between an individual's basic (human) rights and his non-basic (social and economic) rights, and b) *to a confusion of the ways of protecting two different kinds of basic rights of the individual*. The way to protect, for example, the so-called "right to freedom of thought" is assumed to be also the way to protect what is assumed to be an individual's "economic freedom".

"Freedom" with regard to economic rights (or economic freedom) would mean *the absence of limits in the economic activities of the individual*, which would be in contradiction with the very nature of such rights: *that they are themselves limits* set thereto – be they in accordance or not with human rights. It would mean the absence of limits in the economic activities of the individual, whatever their products, or their results, might be. It would amount to demanding that "nobody" interferes with individuals, not only while they are engaged in actualizing special human potentialities, as one kind of human rights demands, but also while they act to protect their own interests, which not only clash inevitably with the interests of other individuals, but in many cases also with their human rights.

Consequently, the demand that the "free" market now brings in the case of non-affluent countries would amount not only to discarding governments, which mostly delineate the limits of economic rights according to private or group interests; but also to discarding *the possibility* of making basic rights determinants in the establishment and changing of economic relations within and among countries.

Thus, a *misconception of freedoms* seems to be at the root of considering the free market as a way out from the current stalemate of poverty, since the free market may function in the economic relations among countries which are, more or less, on the same level of economic development, but it constitutes a *trap* in the economic relations between developed and developing countries.

The same misconception of freedoms seems to be also among the main causes of the spread of fundamentalism, which takes advantage of the so-called freedoms of thought, conscience, opinion and expression, as well as of the much promoted "respect to the ethical and religious 'values' and cultural backgrounds of people" and propagates certain world views and norms, which are essentially contradictory to certain human rights.

*

These and other considerations make necessary to scrutinize our anticipated solutions of the problems we are faced with, as well as to scrutinize the conceptions underlying them; since these problems we are faced with at present are problems which we have created with our own decisions and action in the second half of the Twentieth Century.

This is, I think, the reason why we have to promote not the minimization of the State, but the conception of the State *based on human rights*. Since clearly conceived human rights constitute the ethical principles for – among other things – the establishment, in a given state, of the State under the rule of law *and* of the social State – they also constitute *the content* of the concepts of the State under the rule of law and of the social State – provided that we consider law to be a set of norms enforced in a country in order to *introduce justice* in the establishment of social relations and in the administration of public affairs in the states of our world. This amounts, in practice, to putting the protection of clearly conceived human rights as the main objective of national and international policies in the Twenty-first Century.

Human Rights as Ethical Principles and as Premises for the Deduction of Law*

The most significant achievement of humanity in the 20th Century is its bringing to the fore t h e i d e a of human rights. This occurred especially after the Second World War with the establishment of the United Nations.

But towards the end of the 20th Century human rights have become a fashionable concept, and as a result a slogan empty of content. A chain result of this is the inflation we observe in the number of the a s s u m e d human rights, and another the ever increasing conceptual confusion we observe in the international human rights instruments.

Thus, in spite of the fact that everybody now s p e a k s of human rights, flagrant human rights violations go on in many countries of the world; laws are enforced without any attempt to put them in connection with human rights, i.e., without taking into consideration the foreseeable consequences they bear for human rights; states violate the human rights not only of their citizens, but also those of the citizens of other countries.

Why? So far as I can see, one of the main reasons of this state of affairs – its main theoretical reason – is lack of sufficient k n o w l e d g e of what human rights are. If people really knew what human rights are, most of them – I am sure – would be ready to do everything they can for their protection.

This is why, I think, that before we start dealing with any theoretical or practical issue related to human rights, we need an epistemically justifiable answer to the question "what are human rights?"

*

What are human rights? This simple question is crucial, because its answer also constitutes the c r i t e r i o n used, or to be used, in order to distinguish a human right from other rights.

What we call 'human rights' is first of all a n i d e a, a conception of the human mind: the conception that human beings, b e c a u s e they are h u m a n beings – i.e., because they belong to a species, which, due to its specificities, has produced the bread we eat, has discovered the electricity we use every moment, has written *The Little Prince* which some of us read, has brought the idea of equity (ἐπιείκεια), the institution of *ombudsman,* which some countries establish, etc., i.e., because it has achieved all these – should be treated in a special way, in a way that makes it p o s s i b l e for a human being to actualize such potentialities of t h e human being. It should be treated in this special way,

---

* This is the English version of my "Etik İlkeler ve Hukukun Temel İlkeleri Olarak İnsan Hakları", published in *Ankara Barosu Hukuk Kurultayı* 4. Ankara, 2000, pp. 5-10.

because in life, most human beings deprive other human beings of this possibility.

This is what the art. 1 of the *Universal Declaration of Human Rights* intends to express, by stating that "all human beings are born free and equal in dignity and rights. They are endowed with reason and conscience and should act towards one another in a spirit of brotherhood". This is, if I am not mistaken, the only article which words the conception of human rights underlying the main international human rights instruments.[1]

Human beings should be treated, by other human beings, in a special way, in a spirit of brotherhood, still not as Cain and Abel treated each other. But how?

The subsequent 28 articles of the Declaration are an attempt to answer this how. And the two *International Covenants* and other similar international instruments are attempts – or intend – to put forward the conditions of the possibility of such a treatment, i.e., to put forward norms – basic "universal" norms – to be made effective in the arrangement of social relations: in legislation at various levels and in the administration of public affairs, so that individuals have the possibility to actualize – each one as much as he or she can – the potentialities of the human being, which I mentioned earlier.

What we call human rights are first of all ethical principles for the treatment of individuals, not only in the passive but also in the active sense. They are an attempt – still a very deficient attempt not only in practice but also in theory – to introduce ethical demands in social organization, in law and politics.

Still when we read the various international human rights instruments, keeping in mind certain epistemological distinctions – concerning knowledge, norms, etc., – we observe that the norms (or the rights) mentioned there are of different kinds and of different scope, and that sometimes contradict each other – a fact which bears implications for the actual protection of human rights, e.g., for the question of restriction of rights, for legislation based on human rights instruments and the implementation of the demands (or imperatives) that human rights bring, in general and in special given cases.

This makes necessary to reflect anew on norms in general and on human rights as basic, universal norms (for legislation and the implementation of law) in the light of the present situation of the world – i.e., in the light of what is called "misuse" of human rights – on the one hand, and on the other in the light of violations of human rights through the application of certain laws – a "misuse" which the world community at present tries to prevent by increasing the number of human rights instruments and by trying to reach a consensus in the understanding of single rights. Still little attention is paid to problems which

[1] See also: Ioanna Kuçuradi, "Human Rights. The Idea, the Demands and the Instruments", in *The Idea and the Documents of Human Rights*. Ankara, 1995, pp. 75-92, in the present volume pp. 101-111.

become visible, when we look at these instruments keeping in mind the problems faced in practice and with philosophically clarified concepts of the terms involved, i.e., of the terms which follow the expression "the right to ...".

*

What kind of norms are human rights? To answer this question, let me first say a few words on the concept of norm.

The existence of norms, of different and changing norms, is a (human) fact, related to a specificity of being human: the establishing of social relations, i.e., the creation of social roles, assumed by concrete individuals.

Norms are deduced, undeliberately or deliberately, in order to create an order in a given group, i.e., in order to secure measures for the right and wrong, consequently in order to determine the conduct of individuals or the way how social relations will be established among the individual members of a given group. Whoever assumes or finds himself in a given role, has to behave in accordance with the norms constituting that role.

Norms are usually worded as "ought", "should", "must" or "may" propositions. This means that propositions of norms are not propositions of knowledge, i.e., they have no object independent of those who put them forth. Consequently norms are neither true nor false.[2]

This is the main epistemological specificity of norms and also the origin of the difficulties faced in evaluating a given norm: norms cannot be verified or falsified; their evaluation presupposes a different epistemological treatment.

Compared with propositions of knowledge norms are thoughts, deduced from epistemologically very different premises and by different kinds of reasoning.

The axiological specificity of a norm depends on the epistemological specificity of its premises. Its justification or "foundation" is related to the possibility of going back to its origins – to the premises from which it is deduced – and of seeing their epistemic specificity, i.e., whether the premises from which a given norm is deduced are knowledge or other norms, and what kind of knowledge or norms.

This epistemological evaluation, which every norm has to undergo, is something quite different from the ways of validating or enforcing a norm. The latter are different social or political procedures, aiming at establishing a broad consensus on a given norm. To find out how a moral norm was made valid presupposes sociological research, while to find out how a legal norm was enforced, one has to read the minutes of the sessions of the bodies which the enforcement of such a norm depends on.

[2] For this point see: Ioanna Kuçuradi, "Knowledge and its Object", in Ioanna Kuçuradi and Robert Cohen (eds), *The Concept of Knowledge*, Boston Studies in the Philosophy of Science 170. Kluwer Academic Publishers, Dordrecht, 1995, pp. 97-102.

What we see in the present world, is a search for consensus on given norms, without taking into consideration the epistemological-axiological specificities of the given norms. This is also one of the main dangers of "democratic" decisions in our present world. It makes possible the enforcement, by consensus or by the majority of votes, of norms which are contradictory to human rights.

What I said concerning the epistemological-axiological specificity of norms is true for both moral and legal norms.

What we call 'morals' are systems of norms, which individuals in a given group (or in a given culture) have to follow in their relations with others, in action: of norms of behaviour or conduct, as well as of norms of evaluation. They are the "good"s and the "bad"s prevailing in a given group – a given "society" or "culture".

Now, if we take some distance and look at these moral norms, we easily observe that a part of such norms prevailing in given groups or "cultures" is different, and that it is also changing with the time within the same groups, that even a way of behaviour, once prohibited, becomes promoted or *vice versa*. We also see that the same single action – of yours or mine – is qualified by prevailing different norms on the same issue, simultaneously, as good and bad. This fact, which postmodernism, by losing sight of the specificity of another kind of norms, attempted to justify theoretically, has led some people, and especially the young in so-called "Western society", to the (theoretical) rejection of all and all kinds of norms.[3]

Still besides this observation, we also observe that another part of norms does not show, to a great extent, such a difference or change – for example "for one, to keep one's word". People in each culture or group are expected to obey – to follow or use – both these kinds of moral norms.

In view of this fact, the first distinction we have to make, is between the norms of evaluation – the so-called value judgements – and the norms of behaviour or conduct, though they can be easily translated into each other, since the role they are expected to play is different.

Norms of moral evaluation – or general proposition on what is good or bad – are expected to determine our evaluations, i.e., to be used in order to determine the value of an evaluated object – be it an action, a person, a situation, etc. –; while norms of moral conduct or "ought-should" propositions are expected to determine our actions in life. In other words, norms of evaluation are supposed to lead those who use them as criteria, to the knowledge of the value of given actions of yours or mine – which is not the case –; while norms of behaviour – moral rules or principles – are expected to determine actions carried out in given situations – your actions, my actions, etc.

[3] See also: Jeanne Hersch, "'Cultural Development' a Tentative Answer", in *Philosophy and Cultural Development*. Ankara, 1993, pp. 31-32.

And the "ought" or "should" of these latter norms of conduct or behaviour is deduced from premises of different epistemic specificities and by different ways of reasoning.

For my purpose, I shall confine myself here to pointing only at two kinds of such norms: those deduced in different given historical conditions from experience by induction and those deduced by the comparison of different given (human or historical) conditions in the light of the knowledge of the specificities of *the* human being – or of what is called human dignity. The first kind of norms may be justified – if wished – statistically, the second by a kind of reasoning similar to *reductio ad absurdum*.

At the origin of the first kind of norms (of behaviour) are given natural-social conditions, as well as the conceptions of different cultures concerning the human being. They are norms of behaviour relative to the existing conditions, possessing a practical function, aiming at establishing or safeguarding any order in those existing conditions at the moment they are deduced. So long as the conditions in which they are deduced prevail, if deduced with sagacity, they are functional. But when these conditions change, they lose their function and meaning, i.e., the "ought"s or "must"s they express, lose their ground. Many traditional-customary ways of behaviour transmitted from generation to generation in a given cultural group, belong to this kind of norms. Thus we see that though in time the conditions wherefrom these norms are deduced do not exist any more – which means that there is no more a justifiable reason of the "ought" they express – people in this group try to keep them going. We even see attempts to revive obsolete norms.

Still, in time, new norms on the same issues are deduced from the changed conditions, mostly incompatible with the old ones. And right here we find the point where the so-called "crisis of values", to a great extent, arises from. It seems that those who insist on keeping valid such norms, are unaware of the source wherefrom the "ought" or "must" of these norms is deduced, i.e., that they are unaware of their epistemic specificities.

Norms of this kind – to which many proverbs or products of practical wisdom also belong – are deduced, by evaluating the effects this or that way of behaviour has had, i.e., the benefit or harm they mostly (or often) caused to those who happened to behave in this or that manner. This kind of norms tells us, in fact, so much: when someone behaves in this or that way, the probability of safeguarding his benefit or interests, and sometimes those of the others, increases. In other words: when, in a given case, one is unable to make a right evaluation, but possesses the will to protect what is considered to be in such a case his benefit or interest – or that of the group to which he belongs – it is more probable to protect it, if he behaves in the way the relevant norm (rule, etc.) demands. This does not, of course, exclude the possibility that, in a given case, following this norm one causes harm to his benefit or interest and to those of the others. The different norms which distinguish one culture from another are mostly norms of this kind. This is also the kind of norms which those who advocate equal respect to all cultures invite us to respect and which those who promote cultural identities wish to revive, without evaluating them, i.e., without taking into consideration the implications they bear, in the existing conditions, for the human beings who are born by chance by a mother and/or father brought up in a given cultural group.

As to the other kind of norms (or "ought" propositions), originating in the knowledge of the value of the human being: they are deduced from this knowledge, directly or indirectly, in the face of human or historical conditions doing harm to this value (e.g., "thou shall not kill", "no racial discrimination shall be made").

I would say that the reasoning which leads to the deduction of such a norm (or principle) is made – schematically – as follows: if the value or the specificity of the human being is such and such, or, since the human species possesses such and such potentialities, no one belonging to this species – you, me – should do anything that harms this value, i.e., which abolishes the possibility of actualization of such potentialities. Such norms are often worded in the passive, i.e., they demand that no one belonging to the human species should undergo any treatment which abolishes the possibility of the actualization of such potentialities (for example: "no one shall be subjected to torture", etc.).

A typical example of this kind of norms is what we call human or basic rights. Human rights express – in fact, intend to express – ethical demands concerning how each and every individual belonging to the human species should be treated by and should treat other individuals in general (whoever they might be and whatever their special situation might be), if human dignity is to be protected in practice.

In positive law we find all these kinds of norms. Here, I shall confine myself to saying a few words only on certain differences between moral and legal norms, which is directly relevant to our issue.

Legal norms express, among other things, limits within which real or legal individuals may move, acts that one should-may or should not-may not perform, as well as the treatment which one has to undergo when he transgresses or violates these limits.

They also express arrangements of social relations, i.e., how real or legal individuals, which assume the relevant roles should behave or treat, and be treated by, each other. These norms are what we call rights and their complementary duties.

Rights, in general, are "rights of someone". To use the Platonic concept of right, which I find quite appropriate: a right is something due (ὀφειλόμενον) to somebody by somebody else. In the case of human rights:

they express the treatment which is due to each human being by other human beings.

It usually escapes attentions that human rights demand a treatment not only in the passive, but also in the active sense – something that has negative implications especially in the education of human rights. For example, human rights teaching mostly appears combined with civics, and not with ethics, i.e., it intends to teach people what their rights are and how they shall demand them, rather than to educate people who possess to will to protect human rights and are sufficiently equipped with the knowledge necessary for this protection.

Human rights, as they are worded in the international instruments, intend to express demands concerning what each being and every human being should not suffer, i.e., what direct and indirect treatment should or should not undergo, so that a human individual may actualize, as much as each one can, the human potentialities – ethical ones included – which constitute what we call human dignity.

Still, too often, individuals do not treat other individuals in the way that human rights demand. Then, who will do that?

If we look at the international human rights instruments, i.e., at the addressees in these instruments – with the exception of the *Universal Declaration of Human Rights*, whose addresses are "every individual and every organ of society" – the answer appears to be clear: the instrument which will safeguard – directly or indirectly – the treatment of individuals in the way that human rights demand is the State in each state.[4]

Signing such an instrument is a promise that a (given) state gives to its citizens and to the other states involved. By signing such an instrument a state promises to its citizens and to the world community, that it will implement – i.e., it will make determinant – the demands that human rights express or the relevant right expresses; it guarantees (at least verbally, by a speech act), that individuals in that given country will be treated in the way that human rights demand. It guarantees that laws – legal norms – will be deduced from those basic principles in the conditions of the given country and that these laws will be indeed implemented by those who are responsible of their implementation – by state and public officers, the judges, the police, etc.

But what if there are contradictory norms in these international instruments? I leave this question here aside.

*

Let me now sum up the specificity of the norms or principles we call human rights, i.e., what distinguishes them from moral-cultural and legal norms:

[4] For this point see: Ioanna Kuçuradi, "Der Staat, die Staaten und die Menschenrechte", in Gregor Paul, Thomas Göller, Hans Lenk und Guido Rappe (eds), *Humanität, Interkulturalität und Menschenrecht*. Peter Lang, 2001, pp. 374-393.

a) Human rights are norms (principles) deduced, in given historical conditions, from the knowledge of the value of certain human potentialities. They express the general preconditions deemed necessary for the actualizability of those human potentialities. They bring demands for the treatment of *every* human being. The so-called "universality" of human rights is this specificity of theirs, and not, as it is usually assumed, its worldwide validity. This specificity is also the reason why we should do everything to make these principles *valid* worldwide as much as possible, provided that we re-evaluate our international instruments, since we can made valid worldwide, by the necessary formal procedures, every kind of norms.

Cultural norms, on the other hand, are deduced successfully or unsuccessfully, by induction only from empirical (local) conditions. They aim at protecting the interests of a *given* group, usually against the interests of other groups. Many legal norms are deduced from, or are the legalization of, such norms.

The epistemological-axiological specificity of human rights is the reason why, clearly conceived human rights should constitute the *basic norms* for the direct and indirect deduction of legal norms, i.e., they should constitute the major premises for the deduction of positive law, provided that we are well aware that law exists for the implementation of justice (of human rights) and the protection of human dignity, and not for acrobatic defense of mere personal or group interests, which, as interests, unavoidably clash with each other.

What we see now in positive law is a mixture of legal norms, some deduced from human rights and some others directly from cultural conceptions, i.e., the value judgements prevailing in a given group. And this is what makes possible the enforcement of discrepant norms on the same issue.

b) Human rights are norms concerning the way how a human individual, and every human individual, should or should not *be treated*. This is what it makes such a norm a right and then a *human* right. Thus, considered from the passive perspective, human rights are basic norms for legislation.

c) Still, considered from the active perspective, they are also norms of conduct in interhuman public relations. They express the *minimum conditions* of ethical action in public life.

This is the reason why human rights as principles of action, in order to be effective presuppose that individuals 1) possess *the will* to act accordingly, 2) possess *clear knowledge* of their content, and 3) develop the *intellectual capacity* to find out their implications in a given case.

The knowledge of the epistemological specificities of human rights makes us see, among other things, also the following: All kinds of practical norms (of moral and legal norms), independently of the premises and the way they are deduced, aim at creating *an order* in a given group. And now the question arises: is the *existence* of order – of any order – sufficient for the protection of human rights? If we can overcome the prevailing prejudice, or value judgement, that "order is good", we can see that *not any order* makes possible the humanization of individuals – i.e., the exercising of their human potentialities. What human rights aim at, is the permanent creation of such an order.

This makes us also see that Law is not sufficient in itself for that, but only laws deduced in given historical conditions in the light of human rights. It is very possible – as is often the case – to give damage to human rights through Law, not only because the legislator cannot take into consideration all relevant complicate cases that may appear, but also because laws are often legalization of cultural norms or group interests.

Thus d) considered from the perspective of the State, human rights appear to be demands concerning the basic duties of the State in a given state – i.e., the duties of every state to its citizens. Those duties amount to legislating in accordance with clearly conceived human rights (this is what is called at present adaptation of national law to the international human rights instruments); they also amount to securing the application of such laws and above all to educating those who are expected to apply or implement those laws (State and public officer, judges, etc.), so as to become able to do so.

Such legislation, implementation and education depend first of all on clear knowledge about each human right, i.e., it presupposes that those who are responsible of the implementation and education of human rights, have sufficient philosophical knowledge of the conditions that human rights demand and have become able to put in connection this knowledge with the cases they will face.

THE IDEA OF DEVELOPMENT ITS PAST AND ITS PRESENT*

This paper is an attempt to conceptualize and evaluate an idea that has marked the national and international policies after the Second World War: the idea of development.

But what is an 'idea' – this overloaded term of the history of philosophy? By 'idea', in the context we deal with, I mean a special kind of thought: a conception of the mind, which in distinction from 'knowledge' – each piece of which is related to an object independent from itself – engenders its object; and which in distinction from 'belief' – which also creates its object – is not bound to those who "have" it. Ideas are brought to history, where they remain effective for a while or for good, i.e., they are added to the historical being.

This specificity of ideas seems to be the cause of their obscurity, and consequently of the variety of definitions given of them, or of the variety of their conceptions. Yet this specificity of theirs, at the same time, makes it possible for philosophy to objectify them, i.e., to make them the object of philosophical inquiry and evaluation, the first step of which is to conceptualize them. And this is quite a difficult job, still not as difficult in the case of "development", as it may seem at first glance.

Development o r evolution *(Entwicklung, ἐξέλιξις)* and progress are ideas, which though introduced earlier, were brought to the fore by 19th Century philosophers, still i n c o n n e c t i o n w i t h s p e c i a l b e a r e r s. They have also marked the thinking of our century and indeed in a truthful manner to this past of theirs.

These ideas, be they considered as teleological or causal conceptions of becoming or change, and in spite of the shifts and discrepancies we see in the way they are conceived, have shared a common characteristic during our century: the positive value judgement inherited from the 19th Century, i.e., that development or progress, whatever it be, is something good, something worthwhile, something to wish for. It is this value judgement that has been shaken recently. In this, a part was played not only by practice, i.e., the developmental policies followed all over the world during the past four decades, but also by theory – the theories of development which follow each other.

---

* This paper was published in Ioanna Kuçuradi (ed.), *The Idea of Development. Between its Past and its Future*, Ideas Underlying Global Problems 1, International Federation of Philosophical Societies and Philosophical Society of Turkey. Ankara, 1993, pp. 3-17.

Here I shall not dwell on these theories,[1] nor on the history of this idea. I shall confine myself to scrutinizing, just a little, and submit to discussion, a few interrelated points, which, when we take a look at the philosophical and other theoretical as well as practical treatments of the question of development, appear to need further consideration. So I shall focus here on the question of development in connection with its bearers – i.e., those which are expected to develop – and on the question of goals in connection with the concept of development. This may perhaps help us to better evaluate the proposed "new concepts" of development, i.e., indigenous, cultural, self-reliant, sustainable development, etc., which are expected to guide practice at the turn of the century.

*

Why was the positive value judgement concerning "development" shaken, though its being considered the principal objective of national policies all over the world was not?

A simple answer would be – and, in fact, is – "because it did not answer expectations". Whose expectations and expectations of what? Still neither value judgements,[2] be they positive or negative, nor psychological factors are sufficient in judging a situation, or evaluating a goal or an idea determining practice.

There are, however, facts – different facts in different categories of countries – which allow us to do so. These facts which are, to a great extent, the outcome of national development policies followed within the framework of the given global situation after the Second World War, appear to be closely connected with the prevailing conception of development – especially with the underlying conception of its bearer and the question of goals.[3]

Let me start from the prevailing conception of development in Third World countries, in general, the so-called "under-developed" in the beginning, which seems to be conceptually a more consistent term, and later, more politely "developing countries": previous colonies of European countries or not, and other countries in which "westernization" or "modernization" movements and the relevant debates had started much earlier, starting in some of them, in the second half of the 19th Century.[4]

---

[1] For a review of such theories, see Jan Berting, "The Goals of Development in Developed Countries", in *Goals of Development*. UNESCO, 1988, pp. 141-181.

[2] For this term, see, my "From Revolt to Philosophy", in *Philosophers on their Own Work 1*. Bern, 1984, pp. 109-111.

[3] It is noteworthy to mention for example, that the term 'development' in this context, was translated into Turkish not by 'gelişme', as it is usually done in all other contexts, but by 'kalkınma', which connotes welfare.

[4] For the case of Turkey, see Abdullah Kaygı, *Türk Düşüncesinde Batılılaşma ve/veya Çağdaşlaşma Fikri* [The Idea of Westernization and/or Modernization in Turkish Thought]. Dissertation, Hacettepe University, Department of Philosophy. Ankara, 1990.

Put very briefly, since it is now sufficiently known, "development" in these countries, conceived on the "model" of the West, still reduced only to its economic factors, i.e., industrialization, progress of technology and "high" national product or *per capita* income, gave rise to practices, which have, in fact, secured a slight or considerable increase of the *per capita* income in these countries and led, at least some of them, to make some steps on the way to industrialization, but have, nevertheless, coupled with the rapid increase of population and some other factors, broadened the gap between the rich and the poor, as well as they caused an increase in the number of the poor in these countries, i.e., they sharpened economic disparities and, what is worse, they deepened social injustice.

By 'deepening social injustice' I mean the unfavourable increase in the number (and ratio) of those, whose the indirectly protected basic rights – their rights to a minimum standard of living, to education, health care, etc. – were less and less protected.

Waves of migration to the First World, political agitation, terrorism, *coups d'état* are among the facts we see in many Third World countries during the Decades of Development.

Now, looking at the conception of development guiding practice carried out in various Third World countries, we see that "development" is conceived – by themselves as well as by the so-called developed countries – rather as a goal than as a process. It is conceived as a state of affairs aimed at: the state of affairs in the countries considered already "developed". To reach this state of affairs – as if it were a stable point – and catch up with the West, it would be sufficient to do what "the West" was supposed to have done in this respect – to industrialize and develop or import technology. In this conception of development we see that the goal and the process (that these countries or societies would have to undergo), or better: the goal to be attained and what has to be done in order to attain this goal, amount to the same thing.

Such seems to be, roughly put, at the bottom, the conception of development, which has constituted, with capitalistic and socialistic accentuations, the main objective of national policies in most of the Third World countries – a category, which has recently become problematic, like the "First" and "Second" Worlds.

Now, if what was intended by bringing to the fore the idea of development, was merely progressing in industrialization, technology and increase of national product or *per capita* income, i.e., if what was expected to develop in this sense, were merely t h e c o u n t r i e s under consideration, in other words, if the bearer of development is assumed to be a country, there should be, in the case of many Third World countries, apparently, no reason to complain so much. Being patient would be sufficient. This is, in fact, the way those in power in some Third World countries reason, when they proudly praise the achievements of their development policies; while the great majority in these countries becomes less and less able to meet its basic needs. "Some growth enclaves" observes Louis Baeck, the Belgian economist, "have produced more results than would have been expected. Whoever sees for the first time the wonders of urban-industrial growth in such places as Sao Paolo, Singapore, Abidjan, Caracas, Hong Kong, Mexico City, Taipeh..., will probably be amazed. But as soon as the initial enchantment is dispelled, a more sober assessment prevails. Within the growth enclaves, these harsh modernizers have sometimes achieved spectacular results. But the national product is usually distributed so unequally between classes and regions that social tensions regularly heat up. In order to keep the lid on this seething pot, these regimes are often forced to follow even more an already harsh policy".[5]

These development policies carried out, i.e., financed, to a considerable extent by "foreign aid" (i.e., loans from developed countries) with political implications, have not only broadened the gap between the rich and the poor in these countries, but, with the exception of a couple of countries, also broadened the gap between the few rich and the majority of poor countries. Thus, here it is quite obvious that the policies followed in the "Decades of Development", not only have failed to lead to the state of affairs aimed at, i.e., to catch up with the "developed" countries, but have also created their own facts. The debts of these countries have reached such a point, that it seems improbable, if not impossible, that these countries become able to pay them back at all. A cold-blood – rational, in the sense used in the science of economics – calculation, shows that "developing" countries – if no miracle interferes – are condemned to remain for ever "developing" in the sense assumed.

These and such other facts, as well as reaction to the formerly colonising "arrogant" West, made people in the Third World, and especially in Africa and Latin America, speak of "indigenous development", "self reliant development", etc., and to adopt immediately the idea of the so-called "cultural development", which was introduced also by the West, in connection with its own problems, yet "cultural development" in a special, quite different sense. Right now we are in the World Decade of Cultural Development.

Thus theories and conceptions of development replace each other, each influences practice and produces its own undesirable, but irreversible, facts. And the search for new conceptions keeps on. Do we really need this idea?

To tackle with this question, we have also to take a look in connection with the question of development, at the so-called "developed countries". But even before doing this, though it might sound strange after so many theories and conceptions of development we possess, we have to ask once again: What is development?

[5] Louis Baeck, "Shifts in Concepts and Goals of Development", in *Goals of Development, op.cit.*, p. 41.

*

Now, when we look at the term 'development', within contexts where this term is used in a "natural" way in a few different languages, in view to broadly fix the limits of the concept, so as to distinguish it from, or to put it in a right connection with, other related concepts (e.g., evolution, progress; change, becoming), we get one possible clue for the consideration of its ambiguous uses. We see that it denotes (in English) a) in its active use, a human activity: to frame and work out in full detail a whole, in the light of a guiding end (we develop a project, a plan, an idea, etc.) and b) in its passive or reflective use, an ontical category, a process undergone by a given bearer, yet a bearer that possesses, or is supposed to possess, certain potentialities, which are expected to be actualized *up to a limit* peculiar to that bearer. This limit constitutes the state of conditions that once reached by the bearer, starts for him the process of decaying. Living individual beings, and among them human beings, are examples of this "development". Any interference with this development can be carried out only within the limits peculiar to that bearer.

Thus 'development' in the later sense, denotes a fact, connected with the process of becoming of the aforementioned kind of individual bearers. I think that any conception of development, which does not keep in mind this distinction and its implications – as has been the case up to now – and consequently does not keep itself within these conceptual limits, is condemned, from the beginning, to be one among the many cognitively unjustifiable conceptions – or "theories" – of development. For, such a conceptual frame of development implies, among other things, that any conception of development concerning bearers which do not possess the aforementioned ontical specificity, is condemned to lead to an impasse, for the following reason: such conceptions of development presuppose either an open or hidden teleological approach to becoming – and in our case, to history – i.e., becoming as a linear process possessing an "intrinsic" goal, yet to be never reached; or a melioristic approach to becoming, which amounts to applying the idea of progress, as a non-teleological conception of a linear becoming of a bearer – or supposed bearer – toward better and better states. Both are, however, reductionist approaches to different kinds of (real) being.

It seems that we have made out of a fact – concerning a special kind of process – an idea (in the sense of the German *'Vorstellung'*), a vague idea concerning a desirable state of affairs, that of the already "developed" West in the second half of our century, yet interpreted in a problematic way, i.e., reduced to only a couple of its ingredients; and out of this idea we have made out an ideal and put it as a goal to be attained by the other – "not yet developed" – countries.

Such a conceptual framework, i.e., these minimal conceptual prerequisites of "development", makes us also see on the one hand, that we have confused a process – which is a natural phenomenon – with an activity – which is a human phenomenon –; and on the other, that a) development, as an ontical category –

as a special kind of process – cannot have or be given "goals" and b) what we are trying to do just now, is an attempt to re-evaluate our shaken value judgement concerning development, to question its significance as something that we have wanted, i.e., development as main objective of national policies all over the world. In other words: what we try to question is not "development", but t h e o b j e c t i v e s of the national and international policies of the last few decades; we question t h e a c t i v i t i e s carried out i n t h e n a m e of "development".

"The goals of development" have been an issue of debate during the past few years. After the disappointment to which development considered as a "goal" – i.e., as the main objective of national policies – has led through the facts that these policies created, the question of its value or significance a s o b j e c t i v e was raised. The expression "goals of development" marks a change in the approach to the problem: it expresses the conception that "development" – always economic development – must tend to something else, must mean "the conditions towards which we would like to see development to tend".[6]

This approach is a different expression of the so-called cultural development in one sense, i.e, of the present tendency "to add a cultural dimension to (economic) development", and which has led to the proclamation, by the UN, of the World Decade of Cultural Development.

Still: what was and is meant by 'cultural development'?

*

'Cultural development' represents the present state in the development of the idea of development. It was introduced, by the West, as a way out of the impasse in which it has found itself in the middle of the second half of the 20th Century, and it was immediately adopted by the Third World, yet 'cultural development' in a quite different sense.

Let us take only a look at what happened: the idea of development, put in the fifties as the principal objective of national policies of all the countries of the UN, it was interpreted by the already "developed countries" – and there is nothing to make us wonder in that – as a linear unlimited quantitative increase of industrial and technological production (as "the bigger the better principle"), which, coupled with the political polarization between the First and Second Worlds, has led to unforeseen outcomes in the West, quite diverging, there also, from the expectation of those who had introduced it – to pollution, to the arms race, as well as to what was called the "crisis of values". It is after these outcomes that people in the West started asking "development, what for"? (a rhetoric question, indeed), and started speaking of the need for a "new conception of development", which could lead out of the faced crisis. "Cultural development"

[6] Preface, *ibid.*

has been t h e n a m e of this "new conception" – which is also an idea not sufficiently scrutinized up to now.

It seems that, what Western people have mainly understood from 'cultural development' was the broadening, for the masses, of the possibility to have "access to and participation in culture",[7] i.e., to the activities considered to afford to individuals the possibility to develop their potentialities as human beings – e.g., to artistic, scientific, philosophical activities.

Yet in the Third World countries, which do not partake in the so-called Western or European culture, people understood from 'cultural development', the development of their "cultural identity". In decolonized Third World countries it was understood as developing – i.e., identifying and reconstructing – their o w n culture, which, they assume, was suppressed or forgotten under the influence of Western culture during the colonization era. They started trying to identify the culture – i.e., the conception of Man and the conception concerning what is valuable – which they think is, and wish to be, their o w n. (This is what is going on especially in Africa at present.) While in Third World countries, which are "in the process of modernization" and which have opted for "modernization", 'cultural development' is understood as 'resurrection' or 'revival' of the culture, i.e., of the conceptions of Man and of what is valuable, prevailing among them before they came into touch with the West.

Thus, when we look in this connection at the present situation as a whole, we see that what is called in non-Western circles "crisis of identity", is something coinciding with what in the West is called "crisis of values". The Western people think that they do not know any longer what their "values" are; the Third World people think, either that they do not k n o w who they really are, or, that they are not those who, a t t h i s m o m e n t, in fact, t h e y a r e. Yet all share the view – the value judgement – that 'culture', whatever it be and whatever each one's culture may be, is something "good", something the "basic substance" of which has to be restored in each of them. This is something of which the possibility as well as the necessity seems very problematic. "Affirming and enriching cultural identities" constitutes the second objective of the World Decade of Cultural Development.

Thus we observe an attempt, at global level, to make possible a marriage of "economic and cultural developments" – the latter understood in two different senses. This attempt is very well reflected in the objectives of the Decade, the first being "acknowledgement of the cultural dimension of development", from which the second objective – i.e., "affirming and enriching cultural identities" – and the third one – i.e., "broadening access and participation to culture" – follow. In these two objectives, the term 'culture' and 'cultural' do not denote the same thing. The latter objective appears to be an answer to a need felt by the Western World, the former as an answer to a need of the Third World.

---

[7] This is the wording of one of the four objectives of the World Decade of Cultural Development.

This is the point where the dissatisfaction with the outcome of the Decades of Economic Development has led, and this search is interpreted by some as "emphasizing the [neglected] moral basis of development",[8] to which church organized movements in Latin America and "the cultural reassertion of Islam" are given as examples. This is, to my mind, a wrong interpretation.

I think that the search for "one's own", different "cultural values", "spiritual values" or "meaning", which is going around the world, reflects rather a revolt against the present state of Western culture; and the conviction that religions are the place to find these "spiritual values" reflects a lack of philosophical knowledge concerning what value, values, meaning, and such human phenomena are.

The now open revolt of the people of the Third World against the West, and the unexpected, rapid changes in Europe (the abolishment of the boundary between the First and Second Worlds), have led us at the turn of the century, into a situation, which we have difficulties to evaluate, since we are used to evaluate situations only by models. We have no model right now for such an evaluation. I think we are lucky; since what we need, is a right evaluation of the new situation. On such an evaluation, which has nothing to do with models, depends the setting of appropriate – humane – goals for our small worlds, as well as for our One World.

*

Goals are objects of volition – as objectives, purposes, intentions, aims, etc., are – and as objects of volition determinants of action. Goals and objectives are impersonal objects of volition, while purposes and intentions are rather personal. All of them are closely related with the question of value and meaning. We have to question the value of our proposed goals, not their meaning, because the value and the meaning of something we want, do not always coincide.

Meaning, formally expressed, is the subjective correlate of the knowledge of the value of something. Something is meaningful for somebody. Value, on the other hand, belongs to the characteristics of something; it is an object of knowledge. Still, in life, individuals not only try to know the value of what they evaluate, but also ascribe (or impute) value to it. They do it in the light either of their interests or of something meaningful for them.

Collective value ascriptions to ideas are a fact of the human world. Among the goals set by collectivities – even by mankind at a given historical moment – we see many ideas of this kind.

Goals, in general, are ideas which constitute points of orientation for the deduction of objectives or for action in a given real situation. Viewed from the standpoint of those who set them, they are what they want to become continuously real, or what they believe should become real.

---

[8] Louis Baeck, *op. cit.*, pp. 48-53.

Now when we look at set goals, we can distinguish at least two main kinds, which, as determinants of action function exactly in the same way, but philosophically evaluated have quite different implications concerning the question of value. One kind consists of ideas, which find their origin in the knowledge of the value of Man, i.e., the knowledge of his specificity compared to other beings. Justice and human rights can be given as examples to these ideas. The other kind are goals consisting of ideas, to which a given group has ascribed value at a given time. Collective "ideals" are mostly this kind of determinants, e.g., the unity of the workers of the world, panturanism, etc.

Ideas of the former kind concern, in general, the conditions of the possibility of the actualization of certain human potentialities, which secure to the human species its special place in the universe. Set as goals, they constitute the common determinant of different (special) objectives, and consequently of aims, in different real given situations, i.e., they determine the concrete object of volition in each real situation, which is, each time, of course, unique. Thus they determine action indirectly, through the concrete thing wanted in the given case, and in a quite special way: neither causally nor teleologically, but, I would say, "vertically", i.e., permanently.

As for goals consisting of ideas to which a group ascribed value: they are put forth as answers to different needs felt in given historical situations, by those who set them. They constitute what these people want in general and in each individual case to become real. They determine all action directly and in a teleological way – i.e., without the mediation of a special object of volition in different given situations. Whatever the situation may be, the object of volition remains the same. Here goals and objectives amount to same thing.

There are also other differences between these two kinds of goals – and, of course, of ideas – on which I shall not dwell here.

Development appears to be an idea which has been ascribed value and put as the main objective of the national policies in all the countries in the world, i.e., in countries where often totally different real conditions are observed. We have experimentally seen the deadlock to which it has led. "Cultural development", in the sense of "developing one's own cultural identity", I am afraid, seems to be another such idea. It is right now creating its own facts, which seem to contradict the intentions of the proclamation of this World Decade, and I dare say, also the intentions of a part of those who want it.

The new goals we are looking for – not for "development", but for collective social and political action – have to be ideas of the first kind, in the light of which we could find what right now, at the turn of the century, we want to and we can attain in the existing historical conditions, i.e., to fix our new objectives.

Human rights – clearly conceptualized – appear to be such a candidate. For they demand the permanent creation of conditions – always changing conditions – which afford to individuals the possibility of *developing* their potentialities, as human beings, i.e., the conditions which are normally necessary for human development, or the conditions which make possible for individuals to do their job as human beings, to carry out τὸ ἔργον τοῦ ἀνθρώπου as Aristotle calls it.

PHILOSOPHY QUESTIONING "CULTURAL DEVELOPMENT"*

The purpose of this paper is to put forth some questions concerning philosophical problems which transpire through the attempts to answer the needs that have led the UN to proclaim a World Decade of Cultural Development, and which seem to affect directly relevant practice.

By putting forth such questions, to be answered by philosophers from all over the world, this paper hopes to help the proposed volume to form a whole, and thus make a contribution – of philosophy – to the fulfilment of the intentions that have led to the proclamation of this Decade.

Why has the UN proclaimed this Decade? We find the answer of this question in the relevant UNESCO documents drafted in the early eighties. In the General Considerations of one of UNESCO's earliest relevant documents concerning this Decade[1] we read: "The concept that has dominated international economic thinking in recent decades is that of development, but development reduced essentially to its economic aspects, thereby establishing a questionable distinction between the industrialized and the developing countries, speaking in economic terms." And the following necessity is expressed there: "In actual fact, development has no real meaning unless it enables individuals and peoples to live a better life, in complete harmony with their moral and spiritual aspirations, and makes possible the full flowering of their creative faculties. While it is true that economic development is a crucial requirement, it is also necessary for the economy to have a purpose and a cohesion which it can only find through culture [...]." Is it clear here through what, economy would "find" its "cohesion"? Or: what could 'cultural development' be, when juxtaposed to the economic one?

A bird's-eye view, in connection with our topic, of the world situation before the eighties, could, perhaps, be helpful, as a first step, in dealing with this question.

As a matter of fact, the idea of development given as main objective to the national policies of the members of the UN in the fifties and understood merely as economic development, did not only prove insufficient, but also produced other – its own – undesirable facts. This, however, seems to be only one, although, chronologically, the first, of the main reasons that brought on the

---

* This paper was published in Ioanna Kuçuradi and Evandro Agazzi (eds) *Philosophy and Cultural Development*, joint publication of the International Federation of Philosophical Societies and the Philosophical Society of Turkey. Ankara, 1993, pp. 9-17.

[1] UNESCO General Conference, Twenty-Second Session, Paris, 1983, 22C/94.

international agenda the demand for "cultural development" towards the end of the seventies.

If we trace things farther back, up to the establishment of the UN, we see that the ideal of "development" of the fifties was introduced by the industrialized countries, belonging to the "Western" civilization and believing in "progress"; by countries, two characteristics of which – industrialization and "high" *per capita* income – determined the criterion of being "developed". These "developed" countries had become models for the other countries of the world. No wonder that for these two categories of countries 'development' would not mean the same thing. Thus, roughly put, the economic development has constituted the principal objective of national policies in most countries of the world, though understood as industrialization and increase of the *per capita* income in the so-called developing countries and as unlimited increase of industrial production in the so-called developed ones.

This unlimited industrial production, coupled with the effects of political polarizations in the "developed" countries, led itself soon into a deadlock, by producing its own undesirable results, i.e., an irreversible exhaustion of various natural resources, pollution, and such other results, which constitute a part of the so-called "world problems" or "global problems" today. These results, contradicting the intentions of, and the expectations from, putting development as the main objective to their national policies, made people in the West start feeling the need to bring "a cultural dimension to development" or "a new conception of development". Thus the demand for "cultural development" was introduced in the relevant debates.

Here it is important not to lose sight of the fact, that the idea of bringing a cultural dimension to development, as a possible way to break through this deadlock, finds i t s   o r i g i n in a need felt by the industrialized (Western) world.

Still, there is another important reason that contributed to bringing the question of "cultural development" on the international agenda, though it does not seem to be at its very origin: many Third World countries, which had obtained their independence not long ago, started revolting this time against the "colonization of the minds", and thus joined the motion for "cultural development", although putting on the agenda the question of the development of their "cultural identity". Thus, the question of "culture" put in connection with that of development, led to an explanation of the failure of the developmental policies carried out in these countries by "foreign aid", as a failure due to the lack of taking into account "the culture" or "the cultural values" prevailing in these countries of the Third World. As a result of this explanation the concept of "indigenous development" – i.e., of a policy of development taking into consideration "the culture" or "the cultural values" prevailing in these countries – was introduced.

Thus in the beginning of the eighties we see the question of "culture" and the demand for "cultural development" brought on the agenda of the international community from two different perspectives, or, because of two different needs. Do these demands for "cultural development" ask for the same thing? This is a crucial question, since it is directly connected with practice. How crucial a question it is, can also be seen from what followed during the eighties.

This is why a philosophical scrutiny of the term 'cultural development', aiming at calling attention on what it denotes in various documents drafted in connection with the World Decade of Cultural Development and on the implications of its ambiguity up to now, as well as aiming at putting forth an epistemically justifiable concept of "cultural development", appears to be necessary, provided that we wish to avoid that also "cultural development" produce its own undesirable results, as it happened with "development".

THE CONCEPT OF CULTURAL DEVELOPMENT

The idea of "cultural development" was brought as a complementary conception of development. Now w h a t is it that is expected, in fact, to develop or be developed? And what could it mean to develop t h a t?

As soon as we ask this question, we find a possible starting point in scrutinizing, in connection with our problem, the documents concerning "cultural development", as well as a possible Archimedean stand in order to conceptualize the idea of cultural development in an epistemically justifiable way: t h e b e a r e r of "development".

When we read the relevant documents, keeping in mind the question of the bearer of development in connection with "cultural development", we find different and not rarely irreconcilable answers. A confusion related to the term 'culture' transpires through this fact – a confusion which, inevitably affects, and has already affected, the endeavours of planning the activities of the Decade of Cultural Development. Here is only one example of this confusion from the document mentioned above. In this document in which also the four objectives of the Decade were put forth, we read a definition of 'culture' as "all the distinctive characteristics – spiritual and material, intellectual and emotional – of a society or a social group" (par. 5); and some paragraphs further on we read the following: "all in all, it is vital that culture, that is to say man, should be at the centre of any approach to development problems" (par. 8). Put together, that definition and this explanation of 'culture', make us easily see that the term does not denote the same thing, as well as that its meanings, whatever they are, cannot be considered as its "traditional" and "enlarged" sense, as it is assumed to be.

A careful reading of this and other relevant documents makes possible to distinguish at least two main meanings or 'culture'.

Its first meaning, the so-called "traditional" one, denotes something that can be worded as "the totality of the h u m a n a c t i v i t i e s c o n s i d e r e d to afford to individuals the possibility to c u l t i v a t e – to actualize and/or develop – their human potentialities".[2] This is the idea of *cultura animi*, which has penetrated Western thinking since the beginning of our era. Still the human activities deemed to do so, not only differ from culture to culture, but also show a change during the evolution of one and the same culture.

This latter 'culture', however, does not seem to denote such activities. A possible way to find out what this 'culture' could mean, is to compare what distinguishes one given historical culture from another one – i.e., Greek, Moslem, European, Japanese cultures, etc. Once this is done, it seems possible to word this 'culture' as "the conception of Man and the conception concerning what is valuable, which prevail for a longer or shorter while in a human group, whose limits can be drawn according to varying viewpoints, and which determine the way of living of this group and the expressions of this way of living"[3] (the attitudes in everyday life, in social and political activities, the social and political institutions and their functioning, as well as the so-called modern ideas in arts, literature, the fashionable expressions in language, etc.). These are natural, living conceptions, almost unconscious ones, so long as they have not become the object of scientific research. This is a meaning of 'culture' which reminds us of the Herderian or Hegelian *Volksgeist.*[4]

Such a conceptual distinction once made, it becomes natural to ask: which 'culture' in the context 'cultural development' is expected to be developed? And keeping in mind their positive or negative mutual influence, and especially the fact that there have been conceptions of Man and of what is valuable, which have deprived the members of the groups that possessed them of the possibility of developing some of their human potentialities, is it possible to answer the former question, by simply saying "both of them"?

Such are the reasons why the idea of "cultural development" has to be conceptualized philosophically. The question "what the demand for cultural development could, in fact, be demanding", still appears to need an epistemically justifiable answer.

CULTURAL DEVELOPMENT AND THE QUESTION OF GOALS

The fact that the demand for "cultural development" was originally brought in connection with economic development as the main objective of the national policies of the industrialized countries and understood as unlimited increase of the industrial production and so on, while the demand for developing one's own "cultural identity" was brought by Third World countries in a quite different connection and because of a different need, has not been paid due attention up to now.

---

[2] See also my "Cultures and 'World Culture'", in *Philosophie et Culture,* Actes du XVIIIe Congrès Mondial de Philosophie IV. Montréal, 1988, pp. 457-460.

[3] *Ibid.*

[4] "Das gemeinschaftliche Gepräge".

Thus the main objectives of the World Decade of Cultural Development, determined in the early eighties – i.e., "acknowledging the cultural dimension of development, affirming and enriching cultural identities, broadening access and participation in culture, and promoting international cultural co-operation" – reflect an attempt to find a compromise among these different needs or demands.

The demand for "cultural development" brought by the people of the industrialized countries expressed a revolt against economic development as the main objective of their national policies; it was the demand to renounce considering a larger and larger industrial production as an aim in itself – to renounce "the bigger the better" principle – and put as the objective of their national policies an idea of development containing also "cultural finalities", i.e., it was the demand to give to "culture", or to the human activities that provide individuals with the possibilities to develop their human potentialities, due place in social planification.

This demand seems to have started finding an echo during the past decade. However, if we consider the changes occurred in this respect during the past ten years all over the world, and especially in the East European countries and the Islamic World, a philosophical re-evaluation of human activities appears, right now, to be necessary. The question "which human activities, among those deemed to do so, provide, in fact, individuals with the possibilities to develop their human potentialities" urgently needs an epistemic answer.

As for the demand for "cultural development" brought by many countries of the Third World, it expressed a revolt against the "colonization of the minds" by the "West" or by "Western culture"; it was the demand that they be allowed – by the West – to develop *their own* culture, i.e., *their* "cultural identity". This demand was also put as an objective to the Decade of Cultural Development.

The tendency to ascribe to "cultural development" this latter content has gained ground during the past ten years, still without any scrutiny of the question "what is cultural identity?" and/or "what could developing *one's own* culture mean?". Right now, in the beginning of the nineties, the question of "cultural identity" constitutes one of the burning questions in different categories of countries of the Third World. In countries which came in touch with "Western culture" through colonization and are now independent, this search for identity appears as an endeavour to find out what *their* culture was before colonization; while in the countries which have oriented themselves towards "the West" by their own will, i.e., in countries where modernization movements started in different times and are still going on, we see attempts "to restore" or "to resurrect" the culture, i.e., the conception of Man and the conceptions concerning what is valuable, prevailing – or supposed to prevail – there, before their orientation to or encounter with the West.

In the face of this global situation the following question occurs to the mind: is it possible to think of an objective for national and international policies, which could, perhaps, answer the different needs which brought forth the different demands expressed by 'cultural development'? This also seems to be a crucial question, since it is not impossible that in the absence of such a common objective, cultural blocs replace the political blocs of the present world, which, incidentally, are tending to become less and less pronounced.

This question is also crucial, because it puts in question the very idea of development – be it with or without "cultural dimension" – as the main objective of national and international policies. Up to now, only the need "to bring a new concept of development" has often been expressed, and attempts were made to introduce such new concepts – the latest being "sustainable development".

There is also another point which calls our attention when we read relevant documents and follow the debates around development and cultural development, keeping in mind the question of the bearer of development. And this is the lack of any substantial connection between "cultural development" and human rights. We often meet, in fact, here or there, the expressions "cultural rights", "the right to culture", "the right to development", etc., put forward as human rights, which, however, suffer from the same ambiguity as 'cultural development' does.

The most fundamental intention of the international community in proclaiming the Decade of Cultural Development, namely the will to remind us of "man as the goal of development" viewed in the light of clearer concepts, gives rise to the following question: Is it possible to find not a verbal but a substantial connection between the aspirations that brought the demands for "cultural development" – in whatever sense – and human rights?

CONCEPTIONS OF "CULTURAL DEVELOPMENT" – NATIONAL, GLOBAL, ETC.

There are different conceptions concerning "cultural development" in the sense of "developing one's own cultural identity". Nevertheless, some common elements emerge from these conceptions.

One such common element appears to be the search for what is worded as "one's own values". This is anticipated to be the way to face the "crisis of cultures", in which all cultures admit to be. However we observe that the point of reference in the debates going on is "Western" or "European" culture.

What is this Western or European culture which constitutes, at present, the common "counterpart" of all other cultures? This is a question to be asked, since we also observe that what is called in non-Western circles "crisis of identity" is something coinciding with what, in the West, is called "crisis of values". The Western people think, right now, that they do not know any longer what their "values" are; while the non-Western people think either that they do not know *who, really, they are,* or, *that they are not those who, at this moment, in fact, they are.* Yet all share the view that 'culture' – whatever it is and whatever each considers his own culture to be – is something "good", something which the "basic substance" of has to be restored and developed.

Here are also some issues needing philosophical questioning, one of them being the concept of identity and another one the concept of values.

If we trace the meaning of the term 'identity' in the various contexts where it appears in the debates going one, we realize that 'identity', instead of conveying the meaning of 'self-knowledge', is used in the sense of 'self-conception' or 'self-image' of an individual or a group.

Thus, while 'cultural identity', carefully understood, would mean in the case of an individual, h i s k n o w l e d g e of his conception of Man and of what he thinks is valuable, and in the case of a group, the k n o w l e d g e of the most widespread – still not unique – conception of Man and of what is considered to be valuable at a given moment in that group; it is assumed in non-Western countries to convey the conception of man and of what is valuable that prevailed in these countries before their encounter with the West.

What are the consequences of understanding 'identity' as 'self-image' in this respect? And what could be the implications of understanding 'identity' as 'self-knowledge'? And, in this connection, what sort of thing are these "values" that each culture tries to find or/and restore?

Confusion, in connection with the philosophical question "what are values?", shows through the ongoing debates – a confusion which seems to constitute the heart of the matter.

If we trace the meaning of the term 'cultural values' in the contexts where it appears in various documents, we see that the term 'values' is no less ambiguous than the term 'cultural'. Still in the contexts of "one's own values", 'values' appears to denote everything that a group – or a culture – considers to be valuable, that is, it denotes mainly the "good"s of a culture or 'cultural norms'.

The question of norms, especially their "scientific" justification, has kept especially busy the philosophical community during the past fifteen or twenty years. Still the question of their epistemic specificities does not seem to be given sufficient attention.

Are norms and values the same thing, as it is implicitly assumed in the debates concerning the "discovery" or "revival" of one's own cultural values?

This question is decisive in the treatment of the problems faced not only in connection with the conceptions of national cultural development or that of any other group, but also in connection with "global cultural development", concerning which there are also different conceptions – the most recent being that which is worded as "synthesis of cultural values".

According to this conception what could unify humanity is a global (spiritual) culture. To create this global culture we have to select and "synthesize" what is "good" in, or "the substance" of, each culture.

Another conception of "global cultural development", or a quite different assumption concerning the creation of a global culture, is that which lies behind the debate on "the specificity and universality of cultural values", a debate which has also kept busy the world philosophical community, during the past fifteen years or so, and through which, as well, shows the same confusion between norms and "values".

These and similar observations make necessary for philosophy to try to find the way to conceptualize the idea of "global cultural development" – i.e., to try to determine what it could mean and what in the present world situation it could be –; as well as to inquire into the objective characteristics of a culture which we might wish to become "global", since it seems that there is already a globally prevailing culture. And this globally prevailing culture, i.e., "Western culture" at the present state of its development, appears to be what all peoples of the world revolt against, no matter what their different needs be.

These different revolts against the same thing might be considered also as expressions of a similar aspiration. The people in the West address their demand to those who govern them: they demand an administration which would allow them also to develop their human potentialities; as for the people of the non-Western countries, they address their demand to the Western world as a whole: they aspire to be treated no longer as Saint-Exupéry's Turkish astronomer, or they aspire for the "humanism of recognition", as F. Miro Quesada calls it,[5] and both demand a world order which will secure for them the possibility of bringing their own contribution to the formation of the present and the future of the world.

These demands seem to find an echo, to a certain extent. How to answer them? The question of cultural policies has constituted the theme of several conferences at international, regional and national levels, during the past ten years. What is the outcome?

And another question: if to secure "cultural development" is considered to be the affair of cultural policies, what could it mean, and, at present, how could it be carried out at different levels?

CULTURAL DEVELOPMENT AND CULTURAL POLICIES

It is obvious that cultural policies have to be delineated differently in different countries and at different levels. Still, there are some basic questions concerning the principal objectives of cultural policies and other general points.

One such question is the following: what is that, which cultural policies are expected to plan and develop: the human activities which afford individuals the possibility to develop their human potentialities? Or the conceptions of Man and the "values" that given "groups" consider to be their own? Though it may sound redundant, this question finds its justification when put in connection with some activities carried out by Ministries of Culture – e.g., producing post-

[5] In his "Human Rights in Latin America", in *Philosophical Foundations of Human Rights,* UNESCO, 1986, p. 311.

ers to encourage people "to be thrifty" – or with fashionable expressions floating around, such as "intercultural dialogue", "intercultural co-operation", etc.

And a few other questions: what are the different implications of delineating cultural policies in order to develop human activities, such as literature, various arts, philosophy, etc., and in order to develop "one's own" or specific "values"? Which human activities are directly connected with "cultural" development and consequently have to be given priority in delineating cultural policies, as well as due place within the framework of national policies in general? What is and/or could be the role of NGO's – and first of all of FISP – in global cultural development?

These are some examples of questions concerning cultural policies in general. Different problems faced in this respect in different countries and regions, will, no doubt, give rise to additional questions.

These are only a few of the considerations on the basis of which some questions concerning "cultural development", among other possible ones, were put forward for discussion. They originated in the face of the present world situation, from the original question "what can philosophy contribute to cultural development?", in the hope that this discussion itself brings such a contribution to this issue.

Human Rights Instruments Questioned in the Light of the Idea of Human Rights*

The Problem

The most significant achievement of the 20th Century will, probably, be the priority ascribed to t h e i d e a of human rights. And perhaps the most significant endeavour of the "world community" will be its attempt to codify, through the UN, in declarations, covenants, etc., such rights, i.e., to elaborate documents or "instruments" expected to have "universal" validity.

I need not give here examples of the limited efficiency of these precious normative instruments in protecting human rights in many states and at the global level. Watching the news on the TV affords us plenty of such examples. What are our main shortcomings?

Let us leave aside for the time being the shortcomings due to hypocritical attitudes in politics; let us assume that, amidst such hypocritical attitudes, the will to protect human rights is sincere and let us look at these instruments keeping in mind concrete cases of such shortcomings. Then one main reason of their limited efficiency in preventing damage to human rights, in stopping violations, in remedying violations, etc., appears to stem from these instruments t h e m - s e l v e s: they mostly reflect good and sincere will, but not sufficient philosophical k n o w l e d g e of what we call human rights and of other relevant concepts such as freedom(s), culture(s), development, peace, etc. In other words: they show different confusions, which are "transplanted" to the constitutions of various states, in which articles from these international documents are incorporated – confusions which affect legislation and practice, leading not rarely to decisions and actions discrepant to the intentions in drafting them. And these actions produce irreversible facts, which take time to diagnose and become aware of this discrepancy.

Here are some of these confusions: confusion between the basic *(human)* rights of the individual and collective rights (the so-called "rights of the peoples" included); confusion between the basic rights of the individual and citizen rights (between the rights of an individual as a human person and different social, economic and political rights that states "give" to their citizens, i.e., the different limits that states delineate for their citizens in this respect); confusion between the basic rights of the individual and the so-called "fundamental free-

---

* This paper is the Working Paper for a meeting organized by the International Federation of Philosophical Societies in 1993, in Göreme (Turkey). It was published in Ioanna Kuçuradi (ed.), *The Idea and the Documents of Human Rights*, Ideas Underlying Global Problems 3, International Federation of Philosophical Societies and Philosophical Society of Turkey. Ankara, 1995, pp. 3-12.

doms" (the latter understood, in these instruments, as 'one's not being hindered in...'); confusion between the basic rights of the individual and their (different) implications in (different) real spatio-temporal conditions (implications which, assumed to be basic rights, are given a different interpretation or sense when put into connection with conditions different from those in which they were deduced); confusion between the basic rights of the individual and aspirations, etc. Put in philosophical language: looking at these instruments with epistemological knowledge of principles, we observe confusions between different kinds of norms, as well as confusions concerning the bearers of rights and "freedoms".

As a result of such confusions we are faced with an inflation of "human rights" (what some people call "generations of human rights"); with contradictions in and between these normative instruments, i.e., with "human rights" excluding the protection of each other, something that causes in practice zigzags which produce their irreversible facts.

We also see restrictions of basic rights for the sake of other kinds of norms and lack of restriction of non-basic rights, all assumed to be "human rights", and this makes easier the attempts to protect interests in the name of human rights.

Is it not possible to make these "instruments" correspond more to t h e i n t e n t i o n s that led the world community to draft them after the Second World War and to enforce them as the "foundation of justice" – a correspondence which is a p r e r e q u i s i t e for a more effective treatment of legal issues concerning human rights, i.e., for the deduction of law(s) and its (or their) implementation? If it is possible, then how?

CONCEPTIONS OF HUMAN RIGHTS UNDERLYING HUMAN RIGHTS INSTRUMENTS

What is the conception of human rights in the *Universal Declaration* (1948) and what is the anthropology underlying this conception? What are those of the *Covenants* (drafted in 1953-1954, adopted in 1966 and entered into force in 1977)? And what are the conceptions of some other instruments drafted later, for example those of the *Declaration on the Right to Development* (1986)?

Answering such questions, and showing the differences, could perhaps help us finding out what the world community initially m e a n t or i n - t e n d e d, beyond aspirations, by drafting them, and thus frame an epistemically justifiable concept of, or a criterion for, human rights.

a) The most appropriate document where to look for these intentions appears to be the first drafted one, the *Universal Declaration*, which is an ethical document *par excellence,* up to now probably the best elaborated document of human rights we possess, or, to use a term of the present-day philosophy of language, the most c a r e f u l l y performed speech act of the world community.

In the *Universal Declaration* human rights appear as principles or demands concerning a s p e c i a l t r e a t m e n t of the individuals belonging to the human species. Indeed, 26 of the articles of this *Declaration* are attempts to word such principles and some of their implications in the existing conditions of the world – viewed from a Western perspective – in the middle of the 20th Century.

The underlying assumption necessitating such a treatment is that "all human beings are born free [?] and equal in dignity [?] and rights [?]", because "they are endowed with reason [?] and conscience [?]". For the same reason, i.e., because "they are endowed with reason and conscience", they "should act towards one another in a spirit of brotherhood", since "disregard and contempt of human rights have resulted in barbarous acts which have outraged the conscience of mankind", and since "the advent of a world in which human beings shall enjoy freedom of speech and belief and freedom from fear and want has been proclaimed as the highest aspiration of the common people", etc.

What is intended here is to put forward general (or "universal") principles concerning how human beings should be treated, because the human being (the human species) shows certain specifities, whatever they be (though here they are assumed to be "reason" and "conscience"), which distinguish it from other species. These principles for the treatment of human beings are intended to word the general prerequisites or conditions deemed to afford human beings the possibility to develop their human potentialities, ethical ones included, i.e., to carry out activities, the products of which constitute the value of the human being: the achievements of the human species in history, the blessings of which all of us enjoy.

Who will treat individuals in this manner? The answer in the *Universal Declaration* is only implicit: individuals, i.e., those who recognize "the inherent dignity of all members of the human family", as well as those who don't want that the "barbarous acts" mentioned in the Preamble of the *Declaration* be repeated and those who aspire for a world free from fear and want. But what about those who really do not? And what about those who try to protect their human rights, but not human rights in general, i.e., who try to remedy injustice done to them by doing injustice?

Though worded in the passive, i.e., as principles for the treatment of human beings, human rights in the *Universal Declaration* are conceived mainly as principles of action, concerning how human beings – in fact, those who possess sufficient knowledge of their human identity and the will to carry out its implications – should treat human beings, so that human beings can afford the possibility to develop their human potentialities, and consequently some of them carry out the human activities that constitute what we call "human dignity".

b) The conception of human rights in the *Covenants* is different, but complementary of the above-mentioned conception. Human rights are considered there as basic principles for social organization, as demands concerning the establishment of social relations in a certain manner. They intend to express "legal as well as moral obligations for the states"[1] or principles expected to determine the deduction of all kinds of legal norms, so that individuals can be treated by other individuals – state and public officers included – in the manner that human rights, as principles of actions, demand.

There, the states, signatory of the *Covenants*, "recognize" officially a number of "rights", assumed to be human rights, and promise their citizens, and each other, "to undertake to take steps" for the promotion of these rights.

What they, in fact, promise (i.e., what those in power at the time that a state signed a *Covenant*, whether sincerely or not, promised), is to establish an order determined by a special kind of norms – the principles "recognized" there as human rights – i.e., they promise to legislate in accordance with these principles and not in accordance with other kinds of norms (empirical-cultural, etc., norms); but nevertheless to implement the latter norms within the limits delineated in the *Covenants*.

Thus human rights in the *Covenants* appear to be conceived on the one hand as a special kind of norms for legislation, i.e., as basic norms wherefrom constitutional norms and, in turn, all other norms of more limited scope have to be deduced and implemented in given cases; but, on the other hand, many of these rights are not considered so basic that they cannot be "restricted", i.e., put aside at times even by law in the name of other norms or purposes.

In the *Covenant on Civil and Political Rights* six or seven articles have "a privileged" status in this respect. The article concerning "the right to freedom of thought, conscience and religion" is such an article, though the article concerning the "right to hold opinions without interference" and "the right to freedom of expression" is not.

A comparison of art. 19 with art. 18 of this *Covenant*, among many other things, could make explicit some of the confusions I mentioned above, and be one example of the defects of these precious instruments. Art. 19 states: "1. Everyone shall have the right to hold opinions without interference. 2. Everyone shall have the right to freedom of expression; this right shall include freedom to seek, receive and impart information and ideas of all kinds […]." The exercise of these rights "may [...] be subject to certain restrictions", if necessary, by law. This article is not among those which "in time of public emergency no derogation may be made", while art. 18 is among the latter and states: "Everyone shall have the right to freedom of thought, conscience and religion. This right shall include freedom to [...] manifest his religion or belief in [...] practice and teaching." Now, *first,* what is an 'opinion', the expression of which may be restricted temporarily? What is its difference from a 'thought' which may not be? And what is the difference between both of them and knowledge? *Second,* the exercise of the right stated in art. 19 – assumed to be "a freedom" – can be

---

[1] *The International Bill of Human Rights*, Fact Sheet N° 2, Printed in Switzerland, April 1988, reprinted at United Nations, Geneva, May 1992, p. 17.

restricted, if necessary, for the protection, among other things, of "public morals". What are "public" morals? And what if the prevailing "morals" – the norms concerning what is considered as "good" and "bad" in a country or among the decision-makers – has elements doing harm to human rights, as is the case in many countries? What would it mean, then, to restrict a human right by law, in order to protect "public morals"? Would not this mean to give priority to another kind of norms of more limited scope than human rights? Would not this mean to consider these changing norms more important than the "universal" principles of human rights?

Besides this, in art. 18, from which no derogation may be made in time of public emergency we read: "Freedom to manifest one's religion or beliefs [in worship [...] and teaching] may be subject only to limitations as are prescribed by law and are necessary to protect the fundamental rights and freedoms of others." Does these 'others' include also children to which a religion is taught, with the consent of their parents? And what if a religion has certain elements doing harm to the human rights of those who believe in it?

This difference of approach to the "freedom of opinion and expression" and to the "freedom of conscience and religion", as well as the conditions for their restriction in the articles mentioned, are based not on the knowledge of the rights under consideration, but, probably, on the assumption or value judgement that "morals" and religions are necessarily "good".

This confusion keeps the door open for those in power in various states, to restrict human rights in order to protect group interests and to enforce laws recognizing rights that do harm to the human rights of many of their citizens, and sometimes even of those citizens that are supposed to "benefit" from these rights. At the same time, we see in various states, groups or individuals accusing the State of violations of human rights, because of restrictions of certain desired liberties – liberties which do harm to the human rights of those who wish to have them –; just as we see people condemned, in the name of protecting "public order", because the research they conduct in their field injures prevailing taboos.

c) The conception of human rights in the *Declaration on the Right to Development* (1986) is different from that of both the *Universal Declaration* and the *Covenants*. It reflects a coupling of two positive value judgements: the one concerning "development" with that on human rights.

"Development" is, according to this *Declaration* (art. 1) an "inalienable human right" of both persons and collectivities. This right to development, as understood there, is the right of "every human person and all peoples [what is in fact "a people"?] [...] to participate in, contribute to, and enjoy economic, social, cultural and political development"; and this latter "development" is the prerequisite for the "full realization of all human rights" (i.e., also for the full realization of itself as well!).

What those who drafted it wish to express is, if put plainly, the following: economic, social, cultural and political development (who is to become, or to be, what?) is the prerequisite for the full realization of human rights. Every human being and all peoples are entitled (have the right) to participate in, contribute to, and enjoy economic, social, cultural and political development. Now, what is the difference between 'development' as a right (of every human being and all peoples) and 'development' within the context of 'economic, social, cultural and political development'? Does the latter denote a state of affairs or a process in view to bring forth that state of affairs? Many other questions may be raised.

This *Declaration*, which can easily be used for diverging purposes, is an example of a jargon turned into a leitmotif: the expected (or aspired) outcome from the protection of human rights is itself presented as a human right.

And another example: According to art. 5, "States shall take resolute steps to eliminate [...] threats against national sovereignty, national unity and territorial integrity, threats of war and refusal to recognize the fundamental right of peoples to self-determination." What if "a people" exercising its right to self-determination decides to create an independent state on the territory of another state or other states? Thus the question arises: Are collective rights basic (human) rights? Or, are they implications of basic human rights in given real conditions?

FUTURE PROSPECTS

If the original intention in drafting such instruments (as we can make it out of the *Universal Declaration* and the *Covenants*) is to put forward basic principles of a special kind for a social organization (for an "order") which makes possible for individuals to be treated, by other individuals, so that they may develop their human potentialities, i.e., so that they may, if they can and as far as each one can, carry out certain activities proper to human species; in other words, if human rights express demands concerning the permanent creation of the most basic conditions deemed, normally, necessary for the development and exercise of human potentialities, how could we step forward?

Now, many decades after of the proclamation of the *Universal Declaration*, at the turn of a century in which radical changes have occurred so rapidly that it makes a little easier an overview and more possible for us to learn a few things by our own experience, what do we need for making more effective the principles of human rights?

To answer this question we have to evaluate our human rights instruments and put forth some of the implications of such an evaluation.

HUMAN RIGHTS: THE IDEA, THE DEMANDS AND THE INSTRUMENTS[*]

There is a widespread opinion or acceptance that human rights aim at protecting the individual against the State. This acceptance lies on a conception of the State as an entity in itself, the Leviathan State. This same conception seems to be kept in mind in the elaboration of the international instruments concerning human rights: with the exception of the *Universal Declaration*, the main addressees of the "international community" in these human rights documents are the states. These documents attempt to bring obligations – ethical obligations – for the states which signed them, i.e., they reflect the will or intention to introduce ethical concerns into politics.

As a result of this, we read in many constitutions, that state x is, among other enumerated things, "respectful" of human rights, that is, respectful of the demands that human rights express. Is it possible for a state to be "respectful" of human rights and, on top of it, "respectful" of human rights among other things? A different concept of the State makes such "respectfulness" appear problematic.

If we conceive of the State a human-legal institution, consisting of a network of different organs, established by a group – its citizens – for the administration within justice of what is public and for the protection, when necessary, of the citizens against each other; it is perhaps possible to realize that a state cannot be "respectful" of human rights among other things, but either be or not be based on human rights, i.e., its constitution (in the etymological and technical senses) can be determined by the principles of human rights, or by other kinds of norms and other considerations.

Still, what we often see at present in various constitutions, is a confusion and mixture of different kinds of norms, which, when applied, exclude each other, or lead to opposing practices on the same or factually the same issue.

This leaves ample room, to state organs, for decisions and practices protecting, consciously or unconsciously, group interests – not rarely presented under the guise of rights – to the detriment of basic rights of other citizens, and sometimes even of basic rights of citizens who take advantage of these (group) interests. It also creates the fact which I call the fireman's starting a fire. State organs are also administrated by citizens. Thus the promotion of the idea of deducing positive law, at different levels, i.e., directly or indirectly, from human rights, as ethical principles for social organization and political practice, on the ground of the international human rights documents, is something we need.

---

[*] This paper was published in Ioanna Kuçuradi (ed.), *The Idea and the Documents of Human Rights*, Ideas Underlying World Problems 3. Ankara, 1995, pp. 75-91.

Still, also our human rights documents are not free from inconsistencies or discrepant norms on the same issue, norms which often exclude each other in application and, consequently, leave ample room for the deduction of discrepant laws. This makes possible in practice on the one hand to cause damage, through laws, to human rights, and on the other, to present attempts to restrict group interests as violations of human rights.

Thus, almost half a century after the establishment of the UN with the main purpose of promoting the protection and fulfilment of human rights all over the world, a scrutiny, evaluation and revision of our precious international instrument on human rights, in the light of the experience gained in the meanwhile, as well as in the light of clear philosophical knowledge of what human rights are, of what each right demands, and consequently in connection with the different implications it has in different actual situations, could help to better fulfil the initial ethical intentions which made the world community, after the Second World War, to establish the UN and elaborate, under very difficult political conditions, the Bill of Human Rights. This could also help, in turn, at the international level: to better answer the need, already felt, for a "reform" of international institutions and mechanisms for the protection of human rights;[1] and at the national level to a law making more apt to protect human rights – 'protecting' here understood not only as remedying already perpetrated, or stopping, flagrant violations, but also as preventing violations and contributing to the fulfilment of human rights more and more.

For this we need, as world community, clear philosophical knowledge of what human rights are, not only to know that they are something "good".

Let me here summarize one attempt to put forward philosophical knowledge on human rights.

*

The term 'human rights' expresses an idea, a conception of the human mind: the conception that human beings, because they are human beings – i.e., because they belong to a species which shows certain specificities – possess, all of them equally, certain "rights": each of them should be treated (not to forget: by other human beings) in a special manner.

There is no, or no significant, dispute about that – but only about that. Most of the international human rights documents are attempts to put in black and white this special manner, i.e., to codify fundamental principles or "universal" norms, expected to determine action and the establishment of social relations (of social order) – the term 'universal' assumed usually to denote in this

[1] An international meeting focusing on this need was organized by the University of La Laguna (Tenerife, Spain), in November 1992.

context 'worldwide valid norms', n o t the specificity of a kind of norm distinguished from other kinds of norms.[2]

Now, if we leave aside the other instruments and look, for the moment, at the norms codified in the *Bill of Human Rights*, in the light of philosophical-epistemological knowledge concerning practical norms, we see there norms of different kinds and of different scope – their common feature (what brings them together) seeming to be that they represent the "good"s – the opposite of the "bad"s – or the value judgements of a given culture (of Western culture) at a given historical moment, or the needs felt at a given historical moment – a fact which bears implications in their wording and their restrictions and which has also, w r o n g l y, led to a cultural approach to human rights, and subsequently to the endeavour to look for ways to go beyond this approach.

Thus we observe a dubious increase in the number of "human rights", followed by an increase in the number of instruments, but we see no attempt to evaluate our existing instruments, so that they may better fulfil the intentions lying at the origin of their being drafted: once drafted and enforced, they are taken (almost) for granted and treated like holy scripts. And in spite of this increase in the number of "rights" and instruments, flagrant human rights violation are perpetrated more and more "skillfully", more and more unscrupulously.[3]

Now, what does the *Universal Declaration* i n t e n d to word and declare? And what i n f a c t it words? Let us read art. 1 of this *Declaration*, keeping in mind this aim.

In this article it is declared that "all human beings are born free and equal in dignity and rights. They are endowed, with reason and conscience and should act towards one another in a spirit of brotherhood". The first sentence states an acceptance, while the first part of the second sentence expresses a conception (or image) of Man, though it intends to state an assertion on the "nature" of Man, from which the "should" of the second part of the sentence follows. Both sentences intend to express two specificities of being human.

In this article it is assumed, or accepted, that a l l human beings as h u - m a n beings – i.e., not only as living beings, but as members of one species of the living beings – are b o r n "equal" in "dignity" and "rights", b e c a u s e they are endowed with "reason" and "conscience" (i.e., the *ratio essendi* of their assumed freedom and equality in dignity and rights is their being endowed with reason and conscience – which are considered to be the *differentia specifica* of humans). And b e c a u s e they are (all) endowed with reason and conscience, they s h o u l d act towards one another in a spirit of brotherhood. The "should" here – the only "should" in the *Universal Declaration* concerning how individuals should treat individuals, and n o t how individuals should be treated – is

---

[2] In the *Universal Declaration*, for example, the word 'universal' qualifies the *Declaration*, not the norms.

[3] The number of civilians killed in recent "small" / "regional" wars, is much higher than the number of soldiers killed in the same wars.

deduced from their "nature", which constitutes also the ratio of the claim of their freedom and equality. They should act towards one another in such a spirit and respect human rights, b e c a u s e (justification of the "should") a) "disregard and contempt for human rights have resulted in barbarous acts which have outraged the conscience of mankind" and b e c a u s e b) "the advent of a world in which human beings shall enjoy freedom of speech and belief and freedom from fear and want has been proclaimed as the highest aspiration of the common people (in English, *"de l'homme"* in French, *"der Menschheit"* in German)", etc.

Ergo: 1) if (provided that) human beings don't want that such "barbarous acts, which have outraged the conscience of mankind" happen (again), and if (provided that) the above-mentioned aspiration for such a world exists, human rights s h o u l d be respected. And 2) "it is essential, if man is not to be compelled to have recourse, as a last resort, to rebellion against tyranny and oppression, that human rights should be protected by the rule of law *("par un régime de droit", "Herrschaft des Rechtes").* The first conclusion concerns the individuals, the second the states.

All these express a fuzzy consciousness – of those who drafted this *Declaration* – of being human and a few consequences of this consciousness in the face of the historical conditions of the time. Still to be conscious of something is not the same with possessing a clear knowledge of it. The equality of all human beings is, in the *Universal Declaration*, justified by human "nature" – though this nature is assumed to consist of being endowed with reason and conscience –; but the "should" it brought for action, though deduced from human nature, is justified mainly in an empirical-psychological way.

Various questions can be raised against this conception and justification, e.g.: a) are a l l human beings in fact endowed with "reason" and "conscience", as these terms are understood in Western circles? Are all of them "rational"? b) What about those who have performed, and are now performing, acts outraging the "conscience" of mankind? Aren't they human beings? c) And what about those who think "*après moi* (and now sometimes *avec moi*) *le déluge"*?

This problematic conception and justification appear also to be at the origin of the w r o n g claim, made by many thinkers of non-Western cultures, that human rights are a conception of a culture alien to their own.

Nevertheless, this reading of the *Declaration* affords us a clue, following which it appears possible to transform the consciousness of being human which produced it into knowledge: into the knowledge of t h o s e "things", concerning which human rights bring certain demands.

Put very briefly and simply, the conception underlying the *Universal Declaration*, may be worded as follows: being human, i.e., b e i n g a s p e c i e s possessing certain potentialities or capacities, implies that every individual belonging to this species treats, and be treated by, other individuals in a manner that individuals may actualize – that is, not be hindered from actualizing – potentialities or capacities which mark and constitute the value (the special place) or dignity of the human being; it implies that every individual should have the possibility of actualizing – those who can and as much each of them can – the potentialities of the human being. What the *Universal Declaration* intends to word is the conditions of *this* possibility.

Consequently each human right brings, or is expected to bring, a demand concerning a basic condition, considered normally necessary for the actualizability of certain human potentialities.

Thus knowledge of human rights would mean knowledge of such conditions: of the basic conditions in which an individual may, in general, actualize certain potentialities, including ethical potentialities, of the human species. What each human right demands, or is expected to demand, is the creation or realization of such a condition in the historical reality in which it is deduced. Once deduced such a demand becomes a basic right for every human being – yet a right which may have, and in fact has, different implications in different actual conditions.

How do we gain the knowledge of such a condition? And how such a basic norm or right is deduced? Through an inference, made by a comparison, in the light of a third term – i.e., of the knowledge of the value of certain human potentialities: the comparison of the factual conditions in which at a given historical moment some human beings somewhere are, with the conditions in which some other human beings are at the same historical moment in other places –: the conditions of Man, or of humanity, at the moment of the comparison – viewed in the light of the knowledge of the value of certain potentialities: those potentialities or capacities which made Edison discover the uses of electricity, Saint-Exupéry write *The Little Prince,* an unknown human being to bring the idea of human rights, and many others to achieve what they have indeed achieved, the blessings that all of us enjoy. This is the knowledge of what a human being can become and of the significance, for humanity, of the achievements of those who have actualized such potentialities. Made under the light of this knowledge, such a comparison affords us a hypothetical or conditional knowledge: the knowledge of some conditions, in which it is normally (and there are always exceptions) impossible for a human being to actualize such potentialities. It is from this knowledge that the opposite conditions are deduced, as a conclusion, as conditions necessary for the actualization of such human potentialities.

Thus the starting point in such an inference appears to be the knowledge of human potentialities (or capacities) and of their value. The knowledge of these potentialities we get from philosophical anthropology, while that of their value from the evaluation of what they have produced in history.[4]

---

[4] A considerable number of rights in our international instruments does not seem to be deduced, keeping in mind also this knowledge, but a) directly as the opposite demands of "undesirable" facts or b) by using a third term of a kind totally different from this

What is done during the deduction of the principles of human rights, as a complex knowing activity is, schematically, more or less the following: a) keeping in mind the knowledge of human potentialities, we look at humanity at a given historical moment and we see the stage of actualization of such potentialities, the stage that humankind has reached in this respect at that historical moment: we see the achievements of humankind, or, where humankind stands at that historical moment. This afford us the third term or the basis of our comparison: the knowledge of the value of c e r t a i n human potentialities. b) In the light of this latter knowledge (or third term) we look at different human groups, living at that moment: at this same moment we see groups in which individuals have actualized (or are actualizing) s u c h potentialities to a h i g h e r d e g r e e, compared with the degree to which, in other groups, individuals have actualized them: there are human groups, the members of which contribute more than the members of other groups do, to the possible welfare of humanity, i.e., a greater number of individuals than in other groups, makes such contributions. c) In the endeavour to explain this fact, we connect these different contributions to the difference of conditions existing in these groups: the difference of the determinants in the arrangement of social relations or publicly valid norms for the treatment of individuals in these groups: in this comparative connection certain conditions (in the sense I specified) appear to be unfavourable to, or normally hindering, the actualization of such human potentialities. These unfavourable conditions are either obstacles in general, or historical-local obstacles for the actualization of such potentialities. d) It is from such a comparison that we infer the "opposite" of these existing, generally unfavourable, conditions as t h e necessary conditions or natural prerequisites for the actualization of the human potentialities in question.

These latter "conditions" put a s d e m a n d s for all human beings, constitute what we call human rights. In other words: the knowledge of these general-basic conditions constitutes the most basic premises for the deduction of historical principles and other changing practical norms of more limited scope, i.e., of principles of the kind of *laïcité* or secularism, institutional autonomy, etc., and in turn, of positive law in general.

Such a chain deduction of norms – in different factual situations – I mean, when I point to the need to deduce law from human rights.

This is also a chain to be kept in mind in understanding and evaluating now valid norms, or proposed norms, including those in our international instruments and constitutions.

In other words: if we really care for the actual protection of human rights in practice, we should never lose sight of the fact, that the same human right, or the same basic demand, has different implications in different actual situations: its protection may imply intermediary, and different intermediary, principles.

knowledge, as is the case with "development" (i.e., "national income"), in which one historical outcome is mistaken as a cause.

Thus we can perhaps avoid, among other things, considering conditional implications of human rights, as unconditional (universal) human rights, and finding ourselves at a loss in the face of attempts to present norms deduced, in real situations, from such intermediary historical norms, or deduced empirically, as norms in contradiction with human rights – both of which lead to "democratic" enforcement of contradictory norms.

We have perhaps to learn and try to evaluate e a c h situation for itself, still always in the light of ethical value k n o w l e d g e – an important part of which consists of the knowledge of human rights.

*

Now, if we look at the rights enumerated in our international documents with a concept of human rights put in connection with human potentialities, a different classification of rights can be made, i.e., it is possible to distinguish between kinds of rights and these distinctions might help avoiding, to some extent, confusions such as I mentioned in the "working paper"[5], reflected also in positive law, as well as some confusions connected with fashionable mottos floating around, e.g., "the free market".

*

Considered from the viewpoint of their bearers – i.e., those who have to be treated in a special manner or the object of demands – the rights we find in the *Bill of Human Rights*, may be distinguished as rights of the individual and group rights. The latter (on which I shall not dwell here) concern either natural groups or groups constituted for the realization of given goals (associations, etc.).

Among the rights of the individual we see demands concerning the individual as a h u m a n b e i n g – whatever all its other specificities might be – i.e., the human individual distinguished from individuals of other species, and demands concerning the individual a s a c i t i z e n o f a g i v e n s t a t e, i.e., distinguished from citizens of other states[6]. I think that the term 'human rights' has to be confined to the first kind of the rights of the individual. These are the rights in which all human beings "are" equal.

Now, among the rights of the individual as a human individual, we may distinguish – this time from the viewpoint of the ways of their protection, i.e., exercise and fulfilment – between a) rights or demands connected directly with the e x e r c i s e of human activities by which human potentialities are actual-

[5] See pp. 75-80.

[6] This distinction bears implications, among other things, for the question of "equality in rights": the former are rights in which *all* human beings *are* equal, i.e., they have to be treated in the same way; the latter are rights in which a l l c i t i z e n s o f a g i v e n s t a t e are equal, i.e., they may be treated differently from the citizens of another state. (I would not claim to be my right, as a Professor in a University of the Republic of Turkey, to be paid at this moment a s m u c h a s my parallel is paid in the USA or in Germany.)

ized, i.e., connected directly with the basic conditions affording normally the possibility of exercising such activities, and b) rights or demands connected with the prerequisites affording an individual the possibility of developing his or her human potentialities.

What the first set of rights demands is that the individual be not "hindered" while exercising certain activities proper to humankind, those I mentioned earlier; in other words, that "nobody" (State organs included) "touches" – i.e., gives damage to the other rights of – an individual who exercises such activities.

To protect these rights amounts to codify them, i.e., to put them under the guarantee of international instruments, constitutions and national law in general. Since we can speak of protection of these rights in life, when and where there are attempts to violate them (i.e., not after they are violated), to 'protect' these rights amounts to try to prevent such violations by putting these rights in the constitutions and by more specific laws, deduced as implications in the real conditions of a given country, and in case of violations or attempts of violation, intervene through various international and State organs, created for such purposes.

Thus the "natural" protector of this kind of human rights appears to be the State. In spite of this fact, State organs in many countries are among the violators of such rights. Consequently the possibility of their protection depends on the one hand on appropriate laws, but on the other on the education of human rights as a part of a broader philosophical education, especially of public officers, judges, and the makers and appliers of decisions in general, which can help them – at least a part of them – to become able to connect individual cases, at different levels, with the demands of these human rights.

There are various problems connected with this kind of human rights in our human rights documents. Here I shall confine myself to pointing to only one, a quite general one:

Some rights belonging to this kind of human rights constitute what is traditionally called "fundamental freedoms" and a number of them are worded as "the right to freedom of..." or "the right to freedom to...".

Seen in the light of the aforementioned concept of human rights and after a philosophical clarification of what 'freedom' is – as we see it in philosophical works through the centuries – the equation of the so-called fundamental freedoms with rights – i.e., considering freedoms as basic rights of the individual – appears as a confusion, which bears crucial implications connected with their restriction and the application to individual cases of such restrictions.

When we look at the wording of freedoms in such documents, the term 'freedom' there appears to denote the demand that individuals be not hindered – not in exercising activities which develop the human potentialities I mentioned, but – in doing "things" which are considered as "good", i.e., about which there exists a positive value judgement, without taking into consideration whether those "things" are connected or not with the exercising of human potentialities.

I shall not repeat the example I gave in the working paper. I shall only say that what this kind of rights demands is *not* that an individual be not hindered in *doing* something specified or *acting* (behaving) in a specified way, but in exercising and developing *certain* potentialities of the human species by acting in *very different ways* or doing *different things* which cannot be specified once and for all. 'An individual's not being hindered' means, here, that other basic or non-basic rights of that individual are not damaged, because this individual by carrying out such activities *has done* something (e.g., has brought new knowledge on a given issue) which is not in conformity with a prevailing taboo. Where such demands determine – and as much as they determine – social organizations and practice, *there* the correlative freedoms exist, their *bearer* being the country under consideration, i.e., a country in which the possibility exists for individuals (citizens or not) to actualize and develop those certain potentialities of the humankind. Otherwise, restrictions of these unrestrictable rights are inevitable, as well as in the face of claims of violations of human rights against restrictions of certain acts, running into a deadlock is unavoidable.

This differentiation of bearers and this understanding of freedoms makes, among other things, possible, for example, to distinguish between the basic rights to shape and express one's own opinion from making propaganda. When these are confused in individual cases, this confusion leads – it has so many times led – on the one hand to putting in prison or damaging other rights of individuals whose research was shaking prevailing taboos, and on the other, to easily disguising propaganda ("teaching") of ideas which had and have damaging implications for human rights.

There is also another group of basic rights of the individual, which can neither be respected nor violated, like those mentioned before. They are demands concerning prerequisites affording – or deemed normally to afford – each individual the possibility to develop his or her human potentialities – the right to a standard of living adequate to one's health, the right to education, etc. These rights can be protected – i.e., fulfilled – only indirectly, through other rights "given" by laws – through social and economic rights and public institutions. Their protection depends on *appropriate* – different – legislation in different countries, i.e., on *how* the limits of these rights are drawn: by taking or not taking into consideration their implications for the basic rights of individuals in a given country at a given historical moment. These social and economic rights are rights in which not all human beings, but all *citizens* in a country are equal – or are expected to be equally treated. Where the limits of these rights are drawn without taking into consideration their implications, in the given conditions, for the basic rights of the individual, i.e., where the delineation of these limits is not determined by the principles of human rights but by other determinants, there we are faced with social injustice.[7]

In our human rights documents, the second kind of basic rights of the individual as a human being and social and economic rights of the individual as a citizen of a given country appear under the same heading; e.g., the right of everyone to work (understood as one's having "the opportunity to earn his living by work which he freely chooses or accepts") and "the right of everyone to form trade unions". Do all human beings need to form trade unions in order to protect their "economic and social interests"?

Keeping in mind the difference between protecting r i g h t s and protecting i n t e r e s t s – i.e., possessing clear concepts of "right" and "interest" and consequently knowing that the concept of one's interests always includes clashing either with other's interests or rights – we can perhaps see that this demand (concerning trade unions) does not concern every individual as a human being, but is conceived as a solution, in given historical conditions, for the protection of rights of a category of working human beings in a social-legal order determined by other principles than human rights, determined by clashing interests – in other words, that it is a special form of the right to form associations with a given purpose, in a given type of society.

This conception of economic rights, or "economic freedoms", of the individual as human rights, seems to underlie at present the fashionable world-wide promotion of the so-called free market economy in various non-affluent countries (those on the way to demarxization included) – a promotion, which probably will not contribute to the promotion of, but will give damage to, the basic human rights of the majority of the individuals in these countries.

Also the conception of collective rights as human rights creates similar problems.

It seems to escape attention that the same basic (human) rights have different implications in different real, historical conditions – implications to be deduced carefully in those conditions. This leads to not differentiating between kinds of norms, i.e., to using all of them as f i r s t premises, in different real conditions. This appears to be, so far as I can see, one of the main origins of the contradictions that our human rights documents bear.

Most of those working in international institutions and in other bodies established for the protection of human rights are eager to find new m e c h a n i s m s for the protection of human rights and underestimate philosophical questioning of human rights and human rights issues. In the face of the flagrant violations and disparities in the protection of human rights I do share their concern and their haste.

It should not nevertheless escape attention, that rights and human rights are conceptions of the human mind, which, if they are not conceived clearly

---

[7] See also my "Philosophy and Social Injustice", in *Philosophy and Cultures*. Nairobi, 1982, pp. 47-52, in the present volume pp. 25-35.

enough – i.e., if we do not see clearly what they demand – and if those among the decision-makers who really possess the will to protect human rights are not sufficiently equipped so as to find out, by evaluating each situation independently, their different implications in different conditions, for a chain-legislation based on human rights, this most precious achievement of the 20th Century could turn into a "myth" of our age, as some disappointed people already claim.

After fifty years of the establishment of the UN, at the turn of a century which has brought to the fore the idea of human rights, much and organized work remains to be done, urgently, so that at present and in the coming century, more and more human beings may live as h u m a n beings, and more and more human beings become conscious of their h u m a n identity, before becoming conscious of other identities of theirs, s o t h a t the demands that human rights express can be more and more fulfilled in the active and passive sense.

Are we – *we*: philosophers, jurists and other related professionals, FISP, UNESCO, UN and some other groups of individuals and organizations –, really concerned with the protection of human rights, are we ready to take over such an organized task? Are we ready, i.e., uncompromisingly sincere and sufficiently equipped theoretically, to take over on a world-wide organized scale such a work?

THE CONCEPT OF HUMAN DIGNITY AND HUMAN RIGHTS[*]

During an interview on human rights in a TV programme made almost ten years ago, the interviewer all of a sudden said that, so far as he could understand, I was establishing a connection between philosophy and torture, and asked me what this connection was. I was shocked. In a couple of seconds I tried to guess how he could have come to such a conclusion. My response was: there is no connection between philosophy and torture, still when you look at the fact of torture with philosophical-ethical knowledge, you can realize that torture does not damage, nor "degrade" the human dignity of the victim of torture, as is usually accepted – e.g., in the formulation of the title of the "Convention against Torture and Other Cruel, Inhuman or Degrading Treatment or Punishment". It causes damage to the human dignity of the person who tortures. We protect or damage human dignity, but o u r o w n human dignity, by what we do and n o t by what we suffer, since we are responsible for what we do and n o t for what others do to us. What we do, or refrain from doing, depends on each of us, i.e., acting in accordance with human dignity in our relations with other human beings is a problem in our ethical relation with ourselves, in spite of the fact that our actions are directed to somebody else.

This is an incident that I often use within different contexts for different theoretical and practical purposes, still mainly in order to reverse the broadly accepted assumption that human beings a r e dishonoured or degraded by the treatment they undergo; i.e., in order to call attention to the fact that we protect, or give damage to, human dignity – our human dignity – not by what we suffer, but by what we ourselves do.

This claim of mine is closely connected with the most basic aspect of human rights – their ethical aspect – which is unfortunately neglected in the present debate on, and in the education of, human rights, which focus only on so-called human rights law. Thus in spite of the fact that the term human dignity is often mentioned in connection with human rights, the point of the conceptual connection between human rights and human dignity is not sufficiently clear.

Here I shall try to show this point of connection, which lies also in the origin of single human rights, by clarifying the concept of human rights and conceptualizing what we call human dignity (*dignité humaine*, *menschliche Würde*, ἀνθρώπινη ἀξιοπρέπεια, *insan onuru*) through the concept of the value of t h e human being. Then I shall also try to distinguish this concept of human

---

[*] This is a paper presented in the seminar on "Droits et dignité de la personne humaine", organized by the International Union of Academies on May 24-26, 2004 in Barcelona and hosted by the Institut d'Estudis Catalanos.

dignity from other concepts with which is often confused in everyday life, such as honour (*honneur*, *Ehre*, τιμή/ὑπόληψις, *namus/onur*), and pride (*fierté*, *Stolz*, ὑπερηφάνεια, *gurur*) – a confusion which leads to the assumption that there are different perceptions of human dignity in different civilizations or cultures.

This latter is a difficult job, because such words have not always equivalents in different languages or, even if they have, these words have not always the same connotation.

*

What are human rights?

What we call 'human rights' is first of all a n i d e a, a conception of the human mind: the conception that human beings, b e c a u s e they are h u m a n beings – i.e, because they belong to a species, which, due to certain specificities that it possesses, has produced the bread we eat, has discovered the electricity we use at every moment, has written *The Little Prince* which some of us read, has brought the idea of equity (ἐπιείκεια) and the institution of *ombudsman,* which some countries establish, etc., i.e., because it has achieved all these – should be treated in a special way, in a way that makes p o s s i b l e for a human being to actualize such potentialities of t h e human being. It should be treated in this special way, because in life, most human beings deprive other human beings of this possibility.

This is what the first article of the *Universal Declaration of Human Rights* i n t e n d s to express, by stating that "all human beings are born free and equal in dignity and rights. They are endowed with reason and conscience and should act towards one another in a spirit of brotherhood". In this wording of the first article of the *Declaration* which, if I am not mistaken, is the only article which words t h e c o n c e p t i o n of human rights underlying the main international human rights instruments, we see the attempt to justify the equality in dignity and rights of all human beings by two natural characteristics of t h e human being – one intellectual (reason) and one ethical (conscience) – from which also t h e n e c e s s i t y to act towards one another "brotherly" is deduced: a l l human beings are e q u a l i n d i g n i t y a n d r i g h t s *because* they are endowed with reason and conscience; and *because* they are endowed with reason and conscience they should a c t to one another in the spirit of brotherhood. Here we see that human rights are also conceived as principles of action as well.

Human beings should be treated, by other human beings, in a special way, in a spirit of brotherhood, still not as Cain and Abel treated each other. But how?

The subsequent articles of the *Declaration* are an attempt to answer this how. And the two *International Covenants* and other similar international instruments are attempts – or intend – to put forward the conditions of the possibility of such a treatment, i.e., to put forward norms – basic "universal" norms – to be made effective in the arrangement of social relations: in legislation at various levels and in the administration of public affairs, so that individuals have the possibility to actualize – each one as much as he or she can – the potentialities of *the* human being, which I mentioned earlier.

What we call human rights are first of all *ethical principles* for the treatment of individuals, not only in the passive but also in the active sense. They are an attempt – still a very deficient attempt not only in practice but also in theory – to introduce *ethical* demands in social organization, in law and politics.

Put very briefly, human rights express, and demand the permanent creation of, the general conditions deemed necessary for the actualizability of certain potentialities of the human being.

This is an anthropological approach to human rights, based on a concept of value, according to which the value of the human being is understood as "the special place of *the* human being (as a species) among other living beings", due to certain different or plus specificities of the human being, besides those it shares with other living beings – specificities which also include its potentialities.

Human rights express the objective conditions of the actualizability of such potentialities which constitute the value of the human being as a species. Put forward as norms they tell us how each and every human being should treat, and be treated by, other human beings, so that he or she has the possibility to actualize such potentialities.

Thus, what we call 'human dignity' denotes *the awareness of the value of the human being*. It is this value that makes every human being worthy (*digne* in French) to be treated so as he or she has the possibility to actualize such potentialities of the human being and live in peace with himself or herself. It is the subjective correlative of the objective value of the human being.

Human dignity consists of the philosophical/anthropological knowledge of the value of the human species, i.e., the knowledge of certain of its specificities and of the achievements of the human species in history resulting from them and which secure its special place in the universe. This knowledge makes necessary for all those who possess it, to treat all human beings, whatever their other natural and contingent specificities might be, in accordance with this value – even those who ignore it. It is also this knowledge that helps an individual become conscious of being first of all a *human* being, become aware of his or her *human* identity – our only common identity – whatever all his or her other identities might be.

Single human rights are practical implications of human dignity. They demand from all individuals a kind of treatment for all individuals, which protects the value of the human being. This is why clearly conceived human rights are "universal" norms.

This universality of human rights is what distinguishes them from cultural norms which differ from society to society and show changes in the same society, and consequently what distinguishes 'human dignity' from cultural conceptions of 'honour', which are usually – though not exclusively – related to the different and changing value judgements (concerning what is good and bad) prevailing in different cultures, societies, religions, etc.

In its most original sense 'honour' denotes the esteem paid to the worth, or assumed worth, of a n i n d i v i d u a l. This worth can consist of the ethical specificities of a person – of his virtues, as for example described in Aristotle's *Nicomachean Ethics* – i.e., the esteem paid may have an objective correlative and be based on the knowledge of the virtues of an individual; but it can also be considered to consist of the correspondence of an individual's behaviour to the value judgements prevailing in a culture, i.e., to the ways or models of behaviour and attitudes deemed "good" in a given society.

Thus while the content of the concept of human dignity consists of anthropological knowledge related to the nature of t h e h u m a n b e i n g, the concept of honour is related to the esteem of worth or assumed worth (of the image) of a n i n d i v i d u a l.

We can also see this difference between human dignity and honour especially by looking at cases of dishonour. You will perhaps remember of a statement of an Iraqi prisoner, reported recently in the press, who was tortured by US soldiers. He said that he preferred to be given electricity, as it happened when he was arrested in Saddam's time, than to be obliged to stay totally naked in front of a wall, because the latter treatment d i s h o n o u r e d him, while the former did not.

Thus, though both ways of treatment ignore human dignity, the prisoner didn't f e e l dishonoured when he was given electricity, but only when he was obliged to stay totally naked in front of others' eyes.

To protect human dignity, by what we do or refrain from doing, depends on each of us, while to be honoured depends on others. Still by attempting to dishonour someone, i.e., to force him to see himself, and be seen, in a position in which he does not want to be seen (as in the case of the Iraqi prisoner), we give damage to human dignity which we share with him, whether he feels dishonoured or not. To be honoured depends on others, who evaluate things in different ways, who, if not sufficiently equipped with ethical value knowledge, honour not only the honourable.

A honourable person is he who knows, or at least is aware of, what human dignity is and acts accordingly.

It is interesting that in English (and French) 'honesty' and 'honour' have the same etymon. Honesty can be conceived as the identity (the sameness) of what someone wants to realize by an action and what he carries out. In other words, it can be conceived as the n e c e s s a r y connection between what a person wants to be realized and what he does to somebody else in a given case. An honest person is a person who does to the others what he wants f o r t h e m, and does not expect, from what he does to somebody else, something "to return" to himself – to use Kant's words, who does not treat the others as means. He is one who protects human dignity. Such a person is an honourable person, whether he is honoured or not. He is honourable because he acts in accordance with human dignity.

I think that what differs from culture to culture is the conception of honour which is often conceptually confused with human dignity.

'Honour', as the esteem paid to worth or assumed worth, is also related to one's ethical relation with himself – as self-esteem or arrogance. Self-esteem is based on the knowledge of one's ethical virtues, arrogance on self-image, mostly shaped through the eyes of others. And this is the point where in certain cultures 'honour' is confused with 'pride'. In this case, if someone is treated, or assumes to be treated, by others in accordance with his self-image he feels proud, if not, he feels his pride hurt or wounded.

Considered from the perspective of the individual: dignity is the subjective correlative – the individual's knowledge or awareness – of the value that individuals as *human* beings *possess* and can give damage only by what they themselves do; while honour or dishonour are *feelings* caused, in the light of self-esteem, by the way individuals are treated by others. Thus it is possible that an honourable person treated in a way *intending*, for some reason independent of himself, to dishonour him in others' eyes, does not feel dishonoured, while another person treated in the same way does.

In the latter case we observe a confusion between honour and pride. From the perspective of the individual honour appears as an individual's feeling which has to do with the way he or she is treated by others who pay esteem to his or her ethical virtues – an esteem which corresponds to his or her *self-knowledge*. While pride is a feeling which has to do with an individual's relation with himself or herself, experienced when treated, directly or indirectly, in accordance with his *self-image*.

Human rights have to do with human dignity – the knowledge of the value of certain potentialities of the human being, which also constitutes the major premises in the deduction of human rights norms. This is the reason why human rights are first of all ethical norms and universal norms, and consequently have to be carefully distinguished from cultural/social norms. And this is also why clearly conceived human rights should constitute the major premises in the deduction of positive law: because they express the conditions of the possibility of actualizing certain human potentialities and live a humane life in the active and passive sense.

This concept of human dignity put forward in its connection with human rights through the concept of the value of *the* human being, implies that it would be more appropriate to speak of different conceptions of honour in different societies or cultures, due to the different conceptions of the characteristics assumed to constitute the "worth" of a person, than of different conceptions of human dignity. How can human beings be equal in dignity and treated accordingly, if dignity is conceived differently in different cultures?

In the face of the different conceptions of the same ideas, we have to conceptualize these ideas philosophically. An appropriate way concerning how we can do this, we find in Plato's dialogue the *Meno* and Aristotle's *Nicomachean Ethics*. Thus, in the light of these conceptualizations we can evaluate such ideas, so that cultural conceptions, and the norms formulated on the ground of these conceptions, are not given priority to human rights and so that we can avoid, as much as possible, that human rights are violated for the sake of cultural conceptions.

LAÏCITÉ AND HUMAN RIGHTS*

'Clash of civilizations' is a fashionable expression we hear everyday, as is 'dialogue of civilizations', 'dialogue of cultures', 'dialogue of religions', which are considered to be its antidote. I find this a quite simplistic approach to the relevant problem we are faced with at present and which appears as one of the most acute problems of multicultural or multireligious societies: to the conflicts due to the discrepancy, even contradiction, between norms on the same issues, be they between norms of different cultures or religions, or between them and legal or human rights norms.

At present *laïcité* constitutes a permanent issue of debate in many countries. It is discussed from various perspectives and is often considered to be a way to face clashes between religious communities, which, according to a prevailing view, necessitates "the equal distance of the State to all religions". But, so far as I can follow these debates, no direct connection is established between *laïcité* and human rights.

On the other hand, even in states which avow – in their constitutions – to be "*laïc*", we see an increase in decisions and practices which contradict *laïcité* and which, unnoticed, creep into, spread in and determine, public life. The well-minded but philosophically unscrutinized promotion of "equal respect to all cultures", during the past few decades, coupled with a misconception of so-called fundamental freedoms, has played, and still plays, a crucial role in this. Thus the need to rethink the concept of *laïcité* has become very urgent, since the prevailing understanding does not help us to face the attempts of desecularization made in the name of freedom(s).

Here I shall try to show that *laïcité* is a *sine qua non* condition for the effectiveness and implementation of human rights. I shall do it by analyzing the two different – yet complementary – terms used in order to express the same idea: *laïcité-laïcism* and secularization-secularism and while doing this I shall keep in mind the intentions in introducing, a few centuries ago, this idea in the existing conditions in Europe.

*

Laïcité is a historical principle concerning the arrangement and administration of public affairs. But what is it? In other words, what distinguishes it from other relevant principles and norms which play – or are expected to play – the same role?

---

* The Turkish version of this paper was published in *Hacettepe Üniversitesi Edebiyat Fakültesi Dergisi*, special issue on the 75th anniversary of the establishment of the Republic of Turkey. Ankara, 1998, pp. 21-27.

According to many people *laïcism* amounts to atheism or to the rejection of religion. To them, being *laïciste* means being irreligious or atheist. Many others, nevertheless, oppose this assumption and claim that it is very well possible for an individual to be religious and at the same time *laïciste*. But since neither of these claims is justified in a cognitively justifiable way, the debate usually runs in a vicious circle.

Considered philosophically, as a principle concerning the arrangement and administration of public affairs, *laïcité* appears to have little or nothing to do with irreligiosity, as well as with religiosity. Because those who possess *a* religion – i.e., one given religion – are individuals, and these individuals, who possess that one given religion, constitute one given "group" from this viewpoint, though from the viewpoints of other characteristics they possess, they belong at the same time to various other groups – i.e., they have many other collective identities.

In today's world each individual – unless he is a *"heimatlos"* – is the citizen of a state, whose law is deduced and public affairs are organized with different principles. In many states the citizens possess different religions and some of them are irreligious, while citizens of different states possess the same religion. In other words, 'citizenship' expresses an individual's relation with a state, while 'religiosity' or 'irreligiosity' express his relation with a given religion – with a monotheistic, polytheistic or non-theistic system of "beliefs".

Each religion consists mainly of a doctrine – a dogma, a world view – and a system of morals (a system of norms of evaluation and conduct) related to that doctrine. An individual's belonging to, or possessing, a religion means that this individual believes in the "truth" of a doctrine taught to him and which is different from similar doctrines, still without taking into consideration the epistemic quality of this doctrine; and that in his life fulfils the demands that the norms of evaluation and conduct related to this doctrine bring, still without taking into consideration their epistemological and axiological specificities.

All systems of morals, be they related to a religion or not, are sets of norms – of different and changing general value judgements and rules of conduct – made valid in given groups and aiming at teaching individuals what is "good" and what is "bad", consequently aiming at determining the evaluations and actions of individuals in their relations with other individuals and with themselves. *Laïcité* is not a principle which can find a place in a system of morals.

It is a principle related to the arrangement of public affairs, to the establishment of legal relations and the administration of law in a state. As a practical principle it too expresses in fact a demand concerning what should, and should not, be done; but the demand that it brings does not concern the determination of interpersonal relations, but the determination of legal relations and public affairs.

According to a widespread understanding *laïcité* denotes the separation of the State and religion: according to some, the "non-interference of religion (of the Church) to the affairs of the State", but according to others, "not only the non-interference of religion to the affairs of the State, but also of the State to the affairs of religion".

This is a quite superficial conception of *laïcité;* it loses sight of its historical context – i.e., of the reasons why this principle was introduced or of its "what for" –, and thus keeps the door open to varying "interpretations". This conception, nevertheless, secures us a clue, which can be used in our attempt to clarify the concept of *laïcité*: it makes us see the essential intention in bringing this principle: that "something" usually done should not be done any more.

If we manage to get an insight of, and put our finger on, this "something", we might perhaps grasp what *laïcité* – beyond the claimed non-interference – demands.

To do this, allow me, please, first to remind you of the etymology of *laïcité*, which probably all of you know, and then use it. The Greek term *λαϊκός* (*laicus* in Latin), from which *laïcité* is derived, is an adjective used as a substantive. This term, which is the relative term of *κληρικός,* denotes everyone who does not belong to *κλῆρος* (to the clergy), the layman, whatever his social status or his other qualifications might be. Now the adjective *laïc* in French is related to this meaning of the Greek term λαϊκός – i.e., of the term used as a substantive and as the relative term of *κληρικός* – though the adjective λαϊκός in Greek has a much broader connotation.

Thus, the adjective *laïc* in French, e.g., in the contexts 'morale *laïque*', 'état *laïc*', 'enseignement *laïc*', denotes a "negative" quality, in the technical sense of the term: the only thing that we learn in connection with that morals, state or teaching is that the morals under consideration – whatever it be – is not a system of norms stemming from any religion, that the constitution and administration of the state under consideration –whatever it be – is not determined by norms stemming from any religion; that the educational system under consideration – whatever its objectives and methods might be – is not developed by taking into account the conceptions and norms of any religion.

This means that when somebody speaks of *un état laïc* the only thing we learn from it, is that this state is constituted and administrated without taking into account the world view and the norms of any religion – though this does not exclude a coincidence of certain norms. In such a state the fact that the citizens, as individuals, have a religion or different religions or no religion, makes no difference in their relations, as citizens, with the State. Still the adjective *laïc* in this context does not tell us on which principles that given *laïc* state is constituted or what its regime in fact is. A '*laïc*' state may have quite different regimes.

Thus, *laïcité* as an idea of the Enlightenment and a principle of the modern State – whose basic unit is the citizen and which is based on citizen's equality in rights – consists of the conception and demand, that the doctrines and norms of (any) religion s h o u l d n o t d e t e r m i n e the constitution and administration of the State, that it should not determine the deduction and application of law in a state.

This amounts in practice to the demand that political organs and public institutions should not be based on religious conceptions and norms, and that public and State officers, while exercising their functions, should not take into consideration the conceptions and norms of any religion.

As it appears from this analysis, *laïcité* is only a negative concept, in the technical sense of the term. And this seems to be the reason that makes possible to ascribe to it different contents, most of which do not contribute to the fulfilment of the intentions for which it was introduced.

Now, keeping in mind that all cultural traditions are infiltrated with religious traditions and *vice versa*, as well as that non-religious cultural norms play the same role, we have to enlarge the extension of the concept of *laïcité* and put forward its positive content.

The following question might help us overcome the difficulties created by *laïcité* as a negative concept: if the doctrine and norms of (any) religion would not determine the constitution and administration of a state or the deduction of law, what kind of conceptions or norms would be appropriate to determine them?

In our endeavour to answer this question, the other term used to express the same idea – the term 'secularization-secularism' – gives us a clue.

In the concept of secularization there is a n a d d i t i o n a l element, which we don't find in the concept of *laïcité:* the term 'secular' etymologically comes from the Latin word *saecularis,* which derives from the word *saeculum.* The latter Latin word means 'century', 'age' (αἰών). This etymology makes me think that 'secularization' wishes to express the change, and thus the adaptation, of "something" to the exigencies of the age, in other words, thus understood 'secularization' appears to be a synonym of 'modernization'.

Now, if we keep this in mind, as well as the historical and factual conditions in which it was introduced, secularization would amount to changing and adapting that which is the object of secularization to the new ideas which humanity has produced at that age. What is secularized is usually an institution determined, until that moment, by the conceptions and norms of a given religion which are discrepant to those new ideas. Secularism brings such a demand.

Thus *laïcisme* and secularism appear to be the two sides of the same coin, i.e., the negative and positive concepts of the same idea. *Laïcité* expresses w h a t s h o u l d n o t d e t e r m i n e the structure and functioning of an institution and first of all of the State, while secularism expresses w h a t s h o u l d d e t e r m i n e i t: these are the ideas shaped by the philosophical thought of "the age". Historically they are the ideas produced as a result of the

Enlightenment in the Kantian sense, i.e., "when man leaves his self-caused immaturity" and "finds the courage to use his own intelligence without the guidance of another [...] and primarily in matters of religion".

Now, if the '*laïc* State' is a form of State, whose constitution and administration is not based on the conceptions and norms of any religion, what would be today, in the beginning of the third millennium, the main characteristic of the "modern", "contemporary", "secular" state?

If we look at the principal ideas of our *saeculum* – of our age – from the viewpoint of their value, i.e., if we attempt to evaluate them, and especially when we compare different norms – cultural norms and human rights norms – on the same issues and the different consequences they bear for human beings; it appears that the most significant or valuable idea of our age in this respect, is the idea of human rights, i.e., the idea that human beings, because they are human beings, should be treated, and treat other human beings, in "a certain way". Single human rights are attempts – unfortunately not always successful attempts – to put forward this "certain way".

On the ground of these considerations we can now formulate *laïcism* and secularism as the demand that the deduction of law *[de droit]*, as well as the arrangement and administration of public affairs – the public institutions – be determined, not by religious-cultural-traditional world views and norms, but by human rights and norms which are implications of human rights in the condition of a given country. We can also say that 'secular State' is the state whose law is deduced from human rights and which is administrated in accordance with human rights: it is the State based on human rights.

Thus *laïcité* appears to be a condition *sine qua non* of the modern/contemporary State, a condition *sine qua non* of the possibility of making determinant human rights.

To put it in one sentence: religious and cultural norms in general should not determine the deduction of law, as well as the arrangement and administration of public affairs, so that human rights can determine them.

In a world in which attempts are made to promote so-called "minimization of the state" in the name of (misunderstood) freedoms – a minimization whose one foreseeable consequence would be desecularization – if we sincerely wish to implement clearly conceived human rights, we have to float against the stream and to keep vigil over *laïcité* as a necessary condition for the implementation of human rights.

ON TOLERANCE AND THE LIMITS OF TOLERATION*

THE PROBLEM

Two main but discrepant tendencies characterize the intellectual climate of our world at the turn of the century. We promote, on the one hand, "respect to human rights", i.e., to certain universal norms, but on the other hand, we equally promote "respect to all cultures", which are differentiated among themselves by their different world views and their parochial norms. Not rarely we see that the demands that such parochial norms bring are contradictory to those of human rights.

We are not sufficiently aware of this discrepancy. Still our simultaneous promotion of these two discrepant tendencies has already produced its own facts, among which we see the revival of racisms, nationalisms, fundamentalisms and other similar intolerables.

How to tackle the problems created by these intolerables without giving damage to the so-called fundamental freedoms? This is the dilemma that humanity faces just at this moment, and especially in the so-called developed countries.

At the beginning of our century pragmatism, to face the problems created by the conflicting "truths" of the time, had suggested "pluralism", as an antidote to dogmatism – the corridor of William James. Instead of tackling the problem epistemologically, it tried to solve it by cutting the Gordian knot, i.e., by making out of fact an ideal and by introducing a new "theory of truth".[1]

This pragmatist ideal has become one of the mottos of our time: the "pluralistic universe" has become now "pluralistic society" or "multicultural society". And now, in order to face the "conflicts of cultures", and especially those within "multicultural societies", we promote tolerance.

Still, in the turmoil created by the spread of postmodernism which claimed the equal value of all world views, norms or cultures, in a world in which the "right to freedom of thought, conscience, expression, etc." is taken for granted and in which unscrutinized pluralism turned out to a *laisser faire, laisser passer* in practice, i.e., in a world in which "anything goes"; when the increase of racist-nationalist-fundamentalist conflicts has led to an impasse in

---

* This paper was published in *Diogenes*, N° 176. Berghahn Books, 1996, pp. 163-174; its French version (trans. by Pierre-Emmanuel Dauzat) in *Diogène*, N° 176. Gallimard, 1996, pp. 143-153; and also in Chinese.

[1] See also Ioanna Kuçuradi, "Introduction to the Seminar", in Ioanna Kuçuradi and Robert S. Cohen (eds), *The Concept of Knowledge. The Ankara Seminar*. Boston, Studies in the Philosophy of Science 170, Kluwer Academic Publishers, 1995, pp. IX-XV.

public life, the question of the limits of tolerance is brought on the agenda of the intellectual world community.

Thus now, at the turn of the century, we feel, as humanity, the need to reformulate tolerance "between intolerance and the intolerable", in other words, we feel the need to determine the limits of toleration.

In our endeavour to do this, there is another recent intellectual development in the approach to human rights, which has also to be taken into consideration: the well-minded, very pragmatic "cultural approach" to, or the quest for a "cultural legitimacy" of, human rights, which has led to the application of the "theory of overlapping consensus" to human rights.[2] This approach seems to be a compromise between the two, if unconditionally promoted, hardly compatible tendencies, which characterize the intellectual climate of our days. Probably it escapes attention that what distinguishes one given cultural group from another, is its own specific, i.e., different, world view and norms of evaluation and behaviour, which secure the existence of that group a g a i n s t other cultural groups; while human rights are demands concerning how human beings have to be treated by and treat other human beings, whatever their specific characteristics – cultural ones included – might be. It escapes attention that cultural norms and human rights – though not all of those demands which a r e n o w c a l l e d human rights – are deduced from epistemologically and axiologically different premises and by different kinds of reasoning.

We have to rethink tolerance in connection with all these intellectual and other[3] developments, which have led to the present situation of the world, and reformulate tolerance in connection with the intolerables of our days, still without losing sight of its historical origin, i.e., the historical conditions, in which the idea of tolerance was brought to the fore, in view to face them.

This is what in this paper I shall partly try to do.

WHAT IS TOLERANCE?

If we take a look at various contexts in which the verb 'to tolerate' and the terms 'tolerance' and 'tolerant' are used in certain European languages on the one hand, and on the other at the historical conditions existing at the time when the idea of tolerance was brought to the fore, i.e., the religious-sectarian conflicts of the time, as well as at the conditions of the present world, i.e., the cultural-

---

[2] Tore Lindholm, "Prospect for Research on the Cultural Legitimacy of Human Rights", in *Human Rights in Cross-Cultural Perspectives*, ed. by Abdullahi Ahmet An-Na'im. University of Pensylvania Press, Philadelphia, 1992, pp. 387-426; and John Rawls, "Lecture IV. The Idea of Overlapping Consensus", *Political Liberalism*. New York, 1993, pp. 133-172.

[3] For these other developments see: Ioanna Kuçuradi, "Les droits de l'homme et la décennie du développement culturel", in *Birleşmiş Milletler Türk Derneği 1988 Yıllığı*. Ankara, 1990, pp. 25-33; or "Cultural Morals and Global Morality in the Light of Ethics", in *WASCO'88 The World Community in Post-Industrial Society* 4. Seoul, 1989, pp. 41-47.

ideological conflicts of our time, we see that it is possible to deal with the question of tolerance at least from two different perspectives: from the viewpoint of the "subject" of tolerance, i.e., to deal with tolerance as a personal attitude and from the viewpoint of the "object" of tolerance, i.e., to deal with tolerance (toleration) as a demand concerning the arrangement and administration of public affairs, or, as a principle concerning an *in abstracto* non-determinable area of different views and practices related to the same issues, still an area delineated by the limits where the intolerables start.

Tolerance as a personal attitude

As a personal attitude tolerance is closely related to a given conception of being human, which may underlie the way a person looks at the others: his looking at the other persons – each of whom is unique, consequently "different" – as human beings, whatever their differences, personal characteristics or conditions might be.

What mainly marks the tolerant person is that in concrete situations he does not give damage, though he is in a position to do so, to the rights of another person, who is "different", i.e., who possesses a view-opinion-norm radically different from that which the tolerant person possesses on the same issue, and/or who takes an attitude, acts in a given situation or behaves in general, in a way radically different from that which he approves.

The following points have to be emphasized:

What the tolerant person "tolerates", is not the radically different views-opinions-norms or attitudes-ways of behaviour or practices and given actions of the others, but the existence of these others. What, on the contrary, the intolerant person does not, or cannot, tolerate, is the existence of views-opinions-norms which are "different" from those he strongly believes to be "true", or the ways of behaviour and practices radically different from those he strongly believes to be "good", no matter who possesses or shows them. The tolerant person does not identify the other person with his ideas and practices, which he strongly disapproves of, while the intolerant person does so.

What determines the actions of the intolerant person to those who possess radically different views or opinions and behave or act in ways he strongly disapproves of – if it is not his personal interests – is his concern to "defend" what he takes for granted to be "true" or "good". To eliminate the "erroneous" ideas and "bad" practices he eliminates those who possess or show them, i.e., he causes damage to their rights, if he is in a position to do so. If he is not, as we often see, the intolerant person has recourse to violence: to eliminate the ideas he annihilates – or threatens to annihilate – those who, he thinks, personify them.

What, on the other hand, determines the actions of the tolerant person, is his looking at the others, be they themselves tolerant or intolerant, as human beings who, for one or another reason, possess different ideas, opinions or norms from those he approves, but which however are not guises of personal interests.

Thus it appears that what the tolerant person "respects" is not "differences", but what is identical in all human beings. Hence he rejects consciously to give damage to their rights, i.e., he "respects" their rights. This seems to be the reason why bigots can easily exploit tolerant persons, as we sometimes observe in public life.

At this point we can also see why tolerance, as a personal attitude, does not imply that the tolerant person should not oppose, or fight against, the views-opinions-norms-practices he disapproves of; or, to use the fashionable expression, that he should "respect" others' different views and cultures. Why, for instance, should one "respect" polygamy or blood feud?

In the light of these considerations it appears that "respecting others' different views" is not tolerance, as it is usually assumed. Tolerance, as a personal attitude, is respecting the rights of those who possess radically different views on a given issue and act in a different way from the way that one approves – i.e., it is causing no damage to their rights, though one is in a position to do so.

Understanding by 'tolerance' 'to respect others' different views' and nevertheless rejecting to tolerate the outcome of some of them, betrays lack of sufficient philosophical knowledge on world views and norms – a lack, which leads many people to conclude from the difficulty to evaluate epistemologically and axiologically given views, norms, etc., the impossibility of such an evaluation. In practice such a "respect" amounts to choosing, in the name of "objectivity", to remain indifferent to any view, opinion, norm, way of behaviour or practice and to let "anything go". It amounts to closing one's eyes to the intolerables.

Tolerance as a principle of public affairs

These considerations, put forward by bringing into the focus to subject of tolerance, i.e., the tolerant person, lead us to the core of our inquiry: the philosophical problems we are faced with, when we bring into the focus the object of tolerance, or, the question of the tolerable and the intolerable.

This question, raised in connection with the arrangement and administration of public affairs, amounts in fact to three questions of different order: One of them is the question of what may be tolerated though strange or unusual, i.e., the question of the permissible; the second is the question of what should not be tolerated and consequently must be prohibited, and the third is the question of what, though not approved by the majority or a powerful minority in a given place at a given time, should be tolerated in public life. The first two questions together concern the boundary between the tolerable and the intolerable, or the problem of the limits of tolerance; the third question, put in connection with the first one, concerns the boundary between the permissible and the non-prohibitable.

It is not possible to formulate positively, in the technical sense of the term, the tolerable, but only negatively, in connection with the intolerable; because to determine whether "something" may, or may not, be permitted it must be evaluated cognitively in connection with the existing conditions, independently from whoever approves or disapproves of it.

On the contrary, it is possible to formulate positively t h e intolerable, i.e., to put forward the common characteristics of the intolerables, because what has to be done in this case is n o t to put forward what should not be tolerated, but what s h o u l d n o t b e t o l e r a b l e f o r t h e h u m a n b e i n g (s).

Intolerable are facts, created directly by, or by concurrence of, human decisions, actions or indifference and inertia. Be they conditions, situations, practices, customs, acts, etc., they a r e intolerable, because in one or another way hinder the actualization of the potentialities, which constitute the specificity of the human being, or they cause damage to what we call human dignity. Still they are there, i.e., at the moment we are faced with them it is no more possible to prevent or hinder them.

To "fight" against them, i.e., to change them or secure that they be not perpetuated, it is necessary to dig out the views and norms that underlie them and evaluate those views and norms philosophically, and subsequently to find and carry out what in the given conditions has to be done – in legislation and education – to make them ineffective.

Thus the question we have to scrutinize may be formulated as follows: what are the specificities of views and norms underlying the facts which are intolerable – be they or not different from the views and norms approved at a given moment by the majority or a powerful minority in a country or in the world as a whole?

This is the question of the epistemically justifiable criteria for selecting norms for legislation on national and international levels, and for the administration of public and world affairs, i.e., of criteria for deciding what, in general and in given conditions, should be tolerable, intolerable or non-prohibitable.

This question of criteria is a crucial one in the present state of affairs, not only because groups possessing different cultures – different and often incompatible views and norms on the same issues – are living intermingled in the same space and because liberalistic pluralism, justified by postmodernism, and our unscrutinized conception of "freedoms" has already led to the dilemma I mentioned at the beginning of this paper; but also because now, after the collapse of the "Second World", the tendency to "minimize the State", as many people call it, and to promote international civil co-operation gains ground more and more, still without paying a special attention to the question "co-operation in or for what?" – as is the case now with the unconditional promotion of the "free market" on national and international levels, which seems to be pregnant with further intolerables.[4]

Viewed philosophically the core of the question concerns the ground to stand on in approving, tolerating or opposing and rejecting a given view or norm; it concerns the problem of the right evaluation of views and norms. This is their evaluation in view to know their epistemological and axiological specificities, and not their evaluation from the viewpoint of any different view or norm on the same issue.

By emphasizing this I wish to call attention to the following: the being different of an idea, view, norm, as well as of a practice, way of behaviour, etc., from the prevailing ones at a given place and time, does not automatically necessitate its becoming an object of tolerance, but only object of philosophical evaluation. What determines whether it may, or may not, or even should at least, be an object of toleration, is not its being "different", but its epistemological and axiological quality. It is not excluded that such an evaluation might even show, that a given norm or practice, which is radically different from the prevailing one on the same issue, not only may be tolerated, but that it should be promoted as well.

If we know the epistemological and axiological specificities of norms, i.e., what distinguishes them from knowledge, and their kinds, we may become able to evaluate single norms and see the limits to be drawn to tolerance in legislation, as well as to distinguish between what may be and what should be tolerated in public life.

In the light of these considerations, it appears that it is possible to conceptualize tolerance, also as a principle of public affairs, only in connection with intolerance, still in connection with two different objects of intolerance, i.e., of those which are not tolerated in public life: those which are not, though they may be, tolerated; and those which are not, though they should be.

This means that it is not possible to develop positive criteria, to use them as touchstones for selecting those ideas, norms, practices which may be tolerated in general. Even the fact that certain practices and ways of behaviour may be tolerated in given real conditions, does not necessitate that they be tolerated in different conditions as well. But it is possible, by looking at the intolerables and finding out what makes them "intolerable", to formulate certain positive criteria to use for distinguishing the views, ideas, norms, practices, etc. – be they different from the prevailing ones, or, be they the most prevailing ones – which should not be objects of toleration, i.e., whose propaganda, teaching, or exercising should be prohibited in public life.[5] In other words, this means

---

[4] See also: Ioanna Kuçuradi, "Economic Disparities and the Fashionable Linking of Human Rights, Democracy and Free Market", in *Violence and Human Coexistence*, vol. V. Montreal, 1995, pp. 330-336.

[5] I am well aware that I say something which sounds discrepant to the widespread understanding of the "freedom of thought" and that I say something dangerous, so

that we have first to formulate the criteria of the intolerables, so that we can distinguish intolerance, which may be shown to anything which differs from what is accepted as "true" or "good", from the intolerable: that which s h o u l d n o t b e t o l e r a b l e for the human being(s).

In the case of views, knowledge draws the limits of the intolerable. This means that if there is a clash between a view and k n o w l e d g e on a given issue, this view should not be allowed to become determinant in public affairs. This criterion is especially important when it is put in connection with our promotion of "democracy", because, though the truth or falsity of a piece of knowledge is not a question of "democratic" decision, its becoming or not becoming determinant in public affairs mostly is, as is the case with a n y kind of views.

In the case of norms, customs, practices, the limits of the intolerable start where cultural-religious and other norms and practices of empirical origin cause direct or indirect damage to b a s i c h u m a n r i g t s. When such a norm or practice clashes with a clearly conceived human right and prevents it, directly or indirectly, to determine the arrangement and administration of public affairs, it must not be object of toleration, i.e., it should not be allowed to determine the course of public affairs.

Thus knowledge and human rights constitute not only the criteria of the tolerable and the intolerable, but also the criteria of what s h o u l d b e t o l e r a b l e, whoever likes it or not: these are the implications and consequences of knowledge and human rights in given real conditions.

Thus, the tolerable – i.e., what may be object of toleration – has to be distinguished from what should be tolerable, because they have different implications for legislation.

Keeping this distinction in mind we may understand of tolerance, as a principle of public affairs, the demand that what may be tolerable i n g i v e n c o n d i t i o n s, no matter how different from what prevails, m u s t n o t be prohibited and the demand that what should be tolerable m a y n o t be prohibited, no matter who approves or disapproves of it.

The issue of tolerance as a principle of public affairs is closely related today with the so-called cultural rights and with the question of group rights in general.[6]

In the present state of affairs tolerance may be formulated as the demand that the transmission of collective views and the collective exercise of practices,

---

l o n g as this understanding prevails. But are we obliged to take for granted this understanding?

[6] For the specificity of this kind of norms, see: Ioanna Kuçuradi, "Normların Bilimsel Temellendirilebilirliği" [The Scientific Justifiability of Norms], in *Çağın Olayları Arasında* [Among the Events of Our Time]. Ankara, 1980, pp. 182-189; and in the present volume "Human Rights as Ethical Principles and as Premises for the Deduction of Law", pp. 65-73.

which are different from the prevailing ones in a given place and which do not clash, directly or indirectly, with knowledge and human rights, should be permitted, as well as that the implications and consequences of knowledge and of human rights at least should not be prohibited in public life.

Some implications and difficulties to be faced

If we look at the issue of tolerance from the two perspectives mentioned above, we can also see that the problem of the limits of tolerance concerns tolerance only as a principle of public affairs, but not as a personal attitude. Tolerance as a personal attitude has no limits.

It has no limits, because its object is not the radically different views, norms or practices of the other person, consequently it is an attitude taken independently from the epistemological and axiological quality of those views and norms, and because there is no limit in respecting others' rights, which have, nevertheless, to be carefully distinguished from others' interests.

This understanding of tolerance, as one's respecting, or not causing damage to, the rights of those who think or behave in a way radically different from that which he approves, secures the possibility of its sincere exercise in life; while its widespread understanding as "respecting the different views, beliefs, behaviour and practices of others", unless equated with indifference, makes such an exercise impossible.

It makes possible its exercise by those who possess conflicting world views and cultural-religious-ideological norms, because it does not expect an attitude in itself impossible: one's "respecting" something that he thinks to be "false" or "bad". It also makes possible its exercise, because it does not exclude intolerance – especially while exercising public functions – against views and norms underlying the intolerables.

As a principle of public affairs tolerance is related to questions concerning the object of toleration and consequently to problems of legislation. Here I shall confine myself to pointing only at a few theoretical difficulties relevant to the problem of the limits of toleration and in fact only to those related to norms.

A bundle of difficulties faced in this respect consists of epistemological problems. Put very briefly, it concerns the concept of "truth" and is due, so far as I can see, to the lack of ontological differentiation among the objects of knowledge. This latter prevents people, among other things, from differentiating epistemologically between universal and parochial norms and leads to understanding by 'universality' not an epistemological specificity of a kind of norms, but 'worldwide validity'. It escapes attention that it is possible, by following the due procedure, to enforce, i.e., to make valid, any norm.

ON THE EPISTEMOLOGICAL SPECIFICITIES OF NORMS

To make clearer my claims on norms, and consequently those on toleration, let me say a few words on the epistemological specificities of two kinds of norms which are directly related to our issue.

The existence of norms, of different and changing norms, is a (human) fact, related to a specificity of being human: the establishing of social relations, i.e., the creation of social roles, assumed by concrete individuals.

Norms are deduced, undeliberately or deliberately, in order to create an order in a given group, i.e., in order to secure measures for the right and wrong, consequently in order to determine the conduct of individuals or the way how social relations will be established among the individual members of a given group. Whoever assumes or finds himself in a given role, has to behave in accordance with the norms constituting that role.

Norms are usually worded as "ought", "should", "must" or "may" propositions. This means that propositions of norms are not propositions of knowledge, i.e., they have no object independent of those who put them forth. Consequently norms are neither true nor false.[7]

This is the main epistemological specificity of norms and also the origin of the difficulties faced in evaluating a given norm: norms cannot be verified or falsified; their evaluation presupposes a different epistemological treatment.

Compared with propositions of knowledge norms are thoughts, deduced from epistemologically very different premises and by different kinds of reasoning.

The axiological specificity of a norm depends on the epistemological specificity of its premises. Its justification or "foundation" is related to the possibility of going back to its origin – to the premises from which it is deduced – and of seeing their epistemic specificity, i.e., whether the premises from which a given norm is deduced are knowledge or other norms and what kind of knowledge or norms.

This epistemological evaluation, which every norm has to undergo, is something quite different from the ways of validating or enforcing a norm. The latter are social procedures – different social or political procedures – aiming at establishing a broad consensus on a given norm. To find out how a moral norm was made valid presupposes sociological research, while to find out how a legal norm was enforced, one has to read the minutes of the sessions of the bodies, which the enforcement of such a norm depends on.

What we see in the present world, is a search for consensus on given norms, without taking into consideration the epistemological-axiological specificity of the given norms. This is also one of the main dangers of "democratic" decisions in our

[7] See also: Ioanna Kuçuradi, "Knowledge and its Object", in *The Concept of Knowledge*, *op.cit.*, pp. 97-102.

present world. It makes possible the enforcement, by consensus or by the majority of votes, of norms which are contradictory to human rights.

What I said concerning the epistemological-axiological specificity of norms is true for both moral and legal norms.

What we call 'morals' are systems of norms, which individuals in a given group (or in a given culture) have to follow in their relations with others, in action: of norms of behaviour or conduct, as well as of norms of evaluation. They are the "good"s and the "bad"s prevailing in a given group – a given "society" or "culture".

Now, if we take some distance and look at these moral norms, we easily observe that a part of such norms prevailing in given groups or "cultures" is different, and that it is also changing with the time within the same groups, that even a way of behaviour, once prohibited, becomes promoted or *vice versa*; we also see that the same single action – of yours or mine – is qualified by prevailing different norms on the same issue, simultaneously, as good and bad. This fact, which postmodernism, by losing sight of the specificity of another kind of norms, attempted to justify theoretically, has led especially young people and mainly in the so-called "Western society", to the (theoretical) rejection of all and all kinds of norms.[8]

Still besides this observation, we also observe that another part of norms does not show, to a great extent, such a difference or change – for example "for one, to keep one's word". People in each culture or group are expected to obey – to follow or use – both those kinds of moral norms.

In view of this fact, the first distinction we have to make, is between the norms of evaluation – the so-called value judgements – and the norms of behaviour or conduct, though they can be easily translated into each other, since the role they are expected to play is different.

Norms of moral evaluation – or general proposition on what is good or bad – are expected to determine our evaluations, i.e., to be used in order to determine the value of an evaluated object, be it an action, a person, a situation, etc., while norms of moral conduct or "ought-should" propositions are expected to determine our actions in life. In other words, norms of evaluation are supposed to lead those who use them as criteria, to the knowledge of the value of given actions of yours or mine – which is not the case – while norms of behaviour – moral rules or principles – are expected to determine actions carried out in given situations – your actions, my actions, etc.

And the 'ought' or 'should' of these latter norms of conduct or behaviour are deduced from premises of different epistemic specificity and by different ways of reasoning.

[8] See also: Jeanne Hersch, "'Cultural Development', a Tentative Answer", in *Philosophy and Cultural Development*. Ankara, 1993, pp. 31-32.

For my purpose, I shall confine myself here to pointing only at two kinds of such norms: those deduced in different given historical conditions from experience by induction and those deduced by the comparison of different given (human or historical) conditions in the light of the knowledge of the specificities of the human being – or of what is called human dignity. The first kind of norms may be justified – if wished – statistically, the second by a kind of reasoning similar to *reductio ad absurdum*.

At the origin of the first kind of norms (of behaviour) are given natural-social conditions, as well as the conceptions of different cultures concerning the human being. They are norms of behaviour relative to the existing conditions, possessing a practical function, aiming at establishing or safeguarding any order in these existing conditions at the moment they are deduced. So long as the conditions in which they are deduced prevail, if deduced with sagacity, they are functional. But when these conditions change, they lose their function and meaning, i.e., the "ought"s or "must"s they express, lose their ground. Many traditional-customary ways of behaviour transmitted from generation to generation in a given cultural group belong to this kind of norms. Thus we see that though in time the conditions wherefrom these norms are deduced do not exist any longer – which means that there is no more a justifiable reason of the "ought" they express – people in this group try to keep them going. We even see attempts to revive obsolete norms.

Still, in time, new norms are deduced from the changed conditions, mostly incompatible with the old ones. And right here we find the point from which the so-called "crisis of values", to a great extent, arises. It seems that those who insist on keeping valid such norms, are unaware of the source wherefrom the "ought" or "must" of these norms is deduced, i.e., that they are unaware of their epistemic specificity.

Norms of this kind – to which many proverbs or products of practical wisdom also belong – are deduced by evaluating the effects this or that way of behaviour has had, i.e., the benefit or harm they mostly (or often) caused to those who happened to behave in this or that manner. This kind of norms tells us, in fact, so much: when someone behaves in this or that way, the probability of safeguarding his benefit or interests, and sometimes those of the others, increases. In other words: when, in a given case, one is unable to make a right evaluation, but possesses the will to protect what is considered to be in such a case his benefit or interest – or that of the group he belongs to – it is more probable to protect it, if he behaves in the way the relevant norm (rule, etc.) demands. This does not, of course, exclude the possibility that, in a given case, following this norm one causes harm to his benefit or interest and to those of the others. The different norms which distinguish one culture from another are mostly norms of this kind. This is also the kind of norms which those who advocate equal respect to all cultures invite us to respect and which those who promote cultural identities wish to revive, without evaluating them, i.e., without taking into consideration the implications they bear, in the existing conditions, for the human beings who are born by chance by a mother and/or father brought up in a given cultural group.

As to the other kinds of norms (or "ought" propositions), originating in the knowledge of the value of the human being: they are deduced from this knowledge, directly or indirectly, in the face of the human or historical conditions doing harm to this value (e.g., "thou shall not kill", "no racial discrimination shall be made").

I would say that the reasoning which leads to the deduction of such a norm (or principle) is made – schematically – as follows: if the value or the specificity of the human being is such and such, or, since the human species possesses such and such potentialities, no one belonging to this species – you, me – should do anything that harms this value, i.e., which abolishes the possibility of the actualization of such potentialities. Such norms are often worded in the passive, i.e., they demand that no one belonging to the human species should undergo any treatment which abolishes the possibility of the actualization of such potentialities (for example: "no one shall be subject to torture", etc.).

A typical example of this kind of norms is what we call human or basic rights. Human rights express – in fact, intend to express – ethical demands concerning how each and every individual belonging to the human species should be treated by and should treat other individuals in general (whoever they might be and whatever their special situation might be), if human dignity is to be protected in practice.

In positive law we find all these kinds of norms.

Another bundle of difficulties consists of axiological problems. These problems stem from the lack of distinction between 'value' –: the value of something – and 'values', as well as between 'values' and 'value judgements', i.e., claims about what is "good" or "bad", etc.

This makes impossible to differentiate among epistemologically different activities, all carried out under the name of evaluation and leads, in the face of varying and not rarely discrepant judgements on a given object of evaluation, to the sceptical assumption of the impossibility of carrying out evaluation as a cognitive activity – i.e., as an activity whose outcome is verifiable and falsifiable, but only "rationally" justifiable (in the sense of the German *begründen*) or unjustifiable.

As a chain result, norms and other kinds of claims become objects of "rational" or "scientific" justifications, which do not take into account their epistemological specificities. It escapes attention that many opposite or contradictory justifications are both made "rationally" or "scientifically", i.e., not "metaphysically", as we see now for example in bio-medical ethics.

The theoretical problems I mentioned concerning toleration, and many other problems, find their origin in the lack of distinction among different kinds of norms, and also in the lack of distinction between propositions of knowledge and propositions of norms. These problems have various consequences for national and international legislation and at this moment, on the one hand lead to the enforcement of norms which exclude each other,[9] and on the other hand prevent the enforcement of certain other norms, e.g., the introduction of obligatory AIDS tests. In other words, these problems make us tolerate intolerables and not tolerate positive or negative implications of human rights.

This understanding of tolerance makes me think that "education for tolerance" cannot be separated from philosophical education – an education for all, aimed at helping those who undergo it become conscious of their human identity through a training in philosophical ethics and the philosophical teaching of human rights.

---

[9] For this point see: Ioanna Kuçuradi, "Human Rights Instruments Questioned in the Light of the Idea of Human Rights", in Ioanna Kuçuradi (ed.), *The Idea and the Documents of Human Rights*. Ankara, 1995, pp. 75-92, in which the art. 18 and art. 19 of the *International Covenant on Civil and Political Rights* are given as examples; and in the present volume pp. 95-100.

Universal Human Rights and their Different Implications for Multiethnic and Multireligious Societies*

Two main tendencies, discrepant and essentially incompatible, characterize the intellectual and political climate of our world at the turn of the century. One of these tendencies is the promotion of human rights, the other is the promotion of so-called cultural identities, in which also ethnic and religious identities are usually included. The way to promote them is assumed to be democracy, and democracy, whatever it may be, is considered to be the *panakeia* of our times.

It escapes our attention that by promoting human rights and cultural identities simultaneously, we promote two different kinds of norms, and that consequently we often promote contradictory norms on the same issues.

Here first I shall try to challenge this simultaneous promotion of human rights and cultural identities as solutions to certain of the global problems or conflicts we are faced with; and then I shall submit to discussion a few points, which, I think, could help us in tackling problems related to our issue in a more humane way, i.e., in accordance with the relevant implications of human rights.

*

If we take into consideration that the existence of multiethnic and multireligious societies is an old fact, as well as is the discriminative treatment of individuals having an ethnic origin or religion different from those of the majority in a given country, in the face of which a metaprinciple concerning human rights was formulated in art. 2/a of the *Universal Declaration of Human Rights*, stating that "everyone is entitled to all the rights and freedoms set forth in [that] Declaration, without distinction of any kind, such as race, colour, sex, language, religion, political or other opinion, national or social origin, property, birth or other status";[1] it seems worthwhile to attempt to put forward the developments which brought on the agenda of the world community the issue of identities, be they ethnic, religious or other identities.

Human rights were brought into the focus immediately after the Second World War with the establishment of the United Nations, while the question of 'culture' was brought on the agenda of the international community toward the end of the sixties. Since then, culture constitutes one of its main items discussed with an ever increasing interest, but also with increasing confusion. For this reason most of the conclusions reached and the decisions and actions based on

---

* This paper was published in Yahya Sezai Tezel and Wulf Schönbohm (eds), *World, Islam and Democracy*. Konrad-Adenauer Foundation, Ankara, 1999, pp. 42-52.

[1] Emphasis added according to the aim of this paper.

these conclusions, appear to be, so far as I can see, contradictory to the intentions which brought the question of culture on the agenda of the world community.

So, let me try to take a bird's eye view of the developments connected with our issue since the Second World War, and start by summarising here an analysis that I have made in the second half of the eighties,[2] before the dissolution of the Second World.

We can trace at least two main reasons that have brought the question of culture to the foreground at the global level. And following the developments since then, we can observe a third one, which has completed the picture that the state of affairs, at the end of the eighties, presented in this respect.

One of the aforementioned reasons appears to be the fact that the idea of development, put in the fifties as the principal objective of the national policies of all the member states of the UN, but understood only as economic-technological development, though, as it was natural, in a double sense – i.e., as linear unlimited quantitative growth of industrial production in the so-called developed countries and as increase of the *per capita* income and industrialization in the so-called developing ones – has led to unforeseen outcomes, in contradiction with the expectations of those who had introduced and put this idea as the principal objective of their national policies: pollution, the exhaustion of non-renewable natural resources in many of the industrialized countries, broadening of the gap between the rich and the poor in the Third World,[3] as it was called at that time.

It is after the appearance of these and such other consequences of the ever increasing technological development in the West, that people started speaking of the need for "a new conception of development", or, of the necessity "to bring a cultural dimension to development". Thus they introduced the idea of cultural development – an idea which was not, and still is not, sufficiently analysed.

What Western people have mainly understood from 'cultural development' was the broadening for the masses of the possibility to have "access to and participation in culture", i.e., to activities considered to afford to individuals the possibility to develop their potentialities as human beings – e.g., to artistic, scientific, philosophical activities.

We have to keep in mind that this demand for "access to and participation in culture" was a demand stemming from a need felt by the people of the indus-

---

[2] For this analysis see my "'Cultural' Morals and 'Global' Morality in the Light of Ethics", in *The World Community in Post-Industrial Society*, The World Academic Conference of the Seoul Olympiad' 88, WACSO. Seoul, 1989, pp. 176-185.

[3] For this point see my papers on "Philosophy and World Problems", in *Philosophy Facing World Problems*, Philosophical Society of Turkey. Ankara, 1988, pp. 59-65; and "Back to the Question of Goals", in *Philosophy, Humanity and Ecology*, The African Academy of Sciences. Nairobi, 1994, pp. xvi-xx.

trialized countries; it was considered to be a way out from the impasse into which industrialization had led them.

Another important reason which brought 'culture' to the foreground at the global level was that numerous Third World countries, which did not, and still do not, partake in the so-called Western – or European – culture and which have obtained their independence in the sixties or seventies, i.e., the people and especially the intellectuals of the decolonized countries, started revolting against the "colonization of the minds", as a result of which they brought on the agenda the question of "cultural identity" as synonymous to "cultural development". Thus they have seconded the motion of "cultural development", still understanding it, mainly, as being allowed to develop – i.e., identify and reconstruct – their own culture, which they assumed, was suppressed or forgotten under the influence of Western culture during the colonization era. They started trying to identify the culture – i.e., the conception of Man and of what is valuable – which they a s s u m e d is, and wished to be, t h e i r o w n. This is what happened especially in Africa in the seventies and eighties.

Meanwhile, the people of the countries which are "in the process of modernization" (colonized or not), and who had opted for "modernization", joined the discussion. What they, usually, conceived as 'cultural development' was the resurrection or the revival – though their claim was that they wished to "restore" and "conserve" it – of the culture, i.e., the conception of Man and of what is valuable, prevailing among them before they came into touch with the West.

Thus we observe that what was called in those years in the non-Western circles "crisis of identity", was something coinciding with what in the West was and is still called "crisis of values". The Western people t h o u g h t that they did not know any more w h a t t h e i r " v a l u e s " w e r e; the former t h o u g h t either that they did not know w h o r e a l l y t h e y w e r e, or that t h e y w e r e n o t t h o s e w h o a t t h i s m o m e n t, i n f a c t, t h e y w e r e. Yet all shared the view that "culture" – whatever it may be and whatever each one's culture may be – is something "good", consequently that cultural identities – whatever this term might include – have to be promoted.

In order to explain how these so-called 'crises' came about, let us first attempt to fix the concept or the term 'cultural identity', which is sometimes equated with religious and some other times with racial-ethnic identity or with both of them.

Within the context of 'cultural identity' the meaning that 'culture' conveys can be worded as: the conception of Man and the conception concerning what is valuable, which prevail for a longer or shorter while in a human group, whose boundaries can be drawn according to varying viewpoints, and which determine the way of living of this group and the expressions of this way of living (the attitudes in everyday life, the so-called "modern ideas" in arts, literature, philosophy, language, the sciences and in other human activities, as well as in social institutions and their functioning); natural, living conceptions, I would say almost unconscious ones.[4] Thus understood, 'cultural identity' covers religious identity, but n o t necessarily ethnic identity.

As far as the meaning of the term 'identity' is concerned, we observe that, instead of conveying the meaning of 'self-knowledge', it is used in the sense of 'self-conception' or 'self image' of an individual or a group.

Thus, while 'cultural identity', carefully understood, would mean, in the case of an individual, h i s k n o w l e d g e of his conception of Man and of what he thinks is valuable, and in the case of a group, t h e k n o w l e d g e of the most widespread – still not unique – conception of Man and of what is considered to be valuable at a given moment in that group; it is assumed in non-Western countries to convey the conception of Man and of what is valuable that prevailed in these countries before their encounter with Western culture.

So, if from 'identity' we understand 'self-knowledge', the question of 'cultural identity' in countries "in the process of modernization" appears to be, at the level of the individual, an artificially created problem, while at the level of a group (at a country's level) as a problem stemming from a reaction.

Since, if a person asks, with regard to the problem under consideration, the question "who am I?", i.e., "what is my conception of Man and what do I consider to be valuable?", he can answer this question – if left alone – by identifying, by his own efforts or through the help of somebody else, the conceptions he possesses j u s t a t t h a t m o m e n t; for those are h i s conceptions of Man and of what is valuable, whether he likes them or not. This is also true for religious identity, but not for ethnic identity. One can learn the latter only from his mother or father.

But if this question is asked on behalf of a group, be it a nation or the people of a given country – in fact only by s o m e members of this group – i.e., if this question is worded as "who are w e ?" or "what is o u r culture, o u r conception of Man?" or "what are the values proper to u s?", things become complicated; since such a question can only be asked w i t h r e g a r d to a group, and its answer can be given only and only through scientific research. Research carried out in some of them, shows that in such countries different cultures co-exist, some excluding the other, and therefore conflicting.

Now if a sub-group within a group claims that its i m a g e of cultural identity is the cultural identity of the group as a whole, we come across the fact called 'crisis of identity', which leads individuals to conflicts within themselves, while in social life it leads to confrontations and even armed conflicts.

In other words: what we experienced in the seventies and eighties in some countries was, and what we experience j u s t n o w in some others is, a reaction to "Western culture", a reaction which has led and still leads these groups toward the search of their "cultural identity" or "their own values", and since it

[4] For the justification of the appropriateness of this meaning of 'culture', see my "Cultures and 'World Culture'", in *Philosophie et Culture*-Actes du XVIIe Congrès Mondial de Philosophie IV. Montréal, 1988, pp. 457-460.

is not possible to identify what they wish to identify in the existing state of affairs, they look backwards and try to find, in order to resurrect it, what they feel or assume to be their own, i.e., the conception of Man and the conception concerning what is valuable, prevailing in these groups before their industrialization efforts began or before their encounter with "Western culture", to which they react.[5] But what they react against apparently is the attitude of Western culture towards other cultures, its attitude towards the Turkish astronomer of Saint-Exupéry,[6] an attitude which seems to have changed, since the Western world too promotes this wave of the search for 'cultural identity', introduced by the peoples of non-Western cultures, under the influence of which wave Europe too started looking for its own identity or its own "values".

We could have understood both these revolts in the West and against "the West", as revolts against the same thing: the state of Western culture in the second half of our century, whose marking characteristics are the victory of the "positivist catechism" and its conception of Man underlying both pragmatism and various Marxist doctrines during the period between the two World Wars; we could have understood them as the common aspirations of the peoples of the world to be afforded the possibility to develop – or to be treated in a way that permits them to develop – their human and humane potentialities. And this could have led us to different global decisions and actions. But we missed the point, as it appears from the developments of the past ten or fifteen years.

Instead of putting in connection the problems of various identities with human rights, we have broadly adopted postmodernism, which claims the equal value of all world views, norms, etc., and for this reason is also cordially welcome by many intellectuals in countries "on the way to modernization", intellectuals who reject human rights and other principles related to them – for example *laïcité* – as products of Western culture, yet adopt postmodernism which is also a product of Western thinking. Thus we have made out of a fact an ideal and promote it, i.e., we promote multiculturalism, assuming it to be *the* way which will lead to the peaceful coexistence of different cultural communities, in which concept we also include ethnic and religious communities.

Instead of trying sincerely to find out the implications of clearly conceived human rights for problems related to identities, we produced a "human right": the right to identity; and in our incapacity to evaluate the different norms on the same issues we promoted the equal respect to all norms and identities.

Thus the crises of identities were overcome to a great extent, yet towards a development quite dangerous for human rights: the unimpeded revival of world views and norms that prevent enlightenment which is an essential prereq-

---

[5] The reaction shown by members of existing group cultures which are alive (for example in states, the boundaries, of which are delineated after a war), i.e., a reaction against ignoring or negating them, has to be distinguished from the reaction I mentioned here.

[6] Antoine de Saint-Exupéry, *Le petit prince*. Bourges, Collection Folio Junior, 1984, p. 19.

uisite for the functioning of democracy. Thus in the past ten or fifteen years we observe the "free" spread of various fundamentalisms and "metaphysical" tendencies all over the world, the revival of racism in Europe, an increase in the defence of communalism, all of which contradict the relevant demands that human rights express and even the very idea of human rights; and whose advocates take advantage of the rhetoric of human rights and the preaching of tolerance in order to get a free hand for diffusing them.

In the total chaos of concepts that prevails at present and which is called pluralism – a situation that shows remarkable factual similarities with the situation at the turn from the Antiquity to the Middle Ages – how can we find a clue to proceed in tackling, among other things, the problems of multiethnic and multireligious societies?

Here I shall confine myself to submit to discussion only a few points, to my mind crucial theoretical points, which could help us in our endeavour to face certain problems of multiethnic and multireligious societies.

One thing to do is to become aware of the epistemological and axiological specificities of human rights as norms for the arrangement and administration of public affairs, i.e., to become aware of what distinguishes them from most cultural-religious norms.

Another thing to do is to become aware of the difference between universal human rights and group rights (or collective rights, or rights of the people, or whatever they are called). Such an awareness can help us to distinguish, in given cases, between group rights, which are implications of human rights, and group interests.

And another one is to become aware of the different implications that clearly conceived human rights bear for political decisions related to problems of multiethnic and to problems of multireligious societies.

In connection with the first point I wish to say, in a nutshell,[7] the following: human rights express norms deduced from premises of a special epistemic quality – from the knowledge of the value of certain human potentialities – and they are deduced by *reductio ad absurdum*. This specificity of theirs constitutes their "universality", that they bring demands for the treatment of every human being independently from his or her "race, colour, sex, language, religion", etc.; while cultural, parochial changing norms are deduced in given real social conditions by induction. The latter aim at protecting the interests or benefits of individuals in the given conditions of the groups to which they belong; if deduced with sagacity, they are useful so long as the conditions from which they were deduced have not changed. The former, i.e., human rights, aim at protecting the value of the human being.

---

[7] For this point see my "Human Rights: The Idea, the Demands and the Instruments", in *The Idea and the Documents of Human Rights*, joint publication of the International Federation of Philosophical Societies and the Philosophical Society of Turkey. Ankara, 1995, pp. 75-92; and in the present volume pp. 101-111.

What multiculturalism promotes is respect, not to all human beings, but to all such cultural-parochial norms, an important part of which consists of religious norms. We have to look at norms independently from whichever culture or religion they stem – including our own – to scrutinize them coolheadedly and evaluate them philosophically before we try to spread or enforce them.

In connection with the second point, also put very briefly, I wish to submit to your attention the following: human rights express demands concerning how individuals should be treated by, and treat, other individuals in public life. This means that they are also principles for the arrangement and administration of public affairs in a country, so that individuals may actualize and develop – each as much as he or she can – certain potentialities of the human being, i.e., so that they may carry out activities the products of which constitute the "pride" of humanity.[8]

Group rights or collective rights however, at least those related to our issue, are implications of basic human rights in the existing real conditions of a country. They are not extra rights or privileges g i v e n to a group, but public arrangements which make possible for individuals belonging to a group of individuals who possess certain specificities different from those of the majority in a country, to develop their own human potentialities.

These two points, mainly, make us see the different implications of human rights in treating problems related to multiethnic societies and in treating those of multireligious societies.

Ethnicity, or ethnic origin, is only one of an individual's identities, since as individuals we have many collective identities, the composition of which is nevertheless unique for every individual. As citizens of a state we have a common identity with the other citizens, who might have, and in our present world indeed have, different ethnic identities, which they cannot change, while they can change their citizenship.

Perhaps the most characteristic, though not absolute, specificity of belonging to an ethnicity in the present world, is one's mother tongue. Using one's own mother tongue for communication with others who possess the same mother tongue is a basic human right. An implication of this right is securing the possibility of developing one's mother tongue. But we should not forget that given cases might be much more complicated than we can imagine when we reflect on such an issue in general, and that we need to evaluate each case in itself in order to find out what this same right necessitates in the given conditions of, and the obligations it brings for, a given state, still without losing sight of the fact that what we call t h e State is constituted first of all in order to secure the equal protection of the human rights of the citizens and that using one's mother tongue is a basic human right.

The implications that human rights bear in connection with the State in multireligious societies are different from those related to multiethnic societies.

---

[8] For this point see *ibid.*, especially pp. 81-82.

The most basic thing that they imply is strict adherence to secularism or to the principle we call *laïcité*. This latter principle brings a "negative" demand – negative in the technical sense of the term – the demand that the arrangement of social relations and legislation, as well as the administration of public affairs in a state, be made without taking into consideration the norms of any religion, including those of the religion of the majority of the citizens.[9]

Thus understood *laïcité* appears to be a necessary condition of the possibility that the principles of human rights become determinant. The discrepancy between, or even the coincidence of, a human right with a religious norm should not play any role in political decisions. To get an insight in this necessity we need to know the epistemological and axiological specificities of human rights as norms.

Some of you have probably already noticed that my insistence on the scrutiny and evaluation of norms before their enforcement is quite diverging from the fashionable approach called overlapping consensus, i.e., overlapping of human rights and cultural-religious norms. This is a very pragmatic solution, yet very dangerous for human rights, as is all compromise related to them.

Instead of looking for "overlapping consensus", it seems more appropriate to reflect on toleration – i.e., in our case not on tolerance as an attitude towards each other, of individuals possessing different religions, but on toleration as a principle in the arrangement of public affairs.[10] Also here clearly conceived human rights and knowledge may constitute the criteria not in order to determine what cultural-religious views, norms and practices which are different from those of the majority may be tolerated, but those which may or should not be objects of toleration.

Regarding views, it is knowledge that draws the limits of the tolerable. This means that if there is a clash between a view and knowledge on a given issue, this view should not be allowed to become determinant in public affairs. This criterion is especially important when it is put in connection with our promotion of "democracy", because, while the truth or falsity of a piece of knowledge is not a question of "democratic" decision, its becoming or not becoming determinant in public affairs mostly is, as it is the case with all kinds of views.

Regarding norms, customs, practices, the limits of the intolerable start where cultural-religious and other norms and practices of empirical origin cause direct or indirect damage to basic human rights. When such a norm or practice clashes with a clearly conceived human right and prevents it, directly

[9] For a broader analysis of *laïcité*, see my "Secularization and Human Rights", in Bhuvan Chandel and Ioanna Kuçuradi (eds), *Cultural Traditions and the Idea of Secularization*. Delhi, 1998, pp. 65-77; and in the present volume pp. 119-123.

[10] For this point see my paper "On Tolerance and the Limits of Toleration", in *Diogenes*, N° 176, Vol. 44/8, Winter 1996, pp. 163-173; and in the present volume pp. 125-137.

or indirectly, from determining the arrangement and administration of public affairs, it must not be an object of toleration: in other words, it should not be allowed to determine the course of public affairs.

To protect the human rights of the citizens and to administrate public affairs in accordance with their implications are the *raisons d'être* of the totality of organs and institutions we call "the State". This is why State and public officers have not only to be well aware of the discrepancy between the two fashionable tendencies of our days – i.e., the promotion of the universal norms of human rights and that of cultural identities, which amounts to promoting changing parochial norms –; but also to be well equipped with the philosophical knowledge of the terms floating around us, so that they can foresee at least some of the inevitable consequences of what they are about to do or decide, provided that they really possess the sincere will to protect human rights in the multiethnic and multireligious societies of the present-day world.

The Concept of Democracy and its Problems on the Eve of the Twenty-First Century*

The history of the idea of democracy is a long one. For Plato, the first philosopher who theorized systematically about democracy, democracy was the least good political order (πολιτεία), because it can easily degenerate into ochlocracy which is a deviation (παρέκβασις) of democracy and thus lead to tyranny which is the worst political order. Democracy is "a delightful political order (πολιτεία), anarchic and motley, assigning a kind of equality indiscriminately to equals and unequals alike",[1] he says.

To Aristotle democracy was a deviation of what he calls polity (πολιτεία) which he considers as the best political order: democracy protects the interests of the poor, i.e., of only a part of the citizens, but like the other deviated forms of public order, does not take care of the common or public good.[2]

In connection with our topic it would be quite interesting to trace the consequences which the inaccurate translation into Latin of some Platonic and Aristotelian terms (like πολιτεία, πολιτική κοινωνία, οὐσία, etc.) had for the history of ideas. I shall not do it here. But I shall take a leap to Kant, who draws our attention to the "confusion" between republican and democratic constitutions.

In his *Perpetual Peace* Kant draws our attention to two different principles of dividing the forms of the State as follows: "the forms of the State (of *civitas*) can be divided", he says, "according to those who hold the power and according to the form of government of the people by those who hold the power: i.e., according to the *formae imperii* and these forms are autocracy, aristocracy and democracy; and according to *formae regiminis* which is related to the constitution (i.e., the act of the general will, by which a crowd becomes a people). Thus according to the way how the State uses the power it possesses, there are two forms of government: republicanism and despotism."

Republicanism separates executive power (government) from legislative power; despotism uses the laws, i.e., the public will, as private will. Thus, Kant concludes, democracy, in the proper meaning of the word, is a kind of d e s p o t i s m, because it establishes an executive power, through which all the

* This paper was first presented at the seventh of the series of symposia organized by FISP on "Ideas Underlying World Problems", held in Ankara in the year 1996. Its Turkish version was published in *Hacettepe Üniversitesi Edebiyat Fakültesi Dergisi*, special issue on the 75th anniversary of the establishment of the Republic of Turkey. Ankara 1998, pp. 21-27.

[1] Πολιτεία, 558 c.

[2] Πολιτικά 1279 b 8-9.

citizens may make decisions about (and indeed against) the single individual without his consent, so that the decisions are made by all the people and yet not by all the people. And this means that the general will is in contradiction with itself and also with freedom.[3]

The idea of democracy has penetrated Western thinking through our century, and since the nineties democratization, human rights, free market and privatization have become the mottos of the world community. They constitute the ideals of our time at the turn of the century. It is now a widespread acceptance that democracy and free market are t h e ways to protect human rights.

It escapes attention that democracy is at present reduced to electoralism, as a result of which political parties, determined by the "everything is permitted" principle, in order to get as many votes as possible and come to power in an assumedly "democratic" way, do not, too often, hesitate to promise and do things which, though "delightful" for many voters, are giving damage to human rights, including the voter's human rights.

Due to this equation of democracy or democratization with multi-party elections people – especially in Western developed countries – often lose sight of the fact that this kind of "democracies" not only cannot guarantee the protection of human rights, but on the top of it might close the door to the promotion of human rights in certain countries.

Here is a spot from the elections in an African country, mentioned by an anthropologist, who was there during these elections:

> At the polling booths democracy was in full swing. One man was being upbraided for not bringing all his wives. "They would not come", "You should have beaten them". I asked [says the anthropologist] several Dowagas what issue they were voting for. They stared at me blankly. You took your identity card, they explained, and gave it to the official over there who stamped it and your vote was marked. Yes, but what were they voting for? More blank stars. They had already explained, you took your card [...] Not one of them knows what the election was for.[4]

The protest of some groups in Turkey (and some other countries) against the silence of the Western World in the face of the *coup d'état* in Algeria, after the "democratic" elections there some years ago, can also be mentioned as an example of additional problems and impasses resulting from reducing democracy to electoralism.

Such a "democracy" does not appear to be the assumed form of government of civic society, i.e., the proper way of governing what is public for the protection of the human rights of all citizens; but only a way which certain groups organized as political parties use to come to power and get a free hand to

---

[3] "Zum ewigen Frieden. Ein philosophischer Entwurf", *Kants Werke in zwölf Bänden* XI. Suhrkamp Verlag, 1969, pp. 206-207.

[4] From K. Tomaševski, *Development Aid and Human Rights Revisited*. Printer Publishers, London/New York, 1993, p. 15.

exercise it "legitimately" for doing things which please their followers, but which prevent the exercising of human rights.

Thus a state in which "democracy" functions only as electoralism ceases to be a *res publica* (a republic), i.e., a legal person which all citizens care for, but an entity considered to belong only to those in power.

These and many other reasons make, I think, necessary to raise once again, at the turn of the century, the question "what is democracy?" and to inquire into the conditions of democracy which could secure the protection of human rights.

*

A first question to be raised in connection with the concept of democracy is whether democracy can still be considered as a form of State – as Kant says – or a form of government (a form of administrating what is public), since today it appears to be considered both of them: there are kingdoms which seem to be governed quite democratically, while there are states governed by an elected oligarchy.

I think that today we have to restrict our understanding of democracy as a form of government (of administrating what is public) in the state type whose constituent unit is the citizen – this 'citizen' nevertheless understood not only formally but in the Aristotelian sense, as "one who has the power to participate in the government of the civic society deliberatively and critically."[5]

This concept of citizen, however, presupposes a different conception of the State – different from the prevailing one.

What is the prevailing conception of the State? It is the conception of the State as an entity in itself, not the State as a *res publica* (as republic), but as an entity which threatens i t s s u b j e c t s (and consequently has to be abolished, as certain Marxists claimed), or an entity which interferes and limits the freedoms of the people (and consequently has to be "minimized", as the advocates of privatization and "free" market claim), or even an entity which is expected to protect its subjects (against whom?) and tell them what they should do. Democracy cannot be the form of government of the State conceived as an entity in itself.

There are certain objective and subjective conditions to fulfil, so that democracy can be a form of government "of the people, by the people, for the people".

Such a main objective condition is a different conception of the State: the conception of the State as a human legal institution, whose *raison d'être* is to protect the citizens against each other and to administrate what is public according to the demands of justice – i.e., the conception of the State as a body of organs established (constituted) in order to make law, i.e., the idea of justice, d e t e r m i n a n t in the historical reality: in order a) to transform social rela-

[5] Πολιτικά, 1275 b 20.

tions – rights-duties or role relations – established in this or that manner, into relations based on justice, or to transform them in a way that human rights can be protected and b) to administrate what is public in accordance with the implications of human rights in those historical, given-particular conditions.

The goals of the State as a human legal institution are not the kind of things which can be decided, but the kind of things to become aware of, consequently they cannot be decided democratically. Democracy can function only in a state whose citizens are aware of the fact that the State (the body of organs that constitute the State) exists in order to introduce justice in the establishment of social relations, in other words in order to protect equally the human rights of the citizens.

Thus conceived the State can have two main functions: to protect the citizens against the citizens, i.e., to arrange relations among the citizens taking into account the demands of human rights, and to administrate what is public in a civic society, so as to provide all the citizens with the p o s s i b i l i t y of answering e q u a l l y their needs related to basic rights.

Democracy, as a form of government, seems to be related with the second main function of the State, i.e., with the administration of what is public.

Thus democracy could be the form a government in which decisions concerning the administration of what is public are taken by the participation of all concerned citizens, still of citizens who are aware of the truth that the State exists for the equal protection of the basic rights of all citizens.

Thus the decisions to be taken democratically concern only the ways to be followed in the given real-historical conditions, so that human rights can be protected in t h o s e conditions. In other words: an objective condition of democracy is putting consciously as main objective of national policies the protection of human rights.

In order that democracy can function in a given state, a first unanimity – like that of Rousseau's social contract – concerning putting the protection of human rights as the main objective of national policies is necessary.

At the turn of the century there is – I hope there is – at least a verbal unanimity concerning the necessity to protect human rights. But we are not aware that human rights in order to be protected should constitute the main objective of all policies. And we are not sufficiently aware what issues can be and which cannot be objects of democratic decision, as well as we are not sufficiently aware that democracy is not a goal or objective, but a form of government concerning what is public in a state.

When in the late nineties the Constitutional Court of Turkey decided to close a political party, one of the most important newspapers announced it as a "defeat of democracy". It would be of use to try to find out what conception of democracy underlies this title. I shall not do it here. I shall confine myself in saying that the main problem underlying the title on that newspaper is a confusion concerning the concept of citizen: the citizen is taken into consideration only as the constituent unit of the State and n o t also as "one who has the power to participate in the government of the civic society – in decisions concerning the administration of the public – d e l i b e r a t i v e l y and c r i t i c a l l y" and is c o n s c i o u s of the *raison d'être* of the State, which is to secure the possibility of the equal protection of the basic rights of all the citizens.

And this leads us to consider the subjective conditions for the functioning of democracy – so that it does not degenerate into mere electoralism, which makes possible to come to power parties advocating principles and views contradictory to human rights, e.g., racism, or what is called today fundamentalism.

The main subjective conditions of democracy, which would be promising to lead to decisions which may fulfil the demands of human rights in the given conditions of a state at present, seem to be enlightenment in the Kantian sense a n d philosophical value knowledge. The former is a formal condition, the latter a material one.

Most of you, I am sure, know Kant's understanding of enlightenment. Allow me, nevertheless, to repeat it here, for those few who might have forgotten it.

Here is the answer that Kant gave to the question "What is Enlightenment?", posed to him by a newspaper in 1784: "Enlightenment is man's leaving his self-caused immaturity. Immaturity is the incapacity to use one's intelligence without the guidance of another. Such immaturity is self-caused if it is not caused by lack of intelligence, but by lack of determination and courage to use one's own intelligence without being guided by another. *Sapere aude!* Have the courage to use your own intelligence is therefore the motto of Enlightenment".

What is important in this definition is that enlightenment is not considered to be a world view, as many assume it to be, but a capacity of the individual – the capacity to judge on his or her own account, still a capacity which has to be nourished by philosophical value knowledge.

Philosophical value knowledge is also a condition *sine qua non* for the functioning of a democracy promising to protect human rights. The capacity to judge on one's own account about what should be done in given cases, so that human dignity can be protected, presupposes, among other things, philosophical value knowledge and knowledge of the constituents of human dignity.

At the turn of the century we observe an increase in the number of those who wish "to do something" for the protection of human rights, as well as we observe a shocking theoretical ignorance about the nature of value, values and human rights, all of which makes it possible to give damage to human rights by using the name of human rights, and by using democracy reduced to electoralism to promote communalism which aims at changing the unit of the State, i.e., at replacing the citizen, by the community – be it ethnic, cultural or religious community.

Democracy presupposes the citizen as a constituent unit of the State – a citizen able to judge and participate deliberatively and critically in the administration of what is public, as well as a citizen conscious of the *raison d'être* of the State as a human legal institution.

Thus the functioning of democracy, i.e., participation of all concerned in the procedures of taking decisions aiming at the protection of their human rights in the given conditions of a country, makes necessary the philosophical training of all citizens.

For philosophical training is training in judging for oneself, in grasping and establishing connections for oneself and above all training in grasping for oneself – so much as each trainee can – where human dignity is at stake in a given case. Because this dignity and its implications – e.g., the protection of human rights – draw the limits of tolerance as a principle in the ordering and administration of public affairs.

In the face of the increasing tendency to communalism which claims equal rights not for all citizens but for all cultural, religious or other communities in a state – a claim that has little, if at all, to do with democracy – the Aristotelian concept of the citizen (: of one who has the power to participate deliberately and critically in the administration of what is public in a civic society, i.e., a society consisting of citizens who think of their State as a *res publica*) could be an *idée directrice* which might help us to revise not only the concept of democracy, but also our priorities in education.

I wish to close with a sentence from Federico Mayor's speech which the Director-General of UNESCO has pronounced in December 1997 in a meeting on Philosophical Horizons for UNESCO in the 21st Century: "In a world where high technology and hungry children still co-exist, where everyday we witness new and often unforeseeable intentions, we must promote personal autonomy, intellectual freedom and ethical judgement. From this viewpoint philosophical education is obviously one of the keys of the Twenty-first Century".

FREEDOM OF THOUGHT – WHAT IS IT?[*]

Let me start with a long quotation:

> Freedom of thought, conscience and religion is an 'easy case' in the human rights catalogue. The right to freedom of thought, conscience and religion has long traditions both in domestic and in international law. There are even grounds to state that the origin of the general idea of human rights lies in the long history of protecting religious minorities.
>
> The unproblematic character of the traditional nucleus of the human right in question is apparently the reason that there has been little research regarding this right and human rights complaints to supervisory international organs have relatively seldom touched on this right.
>
> States have not considered it difficult to allow their citizens the freedom to think. The difficulties start when we come to the right to express one's conviction, the right to organize as a community in order to promote a religion or belief and the right to act in accordance with one's conscience even in cases where a domestic legal system seems to require uniform behaviour irrespective of the different convictions of individuals. The real problems concerning freedom of thought, conscience and religion do not concern the nucleus of the right itself (the freedom of an inner state of mind), but issues that relate also to other human rights [...]
>
> The terms 'thought', 'conscience' and 'religion' together cover "all possible attitudes of the individual toward the world, toward society, and toward that which determines his fate and the destiny of the world, be it a divinity, some superior being or just reason and rationalism, or chance",

says Martin Scheinin in *A Commentary* on *The Universal Declaration of Human Rights*, published in 1992.[1]

I made this long quotation, as a typical example of understanding, and the most widespread understanding, of art. 18 of the *Declaration*, as well as of the *Covenant on Civil and Political Rights* and of art. 9 of the *European Convention for the Protection of Human Rights and Fundamental Freedoms*, in which "freedom of thought" is put together with the so-called freedom of conscience

[*] This paper was presented in a conference organized by the Archives of Legal and Social Philosophy, in collaboration with Goethe Institute, Istanbul, on 5-9 December 1995. Its Turkish version was published in the *Archives 3*, AFA, Istanbul, 1998, pp. 17-26, as well as in *Frankofoni* 12, Ankara, 2000, pp. 327-334.

[1] Martin Scheinin, "Article 18", in Asbjørn Eide *et al.* (eds), *The Universal Declaration of Human Rights, A Commentary*. Scandinavian University Press, Oslo, 1992, pp. 263-264. Emphasis added.

and religion, though in some constitutions we see "freedom of thought" separated from the two other "freedoms" or not mentioned at all.[2]

That the "right to freedom of thought" has not been a problematic one is perhaps true for Western European countries, the United States, and Canada, where a positive value judgement prevailing in connection with this freedom – and with all freedoms in general – is so widespread, that this right, although it is not clear what it demands, was u n t i l r e c e n t l y taken for granted.

However this is not true for the majority of countries which adopted the *Universal Declaration* and signed the *Covenant on Civil and Political Rights*. Nor is it true any longer for many parts of Western Europe, where, in the words of the Director-General of UNESCO, Mr. Federico Mayor, "the embers of hatred" of religious fundamentalism, nationalism, racism and ethnic prejudices were "rekindled by the winds of freedom".

The spread of postmodernism which claims that all thoughts, beliefs, views and norms are equal in value, as well as the fashionable promotion of equal respect for all cultures, and of the so-called "value of difference" or of "the right to be different" – coupled with the unscrutinized demand for freedom of thought – makes it possible to promulgate "thoughts" or norms discrepant from and harmful to human rights.

Besides this trend, the confusion prevailing in the concept of human rights in general keeps the door open for those in power in various states to restrict human rights in order to protect group interests, and to enforce laws recognizing "rights" that do harm to the human rights of many citizens, even of those citizens who are supposed to "benefit" from these "rights". But at the same time, we see in various states, groups or individuals that accuse the State of human rights violations, because of the restriction of certain desired liberties – liberties which do harm to the human rights of those who request to have them –; just as we see people condemned, in the name of protecting "public order", because the research they conduct in their field breaks prevailing taboos. We also see governments unable to prevent racist propaganda, because they are afraid of being accused of violating the right to freedom of thought and expression.

Thus the need to reflect on and scrutinize "freedom of thought" has been brought on the agenda.

*

To show the confusion prevailing in the conception of "freedom of thought", I wish to compare art. 19 with art. 18 of the *Covenant on Civil and Political Rights*. Art. 19 states: 1. "Everyone shall have the right to hold opinions without interference. 2. Everyone shall have the right to freedom of expression; this

---

[2] E.g., in the Constitution of the FRG (1949) we see only the "Freiheit des Glaubens, Gewissens und Religion"; in the Constitution of Turkey (1981) two separate articles, art. 24 and art. 25.

right shall include freedom to seek, receive and impart information and ideas of all kinds [...]". The exercise of these rights "may [...] be subject to certain restrictions", if necessary, by law. This article is not among those which "in time of public emergency no derogation may be made", while art. 18 which is included among those rights exempted from this derogation states: "Everyone shall have the right to freedom of thought, conscience and religion. This right shall include freedom to [...] manifest his religion or belief in [...] practice and teaching".

Now, *first*, what is an 'opinion', the expression of which may be restricted temporarily? How does an opinion differ from a 'thought' which may not? And how do both differ from knowledge? *Second*, the exercise of the right stated in art. 19 – assumed to be a freedom – can be restricted, if necessary, for the protection of, among other things, "public morals". What are "public morals"? And what if the prevailing "morals" – i.e., the norms regarding what is "good" or "bad" in a country, or among the decision makers – contains elements harmful to human rights, as is the case in many countries? What might it mean, then, to restrict a human right by law, in order to protect "public morals"? Would this not mean assigning priority to a kind of norms of more limited scope than human rights? Would not this mean to consider those changing norms more important than the "universal" principles of human rights?

Furthermore art. 18, of which no derogation may be made even in times of public emergency, states: "Freedom to manifest one's religion or beliefs [in worship ... and teaching] may be subject only to limitations as are prescribed by law and are necessary to protect the fundamental rights and freedom of others". Does 'others' include, for example, children to whom a religion is taught with the consent of their parents? And what if a religion contains certain elements harmful to the human rights of those who adhere to it?

This variance in approach to the "freedom of opinion and expression" and to the "freedom of thought, conscience and religion", as well as to the conditions under which these freedoms may be restricted, appears to be based n o t on clear knowledge of the rights under consideration, but rather on the assumption – or value judgement – that morals and religions are necessarily "good".

In the face of this state of affairs, it seems necessary to conceptualize anew what is called "freedom of thought" or "the right to freedom of thought", keeping in mind also the "misuse" of this right. This presupposes *a)* a conceptualization of the idea of human rights, *b)* the clarification of what is called freedoms or "fundamental freedoms" and *c)* the clarification of the term "thought".

Here I shall summarise what I did elsewhere[3] concerning these three points and on the basis of these clarifications, I shall attempt to make a different

[3] See, Ioanna Kuçuradi, "Human Rights: the Idea, the Demands and the Instruments", in Ioanna Kuçuradi (ed.), *The Idea and the Documents of Human Rights,* Ideas Underlying World Problems, 3, joint publication of the International Federation of Philosophical Societies and the Philosophical Society of Turkey. Ankara, 1995, pp. 75-92; and in the

formulation – different from the existing ones – of what is called "freedom of thought".

CONCEPTUALIZATION OF THE IDEA OF HUMAN RIGHTS

The term 'human rights' expresses an idea – a conception of the human mind, a thought: the conception that human beings (because they are human beings, i.e., because they belong to a species which shows certain specificities) possess, all of them equally, certain rights: each of them should be treated, by other individuals, in a special manner.

There is no, or no significant, dispute about that – but only about that. Most international human rights documents are attempts to put in black and white this special manner, i.e., to codify fundamental principles or "universal" norms, expected to determine action, as well as the establishment of social relations (of social order) and legislation in general. In such contexts the term 'universal' is usually assumed to denote the worldwide validity of the norms, and not the specificity of a kind of norms distinguished from norms of other kinds.[4]

Yet, if we leave aside other international instruments and look only at the norms codified in the *Bill of Human Rights*, in the light of philosophical-epistemological knowledge concerning practical norms, we see in these instruments norms of different kinds and of different scope – their common feature (what brings them together) seeming to be that they represent the "good"s – the opposites of the "bad"s – or the value judgements of Western culture at a given historical moment –as well as certain needs felt in this culture at a given historical moment. This is a fact which bears implications for the very wording of these rights and for their restrictions and which has also led, wrongly, to a cultural approach to human rights. This cultural approach, in turn, has led, in practice, to a dubious increase in the number of human rights, to an inflation in human rights and human rights instruments, and in theory to the theory of "overlapping consensus", which is becoming increasingly prevalent.

But despite the fact that the norms expressed in the *Bill of Rights* are not all of the same kind, the conception of the idea of human rights underlying the *Universal Declaration* stems from anthropological value knowledge.

---

present volume pp. 101-111; "Freedom and Social Freedom", in R. Balasubramanian and Sibajiban Bhattacharyya (eds.), *Freedom, Progress and Society*. New Delhi, Motilal Bonarsidass, 1986, pp. 153-160; "Knowledge and its Object", in Ioanna Kuçuradi and Robert S. Cohen (eds.), *The Concept of Knowledge. The Ankara Seminar*. Boston Studies in the Philosophy of Science, 170, Dordrecht, Kluwer Academic Publishers, 1995, pp. 97-102; and in the present volume pp. 101-111.

[4] In the *Universal Declaration,* for example, the word 'universal' qualifies the *Declaration*, not the norms.

And what the *Declaration* intends to formulate – as appears from its first article – is a special kind of norms.

If we read the *Declaration* – especially art. 1 – and try to detect the intention of those who have initiated it, we can perhaps formulate the conception underlying this *Declaration* as follows: being human, i.e., being a species possessing certain potentialities or capacities, implies that every individual belonging to this species treats, and be treated by, other individuals in a manner that he or she may actualize – that is, in a manner that does not hinder him or her from actualizing – the potentialities which mark and constitute the value (the special place) or dignity of the human being. It further implies that every individual should be afforded the possibility of actualizing (those who can, and as much each of them can) the potentialities of the human being. What the *Universal Declaration* intends to put forward is the conditions of this possibility.

Consequently each human right brings, or is expected to bring, a demand concerning a basic condition, considered normally necessary for the actualization of certain human potentialities. What each principle of human rights demands, or is expected to demand, is the creation or realization of such a condition in the historical reality in which it is deduced. Once deduced, such a demand becomes a basic right for every human being – yet a right which may have, and in fact does have, different implications in different actual situations.

When the rights enumerated in various international instruments are viewed in the light of this concept of human rights, it becomes possible to distinguish between kinds of rights, and then of basic human rights. These distinctions help, to some extent, in avoiding confusions – confusions concerning freedoms and their restriction, confusions connected with fashionable mottos floating around today, e.g., "the *free* market", etc.

In the *Bill of Human Rights*, *first*, we become able to distinguish (from the viewpoint of their bearers – i.e., those who have to be treated in a special manner or the object of demands) between the rights of the individual and group rights (collective rights, or the rights of the peoples as they are called). *Second*, we become able to distinguish between demands (or rights) concerning the individual as a human being – whatever its other specificities might be – i.e., the human individual distinguished from individuals of other species; and demands concerning the individual as a citizen of a given state, i.e., distinguished from the citizens of other states. I think that the term 'human rights' must be confined to the first kind of rights of the individual: the rights in which all human beings "are" equal.

Among the rights of the individual as a human individual, we may distinguish – this time from the viewpoint of the ways of their protection, i.e., their exercise and fulfilment – between *a)* rights or demands directly connected with the exercise of human activities by which human potentialities are actualized, that is, rights directly connected with the basic conditions that normally afford an individual the possibility to exercise such activities and *b)* rights or demands connected with the prerequisites that afford an individual the possibility to develop his or her human potentialities (e.g., the right to food, the right to education, the right to health).

CLARIFICATION OF THE TERM 'FREEDOMS'

Freedoms are among the first kind of demands described above. What the first set of rights demands is that the individual be not "hindered" while exercising certain activities proper to humankind; in other words that "nobody" (State organs included) "touches" an individual – i.e., causes harm to the other rights of an individual who is engaged in such an activity.

To protect this kind of rights amounts to codifying them, i.e., to guaranteeing them through international instruments, constitutions and national law in general. Seeing that we can speak of the protection of these rights in life, when and where there are attempts to violate them (i.e., not after they are violated), to 'protect' these rights amounts to trying to prevent such violations by putting these rights in the constitutions and by implementing more specific laws, deduced in the real conditions of a given country, and in case of attempts of violations to intervene through various national or international organs, created for such purposes.

Still, when we look at the wording of freedoms in international instruments, the term 'freedom', there, appears to denote the demand that individuals not be hindered – not in exercising activities actualizing the human potentialities I mentioned – in doing "things" which are considered "good", that is, about which a positive value judgement prevails, without taking into consideration whether those "things" are connected to the exercise of those human potentialities.

What these "freedoms" or kind of rights demand is not that an individual not be hindered from doing something specified or from acting in a specified way, but that he or she not be hindered from exercising and developing certain potentialities of the human species, by acting in very different ways or by doing different things, which cannot be determined once and for all. An individual's right not to be hindered from ... means, here, that no harm is done to the other basic or non-basic rights of that individual, because he or she, by carrying out such activities, has done something (e.g., has brought new knowledge on a given issue), which does not conform to a prevailing taboo. Where such demands determine – and as much as they determine – social organization and practice in public affairs, there the correlative freedoms exist.

Thus, so far as the first category or kind of basic rights is concerned (but not the other), conceptually what is called 'a right' and what is called 'a freedom' are the same thing, simply named from two different viewpoints: when we call something a 'right', we mean that it should be protected, we demand that it be protected; when we call it a 'freedom' we mean that it is guaranteed by law, which assures that it is or will be respected. We mean that individuals, in a given state, enjoy the respective right, or we mean that the demand that a right brings is guaranteed by law. *Where* these basic rights of the individual are *actually* respected – in other words where the relevant laws are implemented, i.e., where the other rights of an individual are not violated by those who can do it, or when there are attempts to violate them they are protected by law – *there* (in such countries) the correlative freedoms of these rights *exist*: people enjoy these basic rights. Where they are not respected, insecurity, anarchy or terror prevails. And where they are violated by State organs, oppression reigns, i.e., these freedoms do not exist.

The bearers of freedoms are not the individuals – as is generally supposed – but the countries. A country, in which public order affords to all individuals living there (citizens or not) the possibility of exercising human activities which lead to the actualization and development of a potentiality which constitutes the value of the human kind, is a country where the relevant freedom exists.

So long as the bearers of freedoms are considered to be individuals, restrictions of these "freedoms", that is of the respective rights, are inevitable – as is now the case. Furthermore, in the face of *claims* of violations of human rights regarding the restrictions of certain *acts*, a deadlock is unavoidable. I fear that as long as we continue to consider individuals to be the bearers of freedoms, we shall be unable to draw a limit between freedoms and their misuses, and, consequently, to distinguish in many given cases whether a basic right has been violated or not.

CLARIFICATION OF THE TERM 'THOUGHT'

In order to conceptualize 'freedom of thought' we also need to attempt to clarify the term 'thought'. In various contexts the term 'thought' denotes (in the singular) a complex *activity* of the human mind (thinking), as well as the *outcome* of this activity, i.e., a kind of propositions or expressions put forward as a result of this activity.

The term 'thought' – meaning an outcome of the human activity of thinking – covers a variety of such products of the human mind: ideas, notions, opinions, beliefs, 'ought' propositions, etc., i.e., all such products of the human mind, but *it does not cover 'knowledge'*; since propositions of knowledge have an object *independent of those who put them forth*, whatever the ontical specificity of this object may be; consequently they can be verified or falsified in various ways. Opinions and beliefs, on the contrary, are *personal*: a belief is always the belief of *somebody*, as is the case with an opinion. Still, an opinion shaped by somebody, when expressed, can become the object of other people's belief. Thus any proposition, whether true, false, or even absurd, can become the object of someone else's belief (e.g., that one has to get rid of the troubles of this world as soon as possible, may become the object of other people's beliefs. As a concrete example one can cite the collective suicide in the United States a few years ago; or that "killing an atheist opens the door to paradise" can become the object of the belief of certain people).

There is no doubt that the advocates of "freedom of thought" do not include *such* beliefs in this concept. For this reason, they try to put limits on this "freedom" – limits which in practice lead to an impasse; for example, while *these* limits inevitably allow for violations of the right in question, they are insufficient for the prohibition of racist or fundamentalist teachings.

For this and other reasons it is worthwhile, even necessary, to try to conceptualize the basic right to which "freedom of thought" corresponds, in the light of a clear concept of human rights.

*

In the light of the concept of human rights that I have tried to put forward here, it is possible to formulate this right as follows: *Everyone has the right to put forward new knowledge and ideas, no matter how divergent they may be from prevailing ones.* This right, when guaranteed by law, constitutes what we call "freedom of thought", which expresses the legal guarantee that *this* right of the individual *will* be respected in the given state, i.e., nobody – neither his superiors, nor any State organ, the judge, the police, etc. – will "touch" him, i.e., will cause damage to *his other rights*, because he has put forward new knowledge or an idea – no matter how divergent this knowledge or idea may be from existing or prevailing knowledge or ideas, *and* independently of the specificity or content of the given idea or knowledge.

Yet the specificity of a given idea that someone has brought must be taken into consideration, when we come to the question of *teaching, propagating, or propagandizing* an idea. Here we are faced with the problem of the limits of toleration in the organization of public affairs.

Those who should not be "touched" – or those who should be protected – are the individuals who bring forth new knowledge or a new idea, and *not* the knowledge or the ideas, the thoughts themselves. Teaching and propaganda of certain ideas or thoughts (that someone has put forward, who should not be touched) may, after appropriate evaluation, be prohibited. And the criteria for the prohibition of those ideas and norms which ought not be tolerated in the organization of public affairs, might be *a)* their collision with *knowledge on the same issue* and *b)* their collision with a human right, provided that this right is clearly conceived.

There are still numerous points to consider and develop in this understanding of "freedom of thought" which I have outlined and, as you have probably already noticed, carefully *separated from* "freedom of religion" and *distinguished from* "freedom of opinion". Be it so. This understanding, which also bears implications for legislation, can help us at least to deal differently with certain problems we are faced with today: it can help, on the one hand, to the better *protection of individuals* who bring forth new ideas and knowledge in various countries, whatever the content of these ideas or thoughts may be; and on the other hand, it could make possible to put limits – not on an individual's right or "freedom" of thought – but on the organized teaching and propaganda *of ideas and norms* which contradict basic human rights and consequently cause harm to the basic human rights of the individuals – teaching and propaganda currently made in the name, or under the guise, of human rights.

THE RIGHT TO LIFE AND CERTAIN OF ITS IMPLICATION IN THE BEGINNING OF THE TWENTY-FIRST CENTURY*

The right to life, this most basic right of the individual, has undergone a considerable extension during the 20th Century. Besides the classical violations of this right, such as the death penalty, torture and slavery, new problems arose with the developments in the sciences, and which threathen, directly or indirectly, the right to life of the citizen of our planet.

These same developments also caused a confusion between ethical and human rights problems, because all human rights problems are ethical problems, no doubt, but not *vice versa*, that is n o t all ethical problems are problems of human rights.

That is why it seems necessary to scrutinize various claims related to the right to life in the light of clear knowledge of human rights.

*

The term 'right' in the context of 'the right to life', as well as when it qualifies any other basic right, expresses a d e m a n d concerning a treatment due to everyone by everyone – i.e., it expresses a demand concerning how individuals should be treated a n d treat all other individuals.

According to a widespread conception, the right to life demands to avoid touching in any way the biological/physical and mental integrity of the individual. This way of understanding the right to life is important. Yet is it sufficient to constitute, in the present conditions of our world, the content of the right to life? Does not hunger too threaten the physical integrity of a person?

If we look at the main international human rights instruments – such as the *Universal Declaration of Human Rights,* the *UN Convention on Civil and Political Rights*, the *European Convention of Human Rights* and the *Charter of Fundamental Rights of the European Union* – we see that in connection with the right to life they mention death penalty, torture and inhuman treatment and punishment, personal security, slavery and servitude, medical-scientific experiments, etc.; and in the *Charter of the Fundamental Rights* (2000) we also see that "the prohibition of eugenic practices, in particular those aiming at the selection of persons", "the prohibition on making the human body and its parts as such a source of financial gain" and "the prohibition of the reproductive cloning of human beings" are also mentioned. And though many articles of this Charter repeat the articles of previous human rights instruments – including their prob-

* The Turkish version of this paper was published in Ioanna Kuçuradi, *İnsan Hakları: Kavramları ve Sorunları*, Türkiye Felsefe Kurumu Yayınları. Ankara, 2011 (second edition), pp. 113-125.

lematic articles – art. 2, related explicitly to the right to life, brings the very important new demand that "No one shall be condemned to the death penalty or executed" and thus gives an end to the compromises of the previous instruments. This is a very important step in the history of human rights.

One of the problems to be discussed in connection with the right to life is the question whether premeditated killing or attacking someone in order to kill him or her, is only a crime, or, more than crime a violation of the right to life.

If we approve the claim, often put forward by certain State representatives in political fora, that a given crime is a violation of human rights only if it is committed by a State official, while if committed by a civilian it is only a plain crime, it is easy to reply: not every killing is a violation of the right to life. On the other hand, if we consider human rights first of all as ethical principles – and not only as law – every killing is a violation of the right to life. Another question: Are terrorist killings violations of the right to life? According to the former assumption they are not, while according to the latter they are. Still they are different from someone's killing his wife or husband for any reason.

As you see, at this point we are faced with the problem of criterion. Thus it appears necessary to discuss what can be the criterion that makes a murder violation of the right to life, taking into account also the questions mentioned above, and to justify any proposed criterion by value knowledge. In order to decide whether a concrete, single act is a violation of the right to life or of any other human right, it is necessary to possess the knowledge of the conceptual content of that right, which in turn presupposes clear knowledge of the content of the concept of human rights, i.e., to possess these criteria which are deduced from each other.

Every premeditated killing is much more than touching the physical and mental integrity of a person; it is to annihilate him or her. And t h a t person will not come to the world once again.

In the international instruments, as well as in the old and new debates related to the right to life understood as "to avoid touching the physical and mental integrity of a person", we find the issues of death penalty, torture, inhuman treatment and punishment, as well as problems of medical ethics and bioethics such as euthanasia, organ donation, abortion, interference with the genes, etc.

What calls our attention in these debates, is that both those who are in favour and those who are against, defend their claims n o t on the ground of value knowledge, but by using d i f f e r e n t value judgements on the same issue. As for the international instruments on these issues:

a) The only important instrument which explicitly considers death penalty as violation of the right to life is, as I mentioned earlier, the *Charter of Fundamental Rights* of the European Union; while in art. 6 of the *Covenant on Civil and Political Rights* it is expressed that under certain conditions death penalty will not be considered as violation o f t h i s a r t i c l e of the *Covenant.*

Still when we read this article together with art. 7 of the same *Covenant*, which states that "No one shall be subjected to torture or to inhuman or degrading treatment or p u n i s h m e n t ", we are shocked by an inconsistency: art. 6 does not prohibit death penalty, but art. 7 prohibits inhuman punishment. Death penalty, isn't it an inhuman punishment?

Now, when we look at premeditated killing from the viewpoint of human rights as ethical principles and consider every such killing as violation of the right to life, the following and similar questions have to be raised and answered: to punish someone who has killed and consequently violated the right to life of someone else by death penalty, is it not to answer a violation of a human right by committing another violation of that right? To approve such a punishment given by a judge, in the name of a whole nation, is it not to approve the principle demanding "an eye to an eye and a tooth to a tooth"? Is it not to consider legitimate the blood feud and assume that the human-legal institution we call the State is a revenge instrument?

If we reject, as an implication of the right to life, to sentence to death someone who has violated the right to life of others, it is necessary to consider, as another implication of this right, the need to take the appropriate steps and precautions so that individuals do not kill other individuals. Such precautions might start from establishing in our countries the system of periodical check-ups – including also a psychiatric check-up – of all citizens and continue through increasing the quality of education – including the quality of the education of ethics and human rights.

b) Euthanasia is also an issue often discussed in connection with the right to life. The discussion is usually made in connection with legal problems. Its ethical aspect is to be seen only in certain films. The prevailing tendency in this respect is to leave the decision to individual countries.

If we leave aside passive euthanasia and understand from active euthanasia: to help someone who is ill and suffers unbearably and for whom, according to the medical knowledge of the time, there is no hope to survive, is euthanasia a violation of the right to life, as those who are against euthanasia claim, or not?

Here I wish to give you two examples which can secure us a clue in looking at the issue of euthanasia: The first one is a case that a medical doctor has faced: this doctor has started doing the necessary to someone whose heart had stopped and when, after three hours her efforts had no visible result, those around her and even the relatives of the patient asked her to give up. Yet this doctor continued her efforts to make the heart of the patient function, because she was seeing a very slight reflex somewhere at his eyebrow and ear. Thanks to her efforts during four hours, that patient returned to life and lived for more 15 years.

The second example is a case that I witnessed in a hospital during the illness of my mother. In the next room of my mother's room was hospitalized a young girl – 19 years old. Cancer had affected most of her organs. Analgetics had no influence anymore and she wished so much to live! An evening that I went to the hospital the young girl was not in her room. She had undergone an appendicitis operation, which if not performed, she would have died that day.

Next day, when I went to the hospital in the evening, the young girl was not in her room again. But this time she had left for ever the room. When later I asked the doctors why they had made the appendicitis operation one day ago, they answered that their job was to help people live.

There is no doubt that the job of a doctor is to help his patients continue to live. I nevertheless think it would be useful to reflect on the difference of these two cases.

Euthanasia does not look like an issue on which law can be developed – because every human being, even when he is ill, is unique. I think that law can only put forward certain general conditions for deciding whether euthanasia m a y be applied to a patient who wishes to die. Still each case has to be evaluated in itself.

c) Giving and taking organs for transplantation from living persons is also an issue of debate, i.e., whether the physical integrity of the donor is touched or not.

When we look at the regulations related to the issue of giving and taking organs, we are faced with a threefold ethical relation: between the donor and the recipient, and between the doctor and each of them. The main conditions mentioned in these regulations are "informed consent" of the donor and prohibition of making his organs a source of financial gain. If these and such conditions are fulfilled, does taking from someone an organ for transplantation violate the right to life of the donor or not? Taking an organ under these conditions: is it a human rights problem or only an ethical problem?

There is no doubt that the person whose organ is taken loses something. But is this a violation of his right to life? I think that it is not possible to give a general answer to this question. In certain cases may be and in other cases is not a violation of the right to life. If the organ taken from a donor is taken without taking into consideration the results that this will bear for him, there is an ethical problem. If in addition this threatens his life, in this case there is a violation of his right to life. The specificity of these problems necessitates that a doctor who does not wish to violate the right to life has to evaluate each single case as a whole, on the ground of ethical value knowledge and professional knowledge. This means that the problems faced in this connection are ethical problems. But if they are not dealt with ethical value knowledge and sufficient professional knowledge, it is possible to lead to violations of the right to life.

d) One of the issues debated also in connection with the right to life is abortion. This is an old debate. Abortion is in fact an ethical problem which those who are against put in connection with the right to life.

In the first article of the *Universal Declaration of Human Rights*, in which the conception of human rights underlying the *Declaration* is worded, states that "all human beings are born equal in dignity and rights". This wording makes us think that there it is assumed that human beings have this right from the moment they are born. In fact the proposal made during the preparation of the *Declaration*, that the protection of the right to life should start from protecting the fetus was not accepted, yet for pragmatic reasons. Of course, this should not hinder the discussion of this issue, yet in the light of ethical value knowledge.

If we take into account that human rights bring demands for each human being, it is possible to raise the following questions:

Does the fetus have an existence independent from the person who naturally bears it? Is fetus a human being or a potential human being?

Here also we are faced with an ethical problem and not a human rights problem: the problem of a person's relation with herself. And as all ethical problems, this too makes necessary to evaluate each case for itself.

e) Another right that is discussed in connection with the right to life in the human rights instruments, is the right called "personal security". It is considered to be a right different from the right to social security mentioned in the 22nd art. of the *Universal Declaration* and which is understood as "the right of being protected against intensive interferences from the State or from non-State actors".[1] Others put this right in connection with art. 9 of the *Universal Declaration*, which states that "No one shall be subjected to arbitrary arrest, detention or exile".

There is no doubt that the demand to protect individuals against violent interferences is among the implications of the right to life: human beings should not be killed, should not be disabled. Yet we have to ask: only these and such treatments threaten the physical and mental integrity of a person? Hunger does not threaten it? AIDS does not threaten it? Has not the Chernobyl accident damaged the life of those who were affected or died because they were living there?

I think that all demands to protect individuals against everything that hinders, threatens and annihilates their lives are among the implications of the right to life.

There is still a difference of kind between the former and latter threats. This means that we have to understand the right to life not only as a negative right, but also as a positive right and to define the right of personal security in a way that distinguishes it from the right to social security – e.g., to guarantee the implementation of the implications of one's basic rights as a whole.

To secure to everyone the minimum conditions necessary for the subsistence of his/her physical existence is also an implication of the right to life. To fight against poverty and to secure these minimum conditions for subsistence are among the duties of the State in every country, as well as among the duties of humanity.

---

[1] See Lars Adam Rehof, "Article 3", *The Universal Declaration of Human Rights. A Commentary,* ed. by Asbjørn Eide, Gudmunder Alfredson, Göran Melander, Lars Adam Rehof and Alan Rosas, with the collaboration of Teresa Swinehart. Scandinavian University Press, Oslo, 1992, pp. 263-264.

To carry out the points mentioned above, as well as many other theoretical and practical consequences of human rights is an implication of being a human being. To protect the right to life of everyone who came to the world as a human being, that is to prevent the violation of his or her human rights and to carry out their implications in the situations in which we find ourselves – even when it is for us very difficult – is an implication of the consciousness of being a human being. We have to protect human rights n o t because our rights, too, might be violated, but because we are h u m a n beings. The way which leads to this consciousness is the ethical education of human rights. Nobody should assume that, when I say this, I think that with this education the world would be transformed into paradise or that human rights violations would be eradicated from our world. Ours is an unending struggle. But we should not forget that we protect or give damage to our human dignity n o t by what we suffer, but by what w e d o in our relations with the others.

PHILOSOPHY FACING WORLD PROBLEMS*

The term 'world problems' has become an almost technical term since UNESCO's Medium-Term Plan prepared in 1982 for the years 1984-89. It denotes problems which mankind faces at present, such as hunger, various inequalities, pollution, arms race, development, peace, etc. In the First Part of this Plan, under the title "World Problems and the Lines of Emphasis of the Medium-Term Plan", many of these problems are stated in a clear and documented way.

In this same part we also find expressed the following observation: "Studies of the present and future situation of the world as a whole have proliferated to such an extent in the past few years that, paradoxically, their very number, the diversity and heterogeneity of the analytical methods and tools used and the influence, frequently unacknowledged of value systems and normative assumptions make it more difficult to apprehend things objectively".[1]

In the face of this situation, a theoretical objective is put to the First Major Programme, which bears the title "World Problems": to attempt "to clarify matters for the international community as a whole".[2] In view of this objective "two complementary approaches" are anticipated: the first is expected to be "an analytical-descriptive" one, seeking "to bring together and examine studies and reports on world problems and the ways in which they are perceived", while the second is expected to be "one of synthesis", which "will lead to the preparation of a future-oriented study" that will highlight and guide the work to be done in connection with the themes treated in the other major programmes. And this part on the Strategy Action of the "Reflection on World Problems and Future-Oriented Studies" ends with the following sentence: "These compelling considerations point to the need for incorporating the dimension of p h i l o s o p h i c a l r e f l e c t i o n[3] in an appraisal of world problems".

This need, felt already for a long time by those who are well aware of the vocation of philosophy, has been thus o f f i c i a l l y expressed, thanks to the clear-sightedness of the author(s) of this part of the Plan.

This First Major Programme seems – at least to me – to be at the same time an attempt of UNESCO to answer c e r t a i n e t h i c a l d e m a n d s, addressed to it by men and women from all over the world. One of these demands was addressed to UNESCO exactly six years ago, in 1980, in this very room. In the Seminar on the Philosophical Foundation of Human Rights, the

---

* This paper was published in *Philosophy Facing World Problems*, Philosophical Society of Turkey. Ankara, 1988, pp. 7-13.

[1] Draft Medium-Term Plan (1984-1989), UNESCO, Paris, 1982, par. 6.

[2] *Ibid.*, par. 1004.

[3] Emphasis added.

inauguration of which was honoured by the Director General of UNESCO, this demand was worded as follows: "What we need now, is to develop a world project, which will put forth the ways through which humanity a s a whole will become able to protect human rights everywhere in the world [...] Since the most comprehensive organization we possess, as humanity, is the United Nations, [...], the place where such a project has to develop is the UN. And taking into consideration the present structure of the UN and the composition of its various organs, this place in the UN could be the UNESCO, whose special task is to promote some of the principal activities which constitute Man's value or dignity: education, science and culture; the UNESCO in which and through which also philosophy can pay its tribute to today's humanity. Couldn't the UNESCO take the initiative?",[4] we asked.

UNESCO's programme on "world problems", in spite of the fact that some consider it, erroneously, to be a "political" enterprise, appears as a whole to be UNESCO's wish to answer such demands, and its part for the years 1984-89 an attempt to pave the way for the "objective evaluation" of world problems. For this reason, it is quite natural that world philosophers feel the urge to contribute, by knowledge and ideas, to the elaboration of this theoretically framed programme.

Still, how? The question of how this contribution can be made, still does not seem to be clear enough in the minds of philosophers. The epistemological views prevailing in our days have proved to be inappropriate in the approach of such a question. Besides, present-day philosophy – when it is not mixed up with ideology – is little accustomed to deal with such questions; such a need in world philosophy has only recently been felt. And I suspect, this is the reason why, despite UNESCO's official statement concerning the need "to incorporate the dimension of philosophical reflection in the appraisal of world problems", world philosophy, during the past six years, has not sufficiently carried out the task philosophy was expected to fulfil.

*

What is the specificity of the philosophical consideration of the so-called 'world problems'? And first of all: what is it that makes any issue a 'world problem'?

These two questions may sound too "abstract" to many. Still, it seems to be necessary to come to grips with these questions, first for the objective exposition and correct explanation of these problems, and then for the discovery of what should and could be done in order to face them in accordance with the aspirations of the whole of humanity.

Let us first have a look at the term 'world problems'.

If we read UNESCO's relevant documents with an eye to what is called there a 'world problem', we realize that this term denotes at least two different kinds of problems: *one* of them is constituted by certain facts of our times: there

---

[4] I. Kuçuradi (ed.), *Philosophical Foundation of Human Rights*. Ankara, 1982, p. 6.

are the various facets of the difficulties in which a considerable part of humanity finds itself – hunger, high percentage of mortality caused by curable diseases, analphabetism, etc.– despite the level of civilization attained today by the same humanity as a whole; there are, if viewed through the value-knowledge, or even value-consciousness we have, the "shame" of our age – sharp inequalities among individuals and groups in the protection of basic rights, torture, etc. –; there are also some deadlocks into which the world today is led without noticing it – the arms race, pollution, exhaustion of non-renewable natural resources and other similar facts.

The *second* kind of the so-called 'world problems' appears as some a s p i r a t i o n s , felt in the face of the facts mentioned above, and/or the anticipated w a y s o u t . Development and peace belong to this category of problems. Also human rights are usually considered to be one of them.

Yet the study of these two kinds of problems – both their position and treatment – presupposes different activities of knowing: e.g., facts need to be explained, while in the case of anticipated ways, it is their adequacy or necessity which need to be justified – provided that we don't approach these problems through ready-made formulas, i.e., both their position and explanation or justification are not made by means of the same assumption, theory, doctrine, etc.

For, if we take a look at various studies made recently on various world problems, we often see one and the same real situation presented as a number of different ones, and this is considered to approach the same problem from "different viewpoints", all of which, it is claimed, have to be equally respected. In other words: because the difference between the right, or even wrong, evaluation of a situation – and in our case of a world problem which is a fact – and the various doctrinal evaluations of the same is not perceived, i.e., because there is a lack of knowledge concerning the difference of the modes of evaluation, both the right evaluation of a problem as well as its doctrinal evaluations, which also vary largely among themselves, are considered as "different approaches" to the same fact.

Besides, when we take a look at the various theoretical treatments of world problems, we observe that this "approach from different viewpoints" which is promoted, conveys two different meanings: the analysis, explanation or justification of a problem through the assumptions of different normative systems (morals, cultures, etc.), or through political theories and ideologies, as well as the existence of various juxtaposed views with regard to the same problem by various human and social sciences, both are taken as treatment of the same problem from "different viewpoints".

The interdisciplinary approach promoted by UNESCO is still usually understood as the independent study of the same problem by various disciplines – not as particular contributions, made by various disciplines to different stages of the study of a problem, i.e., to the point to which each discipline is relevant in one and the same study of a problem, which is a fact we are or are not aware of.

In the face of this state of affairs, one of the main contributions philosophy could make to the treatment of world problems, and a basic one, is to shed a strong light on the way of putting forth and evaluating world problems objectively, i.e., to put forth the chain of cognitive activities which constitute this way – a way leading to the grasping of our object of knowledge.

As it can be seen, if this be done, the study of a world problem, a single study aiming at putting forth and evaluating it objectively, presupposes interdisciplinary work, not to be carried out without philosophy. This philosophy, the need of which is felt in the treatment of world problems, is, presumably, a philosophy which, aware of the points where in such an interdisciplinary study philosophical knowledge is relevant and necessary, tries to contribute to the study of world problems and to the elaboration of solutions which bear but a low probability of creating new world problems.

*

'World problems' are f a c t s, produced by a special entanglement of events which are the outcome of social (including economic) and political relations established in this or that way in various countries and the world as a whole; or they are undesired situations – states of affairs – which we become aware of when we look at what is going on, taking into account also the philosophical value-knowledge we now possess – undesired because they are not favourable to the actualization, or make impossible the development, of certain potentialities of many human beings living in different parts of the world.

Yet a situation is not there, ready, before our eyes, like you or me; it becomes the special situation it is, only when it is put forth, when we name it.[5] 'To put forth a situation' means to become aware of and discover the effect which the entanglement of a number of unconnected yet simultaneous events – simultaneous within the section of time under consideration – produce in common upon a human group, i.e., the knot they create in their independent relationship with it.

What is discovered is a fact – e.g., that today, in the Republic of South Africa, *apartheid* prevails. This fact is *on the one hand* an effect of independent simultaneous events – e.g., of certain laws enforced in this *Republic* during the years 1949-1960 –; and *on the other* it is the common cause o f other independent events – e.g., the common cause, among other special ones, of Mandela's imprisonment, of the execution of the poet last year, of the removal of the Magopa tribe from the land they bought in 1936,[6] etc. The first set of events is what has produced the fact or what has created the existing situation, while the second set makes possible to know and put forth the same fact or situation.

---

[5] This seems to be, probably, the most fundamental reason why one and the same situation is presented as a few different ones.

[6] See "Forced Removals and the Law: The Magopa Case", *South African Journal on Human Rights,* Vol. 2, 1986, p. 91.

To go, by means of the latter set of events, to their common cause, is to put forth a situation in its factuality, i.e., as a human fact; while to find out the former set of events, is to explain the same situation in its historicity, i.e., as a historical, unique situation.

Now, it is among the tasks of philosophy to put forth a situation in its factuality – to give a situation its name – on the ground of the cognitive data afforded by various human or social sciences relevant to the case, yet of a philosophy which has already clarified the relevant concepts. To explain the same situation, i.e., to put it forth in its historicity, seems to be the job of various historical sciences.

To judge that a situation thus put forth is a desired or undesired one, depends on the viewpoint of the judging person who looks at it, on his value-criterion: the criterion he uses may be value-knowledge or principles deduced from such knowledge – e.g., human rights – aiming to protect value in individuals; or it may be a belief with or without cognitive foundation, or even a special need of his, e.g., his interests. Here is the only point where viewpoints may play a role. If such a viewpoint plays any role elsewhere, if, for example, it plays a role during the endeavour of putting forth the fact in consideration, it becomes impossible – unless by chance – to diagnose the real situation or world problem, as well as to explain it correctly.

Still, to judge that the situation constituting a world problem is an undesired one, or its opposite, is not a necessary constituent of its right or objective evaluation. On the contrary, it appears to be a constituent *sine qua non* of the right evaluation of a situation or world problem, to put it in connection with the value of the human being or the basic human rights, which are demands originating from this value in the existing conditions: to disclose the damage this situation causes to those who are in it, and how, it appears to be among the conditions of the objective evaluation of a situation, as well as among the tasks of philosophy.

To relate a situation put forth in its factuality, or a world problem to basic human rights, makes it possible to determine which human potentialities find a favourable or unfavourable soil for development, or even are hindered in this development under the totality of such conditions. Consequently it appears to be a component of evaluation affording the possibility to determine the goals to be put for the future on the ground of this knowledge, and not from other "viewpoints".

On the other hand to relate a world problem or a situation put forth in its historicity to basic human rights, makes it possible to find out what o u g h t t o be done and what c a n be done for the attainment of the goal proposed. Consequently it appears to be an evaluation component which could help that the solution anticipated in order to face a world problem, bear, as solution, a high probability to lead to the goal proposed: to the conditions which today's humanity as a whole aspires at.

Thus the possibility to select such a way to face a world problem seems to depend on our capacity to determine it not with regard to the undesired situation – which may be also desired by some – but with regard to its evaluation, in its factuality and historicity, in relation to basic human rights.

For when we look at the facts called "world problems" today, taking into account the philosophical knowledge we have reached in our age, it is not difficult to see their common characteristic; a l l of them are situations in which human rights are, directly or indirectly, either threatened or violated.

When we look at the conditions of today's world as a whole, taking into account our value-knowledge, the origin of world problems appears to be the disregard of basic rights and their implications in the existing conditions: world problems spring from this disregard due to ignorance or to the priority given to interests. Nevertheless, when we look at the connections established between world problems and human rights up to now, we see that the questions of human rights are usually considered as one bunch of world problems, only one among others; that is, the essential relation existing between human rights and a l l world problems, as I mentioned above, is, I am afraid, overlooked. At present, respect for human rights is counted among the aspirations of humanity, next to development and peace. Nevertheless, as humanity, I am afraid, we are not yet aware of the fact that respect for human rights – if really exercised – would amount to making human rights the criterion as well as the milestone of every social and political decision and action.

Right now the tendency to approach world problems from an "ethical viewpoint" gains more and more ground in world philosophy. Beside such approaches in philosophy we also observe various other attempts made to treat world problems from the viewpoint of value-norms, valid in different morals, religions and cultures. If we take into consideration the natural variety of these norms, we cannot expect that such attempts might ever lead us to a common ethical consideration of world problems. Yet the demands expressed by the basic rights which are deduced, in the face of the existing conditions of the world, from the knowledge of the value of c e r t a i n human potentialities seem at the same time to provide us with the common "ethical viewpoint" we look for.

The ability to adopt and make use of this viewpoint, seems to depend on one's consciousness of being human above everything else one is.

"WORLD PROBLEMS" FROM THE VIEWPOINT OF HUMAN RIGHTS*

THE PROBLEM

The question of human rights – their violation and unfulfilment – is at present considered as a world problem; it is assumed to be o n l y o n e among other problems we face as humanity, a problem like "development", peace, arms race, disarmament, pollution, the exhaustion of non-renewable natural resources in certain areas, communication, racism, etc. Consequently with the exception of a couple of them, such as racism or analphabetism, no connection is usually made between these problems and human rights – neither in theory nor in the debate of social and political questions.

On the other hand, an inflation has been observed in the number of the so-called human rights during the past few years. By simply putting next to various problems the word 'right', people claim to speak of "new" human rights: of "the right to development", "the right to peace", "the right to live in an unpolluted environment", etc.

Thus human rights today remain still a confused question of theoretical thinking, while in praxis-oriented thinking they are considered as a very important question, yet a question which nobody still knows where to place, consequently a question open to political exploitation, and, as a result, a feared question. And every day, every night, the televisions of the countries of the world, and nonetheless our personal experience, make us witness violations and disregard of these rights.

The theoretical confusion takes its source – as I often said – from the fact that philosophers have not s u f f i c i e n t l y tackled with this question, i.e., so much as to have an influence on this matter, although it is the job of philosophy to inquire into the concepts related to human rights as well as into their implications under the existing conditions. This is why even a few studies made on such issues scarcely reach those who decide on questions of human rights in praxis; it is only recently that these circles started becoming aware of the fact that philosophy might contribute to the settlement of such questions.

The main obstacle faced by philosophy in tackling satisfactorily issues of human rights seems, to me, to be the epistemological views prevailing nowadays. The inadequacy of these epistemological views – of logical empiricism with its various ramifications, as well as of Marxism – to treat such questions makes even philosophical circles a) to look on human rights as mere abstract "assumptions" deprived of any cognitive ground, and consequently b) to fail to

* This paper was published in *Philosophy Facing World Problems*, Philosophical Society of Turkey. Ankara, 1988, pp. 57-71.

notice the clarity that some studies, of a different epistemological approach, were able to bring to certain human rights issues.

Yet this lack of clarity has various negative consequences in our world in which material and spiritual interests dominate: a) at the national level it prevents people from seeing the harmful effects that some enforced laws, or certain social arrangements, may have on a kind of basic rights (on those I call "indirectly protected rights"[1]); and at the international level it hinders people from having an insight into the implications that some decisions – e.g., economic decisions – have for the people of the non-industrialized countries, sometimes even for those of the industrialized ones, or from realizing the effects of such decisions even after they have started making themselves felt. b) In the case of another kind of basic rights (of those I call "directly protected rights"[2]) this same lack of clarity seems to be at the national level the cause of social arrangements which make impossible the protection of these rights; and at the international level the reason why some states are able to find ways of defending violations of human rights or accusing other states for such violations without seeing their own humps – to use the Turkish expression – or, even, as it is put in paragraph 65 of UNESCO's Medium-Term Plan 1984-1989 (Draft), the reason why "the very people who habitually express indignation at certain actions [can] tend to minimize others that are equally serious, because the regimes responsible for them share their view of the world or serve their interests".

In other words, this lack of conceptual clarity in questions of human rights a) makes it often very difficult to realize the close connection existing, in fact, between world problems and basic human rights: for example, it constitutes an obstacle in the r i g h t or "objective" evaluation of problems which are already diagnosed, owing to the immediate troubles they cause, so that in spite of the fact that the "studies of the present and future situation of the world as a whole have proliferated in the past few years", it has become "more difficult to apprehend things objectively";[3] or it makes impossible the diagnosis of the problems underlying the experienced troubles, and as a result the feeling of helplessness spreads out more and more among the people, and especially the young people, of our world.

b) This conceptual confusion is not only an obstacle in realizing the connection which exists between world problems and basic human rights, but also the cause that the solutions anticipated to face such problems become, in the long run, the origin of new "world problems": economic development as the

---

[1] For this classification see my "Philosophy and Human Rights", in *Philosophical Foundation of Human Rights*. Ankara, 1982, pp. 49-51; and in the present volume pp. 19-24; or my "Philosophy and Social Injustice", in *Philosophy and Cultures*. Nairobi, 1983, p. 64; and in the present volume pp. 25-35.

[2] *Ibid.*

[3] Medium-Term Plan 1984-1989 (Draft), par. 6.

main objective of national policies seems, to me, to be a typical example of that; another is the measures taken in the name of "security".

I shall not expose here the conceptual framework which constitutes the ground on which I base my considerations and which makes possible to see the connection existing between world problems and basic rights;[4] but I'll only attempt to show, by means of a world problem which is not yet considered as "a world problem", the connection existing between basic human rights and certain world problems created by the endeavour to fulfil two widespread aspirations, which are, in fact, considered as "world problems". In other words, I shall try here to call attention to the connection existing between basic human rights and certain facts created by the attempts to promote "development" and "peace", by means of another fact – the deviation of most of existing states from the *raison d'être* of the State as a *legal human institution*. Than I'll point at some of the implications.

DEVELOPMENT AND SOCIAL INJUSTICE

The Second World War constitutes an important turning-point in the history of the 20th Century. The peoples of the countries which had participated in this war, as well as the peoples of some other countries – the peoples of the United Nations – "determined to save succeeding generations from the scourge of war, which twice in [their] life-time has brought untold sorrow to mankind; to reaffirm faith in fundamental human rights, in the dignity and worth of the human person, in the equal rights [...] of nations large and small; and to establish conditions under which justice [...] can be maintained; to promote social progress and better standards of life in larger freedom", have resolved, forty years ago, to combine their efforts to create a world free from fear and want, and thus they established the United Nations Organization.

These nations, which in spite of this proclaimed resolution of theirs, had in the meanwhile signed pacts and created "blocs" against each other, put forward the ideal expressed by the word 'development' as the best way to fight poverty and secure social progress. This idea put as the main objective of national policies of the countries of the world, had, as an implication, their division in "developed" and "underdeveloped" or "developing" ones.

Since the criterion used in this dichotomy was high national income and industrialization, in the countries falling under the category of "developing countries" increase of national income and industrialization became the main objectives of their national policies – objectives to which they didn't hesitate to sacrifice everything else –; while in most of the industrialized countries "further development" or "progress" turned into a deadly competition or "race" in in-

---

[4] My view on the question of "right evaluation". For this see my *İnsan ve Değerleri* [Man and Values]. Istanbul, 1971; and more specifically the chapter 1a in my *Etik* [Ethics]. Ankara, 1988.

creasing industrial production – a race to which they had subordinated almost everything else.

Still, the experience of the past few decades, i.e., some facts which are the outcome of these "developmental policies" followed in both the "developed" and the Third World countries, and which are counted among the so-called world problems, suffice, I think, to make us see the impasse where this idea of development – not alone, no doubt – has led most of these countries. Even a blind man could see this outcome.

Thus, this idea, which has been introduced and adopted as the most appropriate way to get rid of poverty and to promote justice, has created results contradicting the expectations of its introducers. But since it has become an *idée fixe* of our times, nobody is still willing to give it up, despite the fact that a considerable part of the world problems we face is its outcome:

In most of the so-called developed countries this competition for more and more industrial production and technological progress, has led to an unchecked use of natural resources which got nearly exhausted in various parts of the earth, to pollution, to the threat of nuclear energy, etc., and, besides, to various unexpected social problems such as that of foreign labour, the spread of alcoholism and of drugs, the emergence of marginal groups, etc.

In many Third World countries, on the other hand, the idea of development, while it caused the slight increase of national income we observe if we look only at figures, it also intensified social injustice, i.e., it broadened the unequal distribution of deprivations, and this coupled with other factors, gave birth to the various political disturbances upsetting these countries. This situation or world problem is described in the UNESCO document mentioned before, written in 1982, as follows: "In the Third World, vast populations frequently enjoy none of the benefits of the progress and towns and cities – in many cases and at least as regards certain categories – are like islands of modernity cut off from the hinterland."[5]

Broadly calculated 1.300 million people have no access to drinking water. This is a striking figure we find in the same document. The *idée fixe* of industrialization and technological development prevents some Third World governments even from reflecting on the possibility of taking some very simple precautions aiming at a little more protection of the basic rights of their citizens w h o a r e l i v i n g and will probably not be alive when these countries become industrialized one day. A friend from a southern African country gave me the following example: there is a district in his country, where people, in order to go to and come back from their fields, have to walk at least 6-7 hours carrying their products on their back. In this country where motor vehicles are not imported, owing to economic difficulties, and where no horses or mules are to be found, nobody thought of breeding such animals, to use them for the time being in transport and in the cultivation of the soil. An indication made by a

---

[5] Medium-Term Plan 1984-89 (Draft), par. 19.

Western scientist in this respect was met by strong protest, claiming that this was a Western invention for keeping that country underdeveloped.

Another fact resulting from the idea of "development" at the global level is described in the afore-mentioned UNESCO document as follows: "[...] in 1979 four industrialized countries alone accounted for just over half of the world gross product, and in 1980, whereas the average per capita product in the industrialized market economy countries amounted to 10.660 dollars, in the so-called low-income countries it came to only 250 dollars – or forty-two times less".

What I wish to point at, by using these spots selected from three different perspectives, is that the way anticipated and followed up in order to abolish social injustice at national and world levels, i.e., development, as main objective of national policies and "foreign aid" made by rich countries to the poor ones, has led – as it can now be easily seen if we look at the situation as a whole – to the widening of social injustice; while it afforded to a few people the possibility of living on "islands of modernity", together with the increase of population in these countries it did increase the number of those who are deprived a some of their most basic human rights.

Why did this happen? Why has the path followed in order to abolish social injustice led to its opposite?

So far as I can see, what has caused this outcome – and let aside the "how" – appears to be the conception of the State prevailing at present – a conception which considers the State as an entity in itself, which equates it with "power", and without taking into consideration the distinction between 'benefit' and 'interest' it gives priority to the 'interests' of this entity against not only the interests of the citizens, but against their benefit as well. And, so far as I can see, *this* conception of the State, which was shaped empirically during the past few centuries and which ignores the goals of the State as a legal human institution, constitutes now, perhaps, the most fundamental world problem, i.e., it constitutes – together with the other causes peculiar to each world problem – the most fundamental common cause (the "factual cause") of the deadlock to which we are led.

Becoming aware of that, and consequently becoming aware of the connection existing between the goals of the State as a legal human institution and the idea of justice conceptualized in view of the existing conditions today, enables us not only to see why developmental policies have led us to a deadlock, but also it can highlight our search for ways out.

Or: it enables us to determine, under the existing conditions on the ground of philosophical knowledge, the content of the demand "to bring a cultural dimension to development" – a demand that the Western World has introduced recently as a way out from this deadlock, and that it translates as "to put Man at the heart of development", since this world does not seem to be willing to give up the idea of (or the term?) development.

THE STATE AND SOCIAL INJUSTICE

Let us take a look at the connection existing between the widespread conception of the State, which I mentioned before, and injustice as it appears nowadays.

Injustice appears in general as violations or disregard of rights. Still, if we try to find out how it emerges today in various countries, we see that it appears a) in case the State either has not put under legal guarantee most or some of the basic rights of its citizens, i.e., their directly protected rights, such as the right to security of the person, the right to privacy, etc.; or, though it has done so, it has enforced laws discrepant with this guarantee, or even itself through its own organs violates these rights; b) in case the State does not carry out, for a great or small part of its citizens, the implications of another kind of basic rights, such as the rights to education, to medical care, etc., in the existing conditions; and c) in case the State does not interfere effectively, through its appropriate organs, with such violations or disregard, etc. What in legal terminology is called "the rule of law" and "the social state", are demands introduced in the face of the above-mentioned appearances of injustice.

In other words: injustice, as it appears today in general – social injustice, included – is a state of affairs, created when the States do not (or cannot) fulfil the goals of the State as a legal human institution.

Still, the State, which is now considered only as a political institution in the narrow sense, is, nevertheless, a legal human institution, i.e., a kind of institution which finds its foundation in the ontical conditions of the human being (in his being a biological, social being, a being bringing demands to itself, etc.), and not in historical conditions, as social institutions do. This characteristic of the State distinguishes it from social institutions, the function of which coincides with the purpose of their establishment. This characteristic of the State also determines its goals as a human institution, which are: a) to transform social relations – relations of rights and duties, or role relations – established, in one way or another, among human beings living in groups, into legal relations – relations determined by the idea of justice, and b) to administrate the *res publica,* i.e., what belongs to everybody and to each one in a group, in view of the idea of justice. From the viewpoint of this goal the State is a legal institution – an institution established in order to add to what happens by itself the implications of the idea of justice.

Now, if starting from injustice as a state of affairs we face today, we formulate the idea of justice as the demand to afford to individuals the possibility of fulfilling their basic rights, or to carry out, at the national and global levels, the implications of these rights in the existing conditions; we may thus reach the following conclusion with regard to the functions of the State as a legal human institution: a state established and functioning (i.e., the Constitution of which is made and implemented) in accordance with the goals of the State as a legal human institution, is expected to exercise at least the following two functions: to guarantee, and afford the possibility, to its citizens to exercise their basic rights. The analysis of these two functions in view of the existing condition – which means also to try to create for the citizens the conditions which will allow them to develop their human potentialities – also determines the duties of the State, of every state, in domestic affairs. What is politics for, if not to fulfil such duties?

And we may say that every constitution made, every law enforced, or every institution established without adopting as its foundation the protection of basic human rights, is a misuse of positive law; and that it is to be expected that every national policy, which does not have as its principal objective the protection of basic rights in the existing conditions of a country, will be led to a blind alley through some results that sooner or later will occur.

In the face of this "world problem", seen under the light of the knowledge of basic rights, the possibility to break through this deadlock seems to depend a) on giving a place to the teaching of human rights at all levels of education, and especially in the curricula of programmes training students for public offices, and in extramural education as well, b) on trying systematically to generalize the concept of the "State based on human rights" instead of that of the "State respectful to human rights", which is very well compatible with the entity-State conception, and c) on putting as the principal objective of national policies – i.e., as the objective determining permanently every public and political decision within a state – the protection, in the existing conditions, of basic human rights, etc.

This does not, in fact, mean that the poor countries will have to put aside economic development; it only means that economic development as the principal objective of their national policies should be replaced by human rights. As for the rich or the so-called developed countries, this would imply that, if they wish to compete at all costs, they have to find another object of competition – something connected with the protection of human rights.

Another implication of what I said would be to give up using the high rate of their *per capita* national income – and even industrialization – as the criterion of "being developed". Yet, if we don't wish, as humanity, to give up this *idée fixe* of ours – as it seems to be the case – it would be appropriate to give it a different content, i.e., to start "measuring" the degree of development of a country, by how much it has actually guaranteed and made possible the fulfilment of the basic rights of its citizens.

DEVELOPMENT AND GLOBAL INJUSTICE

The problems I mentioned up to now are some of those which constitute the bunch of "world problems" we face as an outcome of considering economic development as the principal objective of national policies.

There is also another fact which belongs to this bunch of problems: the fact that in a few countries of the world the indirectly protected rights of the majority of the citizens are "protected" much more than human dignity requires, while in most countries of the world the basic rights of most of the citizens are protected very little or not at all. This is the fact, or, world problem called 'global injustice'.

This problem, too, is usually considered to be only an economic fact, and consequently it is expected to be solved by introducing a new global economic order and by economic aid which rich countries extend to poorer ones – an "aid" mostly effectuated by giving loans.

Still, we observe that the rich countries, which extend this "aid", usually, are not willing to make the least sacrifice in "protecting" the maximum of their economic interests, and that their "aid" consists in loans with high rates of interests, given, usually, in view of their economic and especially political interests. Some international economic projects elaborated with a more humane concern – like that of the North-South dialogue – seem to bear the danger of deepening even more the already existing social injustice in these countries, because they seem to be elaborated without evaluating correctly the social conditions of these countries.

Paul Trappe,[6] in his evaluation of the Brandt-reports concerning "urgent" aid to developing countries, after a comprehensive analysis based also on statistical data, shows how foreign "aid", as it has been extended to such countries for thirty years, has created conflicting classes which did not exist before; and he concludes that every aid which will be extended to them without taking into consideration their social conditions, could only but make the already existing chaotic situation even more chaotic – the Gordian knot totally unsolvable – consequently "the plea of the many" should not be presented so as to evoke the feeling of obligation to give to these countries an aid, which, since it does not reach the many, would make the situation even more chaotic.

Besides Trappe, who attempts to highlight the question of development in its connection with "foreign aid", Odera Oruka, in his very interesting paper on "The Right to Self-Preservation and a Global Ethical Obligation", attempts to highlight the question of foreign aid to "developing" countries from the viewpoint of its principles and calls attention to three principles underlying this aid, which he calls "the law of international trade", "historical rectification" (i.e., compensation of the damage caused to some of these countries in the time of colonization) and "international charity". As a result of the first principle poor countries are obliged, in order to meet their urgent needs, to accept aid-conditions which in the long run are harmful for them. The second principle could lead rich countries to consider aid as an obligation only for those poor countries with which they had a colonial past. As for the third principle, it makes the giving countries see themselves as superior to those which receive; while it makes the latter feel pity for themselves and resentment for the giving. And he suggests that "we need a principle which would make it ethically obligatory for affluent nations to aid the poor ones as unqualified moral duty for humanity, and for the latter to receive such aid without feeling self-pity. Such a

[6] See his *Entwicklungssoziologie*. Basel, 1984, pp. 3-18.

principle should also help to invalidate the use of 'national supererogation' in the relations between nations without thereby discrediting the principle of national sovereignty and equality of nations".[7] He names this principle "a global ethical obligation", by which he means the obligation to provide to the peoples of the world the possibility to meet the minimum of their basic needs.

Here I wish to elaborate a little further this principle in its connection with human rights and consequently to show why it is an obligation – be it felt or not – to put basic human rights as the main objective and as a criterion for the evaluation of world politics.

To show this means to show "the place" where the demands that human rights express originate from, or to show the cognitive ground they are deduced from.

THE ANTHROPOLOGICAL ORIGINS OF HUMAN RIGHTS AND THEIR IMPLICATIONS

Here I shall summarize the "place" I just mentioned as follows: the origin of the idea of basic human rights appears to be the knowledge of the value of certain ontical human potentialities which made Edison discover the uses of electricity, Saint-Exupéry write *The Little Prince* and thousands of others to achieve what they have indeed achieved, blessings all of us enjoy. This is the knowledge of what a human being can become, and of the significance, for humankind, of the achievements of those who have actualized up to now such potentialities. This knowledge implies, on the one hand, the necessity to create for every human being the preconditions which make possible the actualization of these ontical potentialities of the human being, since, when we look at the world as a whole, we see that the conditions in which the majority of human beings find themselves are unfavourable for such an actualization. This same knowledge, on the other hand, involves the obligation for every human being that possesses it, to work for the creation of the preconditions just mentioned. But to take over this responsibility and bear it in concrete situations, i.e., to try to carry out its implications, proves to be the mark of those who possess a clear consciousness of their human identity and not of those who give priority to any group identity of theirs, be it cultural, religious, national, etc.

Yet though this knowledge or consciousness is necessary to make one carry this obligation, it is not sufficient for making one find out what should be done in a given situation, for example, what we have to do in order to face a world problem today. One needs also to know to evaluate correctly a given situation, event, etc., and to try in every case to do that. In the face of the "world problem" of global injustice, the way out appears to depend on making,

[7] From his paper read in a symposium on "Ethical Issues in International Development", in the VIM World Conference on Future Studies. San Jose, Costa Rica, December 9-14, 1984.

in earnest, the protection of human rights the point of orientation of world politics. In our world where more than the half of those who live today fail to enjoy the minimum of protection of their basic rights, any attempt to establish a world order which could provide this minimum, makes necessary to reflect on and find out ways, I believe, essentially different from those followed or anticipated at present by our economic policies – ways which take into account the special complex conditions of individual countries within the framework of the world as a whole.

The possibility to make just now human rights the guiding principle of world politics does not seem, in fact, very probable. Still, in connection with this problem, there is something that could be done today: we might put as main objectives of education to make young people acquire the consciousness of being human and able to make right evaluations of situations, events, etc., they come across. This seems possible even today, provided that we wish it sincerely.

POLITICS AND HUMAN RIGHTS

The bunch of world problems we have glanced at until now, rather covers problems which are the outcome of the manner of arranging and implementing economic relations at the national and international levels. Their common factual cause is, as far as I can see, the conception of the State prevailing nowadays.

There is also another bunch of world problems, which, without being independent from the ones already mentioned, are the outcome of the manner of arranging and implementing *political* relations at the national and international levels. The common factual cause underlying them seems to be *the conception of politics* originating from the prevailing conception of the State: that of politics, as the arrangement of group interests. In spite of their innumerable appearances *political* world problems today seem to be the outcome of conflicts between diverging group interests, but *also* between group interests and group rights.

'Interest', in distinction from 'benefit', denotes the *calculation* we make when we act in order to carry out something we wish, without taking into consideration its implications for the basic rights of others – 'others' in the broad sense – in the existing conditions. As a result, we take more than we deserve in that case and this "more" is reduced from the other's part.

At present, the idea of "international understanding and co-operation" has been introduced as a way to face the conflict of group interests which are threatening "peace" or are causes of war, as well as the idea of "group rights" as a way to face conflicts between rights and interests.

This idea of, or demand for, group rights itself, being introduced without first clarifying the concept of human rights, which are rights of the individual, is a dim concept, too; consequently it is open now to multilateral misuse.

What are "group rights"? Or to use the denomination we find in international documents, what are "collective rights" or "the rights of the peoples"? In those documents these rights which are often confused with human rights, amount to three or four. In order to be able to answer this question, let us first look for the fact in the face of which this demand has been introduced:

As a result of the political geography delineated in the recent past – especially after the First and Second World Wars, after the era of colonization, after various emigrations and other events – various large or small groups, possessing different characteristics, were obliged to live together with other large or small groups as the citizens of the same (nation-) State or as the peoples of the same country, and they are still obliged to do so. This situation, together with the prevailing conceptions of the State and politics, has led and still leads the groups in power to policies delineated to serve their various interests as a group, i.e., policies which neglect the basic rights, or ignore the implications they bear for the rights of the individuals of the other groups possessing characteristics other than those possessed by those in power.

In other words: the reason for introducing the demand that group rights express is the fact that in many countries of the world, the group in power which possesses certain characteristics of its own hinders, directly or indirectly, the other groups which are not in power, and which each as a group possesses different characteristics, to exercise their basic rights *because* of this difference.

Thus, the demand that group rights now express appears to be an implication of the basic human rights under the existing national and international conditions – an implication in the face of the consequences of the policies which many states follow in this respect and which contradict the *raison d'être* of the State as a legal human institution.

We have to respect the group rights which are implications of the basic rights of the individuals under the existing conditions in the world, yet, we have to respect only them. Still, notwithstanding that such group rights are not sufficiently respected in many states of the world, I have to confess that the tendency this respect has created does not seem to be, in the long run, a way which could lead to a more effective protection of basic rights in the world. The oppression of colonialism and of various discriminating policies has led and still leads various groups to establish their own independent states, and at the international level to the creation of new – cultural – blocs.

Nevertheless in various states established recently, we observe that shortly after the proclamation of their independence, i.e., shortly after the unifying "common enemy" has left, these states fall in the trap of minor divisions, rather then trying to protect the basic rights of their citizens. Thus human rights are still disregarded as previously; for, these states, too, are established with the same State conception.

Thus we may say that, so long as this prevailing conception of the State shows no change in the minds of the people of the world, in which political units keep on increasing, and so long as the protection of the basic rights on world scale does not become the common objective of international efforts; what we have to expect for the future is not "one world", but rather a hardening up of the bloc-creating tendency, i.e., we have to expect the increase of "worlds" in which it will be even more difficult for more and more human beings rapidly increasing in number, to exercise their basic rights – of "worlds" which though perhaps different, nevertheless are all far from affording those who live in them the possibility of actualizing and developing their human potentialities.

ARMS RACE AND PEACE

"International understanding and co-operation" and "disarmament" are the mottos expressing today the ways anticipated in order to face international conflicts of interests in the world. They are considered to be the way to maintain "world peace".

Still, who is to become "disarmed"? And what is this peace they wish to maintain?

It is obvious that those who are to be disarmed are not the 160 countries of the world. Everybody knows, surely, who they are. This is why I'll not dwell on this point. Yet, I think, there is, among others, a point, which is forgotten owing to the pessimism caused by the alteration of hope and disappointment which disarmament conferences create: the initial responsibles of the start of nuclear arms race and of its going on. Rather than the politicians of yesterday and today, responsible of this race are the scientists, who, either by error or deception, or any other reason, have deviated science, as a human activity, from its goal, affording thus to those politicians the possibility to conduct this race or the cold war.

It is estimated that at least a quarter of world scientific research expenditure is for military purposes; and the number of scientists and engineers currently engaged in military research and development activities is between 400.000 and 500.000.[8]

Thus, if we take into account the origin of this race, run in the name of security, i.e., if we keep in mind how it was made possible; we may say, a radical way to break through this vicious circle of arms race would amount to making possible, first of all for the scientists of the countries which run this race, t o r e j e c t t o g e t h e r to work on military research and arms development, and t o w o r k t o g e t h e r in order to find ways of annihilating the already stored arms. This is a way which relevant international scientific organizations could open, provided that they share the will to do so.

WORLD PEACE

At present the problem of the so-called "world peace" is considered as a question of the disarmament of those who possess nuclear weapons and are involved in this race. Such an approach is an obstacle hindering people from seeing the connection existing between the question of "world peace", or peace in general,

---

[8] See Medium-Term Plan 1984-1989 (Draft), par. 55.

and human rights, and leading people to equate the 'maintenance of peace' with the 'prevention of a hot war'.

The "efforts for peace" exercised by those who are now in the position to proclaim a world war, reminds me of Kant's following remark about the "harmony" existing between those who have the same object of will: "In this way a harmony may result resembling that depicted in a certain satirical poem as existing between a married couple bent on going to ruin 'Oh, marvellous harmony, what he wants is what she wants'; or like the pledge which is said to have given by Francis I to the Emperor Charles V, 'What my brother wants (Milan), that I want too'".[9]

But what is peace? We have to keep in mind the truth which twenty-five centuries ago Socrates tried to teach to his contemporaries, that it is impossible to answer any other question about anything unless we know what it is (and in the case of an idea unless we determine its positive content); otherwise the opposite of any claim would be always possible. We have to keep in mind this crucial truth and attempt, in this Year of Peace, to give an answer to this question.

Here I'll communicate to you my attempt:

Peace, as a concept, is the relative concept of war. Still, when we look at reality, at the wars going on or those once fought, we see that each war is an event: it starts, i.e., it is declared at a certain moment, it goes on for a while, short or long, and comes to an end one day.

Viewed within historical dimensions war appears as a chain of events; while, if considered as a human fact, it appears to be a state of affairs, or a total of certain conditions, created by the emergence and confrontation of two sides in their relation to the same thing (to Milan, for example), i.e., by events which each side, in its endeavour to eliminate the other in order to fulfil its own wish, starts and continues through actions which know no limits.

Thus, though peace as a concept is the relative or opposite concept of war, in reality it is not its "opposite" state of affairs. Still we cannot determine what peace is by looking at reality, as we do with war, i.e., by looking at single wars, since in reality we don't encounter "peaces", as we do with wars.

We can, nevertheless, obtain the negative concept of peace – 'negative' in the sense of philosophical terminology – by considering the fact of war: we can tell which characteristics should be absent from this total of conditions. Thus taking as a point of departure war as a fact of the human world, we may define the concept of peace as: the state of affairs or the entirety of conditions, which does not give birth to "sides" in connection with the same thing, which, owing to its nature, does not lead to confrontation those who are in relation to one and the same thing; it is a state of affairs or an order

[9] *Critique of Practical Reason,* 4, Theorem II, Remark (from Lewis White Back translation).

of things, which, owing to the principles of its establishment, does not itself cause the confrontation of two sides.

Considered as such an order or entirety of conditions peace is a juridical state, or a state of affairs in which Law prevails.

In the historical moment we live, how can we shape a positive concept of this state of affairs we tried to determine negatively? Or, how can we word the positive concepts of peace at the level of countries and at the global level?

I think, 'peace' at a country's level, or domestic peace today, is the name we could give to the state of affairs reflecting the existence of social freedom in a given country. Let me make just a little clearer this point:

Compared with the other kinds of freedom,[10] social freedom appears as an idea: as a demand that the social relations in a country be so arranged as to protect human dignity, i.e., those potentialities that distinguish Man from other living beings; so arranged as to provide individuals with the possibility to be determined also by value knowledge. For, individuals are those who make these arrangements, who enforce and implement laws, regulations and positive Law in general. And individuals can do all that taking into account value knowledge and principles aiming at protecting value; or, they can do all that, being determined by other motives – more than anything else by their personal interests, or those they consider as their own too.

The most basic principles aiming at protecting value that we, as humanity, possess today, in connection with the organization of social relations, are the principles we call basic human rights. These rights, when put under the guarantee of Law in a country, become the freedoms which constitute the content of the concept of social freedom.

Thus, we may say that, if the principles expressing basic rights are under the guarantee of Law and if the demands they express are constantly fulfilled in a country, i.e., if in a country all enforced laws, all established institutions aim at providing all citizens, permanently, with the possibility of an equal and dignified protection of their basic rights; then in this country social freedom exists. Such is, I am afraid, the state of affairs we may call 'peace'.

A fact of our times – a fact which we may call a world problem – is that most of the basic rights, though put under the guarantee of Law in most of the countries of the world, i.e., though the names of the basic rights are to be found in their constitutions, a small or large part of their citizens is unable to exercise these rights. And this leads to various conflicts, civil wars included.

Thus peace must be the state of affairs that can be created not only by including basic rights in positive Law, but also by fulfilling the implications these demands have in a given country, i.e., by constantly trying to make social freedom a reality; the state of affairs in which basic rights do not very often remain black on white.

---

[10] See my "Freedom and Social Freedom", in *Freedom, Progress and Society*. New Delhi, 1986, pp. 153-160.

In this Year of Peace, a contribution that the people of the countries of the world, and especially their public or State officers, could make to the efforts for peace, could be to review the conditions of their countries as a whole, from the viewpoint of such a concept of peace, and try to determine their own part for the creation of this state of affairs.

There is no need, I believe, to put in words, on the ground of the concept of peace I put forward here, what kind of a state of affairs "world peace" could be. Each of you can make this deduction. Besides, if I did that, I might cause a thickening of the widespread pessimism in view of world peace.

Nevertheless, if we look at the efforts exercised at present – at those efforts exercised up to now, at least – with respect to "world peace", keeping in mind such a concept of peace, this latter helps us to realize, among other things, the following points:

a) These efforts appear to be rather the efforts of two sides, which, both being in quest of Milan, mutually try to prevent eliminating the other by use of arms. It would be more correct to call these "efforts to prevent a war from flaring up", instead of "efforts for peace".

b) Considered under the light of such a concept of peace "world peace", as it is being dealt with, i.e., in connection with the question of disarmament, it does not appear as a world problem, but only as a problem which only the two worlds (the First and Second Worlds) immediately face, and which concerns many other countries only through its consequences, actual as well as probable.

c) Considered from the viewpoint of such a concept of peace, no efforts but only those exercised in view to contribute to the creation of the conditions which could afford all the citizens of all the countries of the world the possibility to exercise both kinds of their basic rights, could be, or might claim to be, earnestly called 'efforts for peace'.

d) Still, under the light of this concept of peace, we also see some sincere efforts shown in this respect. But nobody calls them "efforts for peace".[11]

CONCLUSION

If we look at the world problems – at any problem – of our day, in the light of philosophical knowledge, all of them appear at present closely connected with questions of human rights.

The possibility to realize this connection seems, nevertheless, to depend on the clear knowledge of what human rights are and consequently of the reason why they should be protected.

But the possibility to introduce, on the ground of this knowledge, the protection of human rights as the main objective of social and political activities, depends on whether those who are, at various levels, in a position to make this change, are conscious of being human – a consciousness which often, in the

[11] WHO is such an example.

conditions of the present-day world, paralyses those who possess it while in action.

Goals and Traps in the Ways out of the Current Stalemate of Poverty*

In the Draft Declaration of the World Summit for Social Development, held in Copenhagen in March (March 6-12, 1995), we read that the Heads of State and Government have committed themselves, among other things, "to the goal of eradicating poverty in the world, through decisive national action and international co-operation, as an ethical, social, political and economic imperative of humankind" – in a world in which today "over 1 billion people live under unacceptable conditions of poverty". "To this end", they say, they "will [...] focus [their] efforts and policies to address the root causes of poverty and to provide for the basic needs of all".[1]

Do these leaders really possess the sagacity and the courage to do so?

Also 50 years ago "the peoples of the United Nations determined [...] to promote social progress and better standards of life in larger freedom, and for these ends [...] to employ international machinery for the promotion of the economic and social advancement of all peoples, ha[d] resolved to combine [their] efforts to accomplish these aims"[2] and thus create a world "free from fear and want".[3]

What became of these efforts shown during the past fifty years? How did these efforts lead to the "current stalemate of poverty", to the eradication of which the Heads of State and Government have committed themselves in Copenhagen?

Here I shall try first to summarize a critical analysis of problems related to our topic, which I started making in the beginning of the eighties, in order to show two traps which the current anticipated solutions bait – traps mainly due to the fact that although we are now well aware of the deadlocks to which our policies for economic and social development have led us, we are not sufficiently aware of the fact that we are trying to break through these deadlocks by solutions based on the very same approach, which has led us to them. After this analysis, I shall attempt to sketch a vision, based on a different approach, resulting in fact from this analysis.

---

* This paper was published in *Futures Beyond Poverty – Ways and Means out of the Current Stalemate*. Turku-Finland, 1997, pp. 88-89; its Turkish version in *İktisat Dergisi*, N° 368, 1997, pp. 119-125; and its Polish version in *Transformacje* 1-4, 1998, pp. 99-107.

1 Draft Declaration of the Copenhagen Summit, Commitment 2 (emphasis added).

2 Charter of the United Nations (emphasis added).

3 Universal Declaration of Human Rights, Preamble.

ECONOMIC DEVELOPMENT AS MAIN OBJECTIVE OF NATIONAL POLICIES

The first thing that those who established the UN did, in connection with our issue, was to put forward the ideal expressed by the word 'development', as the way to fight poverty and secure social progress – an ideal, which was put as the main objective of national policies of almost all the countries of the world and which the division of the countries of the world into developed and under-developed, or developing, countries is based on.

Since the criteria used in this dichotomy were "high" national income and industrialization, in the countries falling into the category of "developing countries", the increase of national income and industrialization became the main objective of their national policies; while in most of the industrialized countries the efforts for "further development" or "progress" turned into a deadly competition, or race, in increasing industrial production – a race to which they had subordinated everything else.

The experience of the past few decades – i.e., certain facts or "global problems" which are the outcome of these developmental policies followed in both the "developed" and "developing" countries – makes us see the impasse or the stalemate where the ideal of development as the main objective of their national policies – not alone, no doubt – has led most of these countries.

In most of the so-called developed countries, the competition for more and more industrial production and technological progress has led to an uncontrolled use of natural resources which got nearly exhausted in various parts of the earth, to pollution, to the threat of nuclear energy, etc., and besides, to various unforeseen social problems.

In many developing – or Third World – countries on the other hand, developmental policies, while they caused the slight increase of national income we see if we look only at figures, also deepened social injustice, i.e., broadened the unequal distribution of deprivations in those countries and intensified various political disturbances in most of them.

This situation or global problem is described in a UNESCO document, written in 1982, as follows: "In the Third World, vast populations frequently enjoy none of the benefits of the progress and towns and cities – in many cases and at least as regards certain categories – are like islands of modernity cut off from the hinterland".[4] "In 1979 four industrialized countries alone accounted for just over half of the world gross product, and in 1980, whereas the average per capita product in the industrialized market economy countries amounted to 10.660 dollars, in the so-called low-income countries it came to only 250 dollars – or forty-two times less". "Broadly calculated 1.300 million people are without access to drinking water". All these are striking figures we find in this document.

[4] Draft Medium-Term Plan 1984-89 , par. 19.

It is obvious that developmental policies have not only deepened social injustices, but global injustice as well. These policies carried out, i.e., financed to a considerable extent by "foreign aid" or, as it was later called, "development aid", i.e., loans from developed countries, with political expectations, have not only broadened the gap between the rich and the poor within these countries, but (with the exception of a few countries) also broadened the gap between the few rich and the majority of the poor countries.

The debts of these latter countries have reached such a point that it seems improbable, if not impossible, that these countries will be able to pay them back at all. A cold-blood – rational, in the sense used in the science of economics – calculation shows that most of the developing countries – if no miracle interferes – are condemned to remain for ever developing in the sense assumed.

The situation in 1995 does not seem better. In the document of the Copenhagen Summit, i.e., after 15 years, we read exactly the same sentences: "a) within many societies, both in developed and developing countries, the gap between rich and poor has increased. Further, and despite the fact that some developing countries are growing rapidly, the gap between developed and many developing countries, particularly the least developed countries, has widened; b) more than one billion people in the world live in abject poverty, most of whom go hungry every day. A large proportion, the majority of whom are women, have very limited access to income, resources, education, health care and nutrition, particularly in Africa and the least developed countries".[5] Put together these official statements mirror the current stalemate.

Thus 'development', which was introduced and adopted as the most appropriate and promising way, i.e., as the way *anticipated* and followed up, in order to abolish social and global injustice and to get rid of poverty; in other words, development as the main objective of national policies based on "foreign aid" or "development aid" made by rich countries to the poor ones, has created results contradicting the expectations of its introducers. While it afforded a few people the possibility of living on "islands of modernity", together with the increase of population in these countries it also increased the number of those who are deprived of the means to answer even their most basic needs.

"CULTURAL DEVELOPMENT" AS A REMEDY

The impasse to which developmental policies had led throughout the world, *but mainly* the global problems faced in the industrialized countries (pollution for example), i.e., the consequences of the ever increasing technological development in the developed countries, made people in those countries start speaking of the need for "a new conception of development" or the necessity "to bring a cultural dimension to development". Thus they introduced the idea of "cultural development".

---

[5] Draft Declaration of the Copenhagen Summit, par. 16a and b.

What people in the Western-industrialized countries have mainly understood by 'cultural development' was the broadening for the masses of the possibility to have "access to and participation in culture", i.e., to activities considered to afford individuals the possibility to develop their potentialities as human beings – e.g., to artistic, scientific, philosophical activities.

We have to keep in mind that t h i s demand for "access to and participation in culture" is a demand s t e m m i n g f r o m a n e e d f e l t b y t h e p e o p l e o f t h e i n d u s t r i a l i z e d c o u n t r i e s, considered to be a way out of the impasse to which industrialization has led them.

Yet another important reason which brought 'culture' to the foreground at the global level, was that numerous developing (or Third World) countries, which do not belong to the so-called Western or European culture and which have obtained their independence a few decades ago, i.e., the people and especially the intellectuals of the decolonized countries, started revolting against the "colonization of the minds", as a result of which they brought to the agenda the question of "cultural identity" as synonymous to 'cultural development'. Thus they seconded the motion of "cultural development", still understanding it, mainly, as being allowed to develop – i.e., to identify and reconstruct – "their own" culture which, they think, was suppressed or forgotten under the influence of Western culture during the colonization era. They started trying to identify the culture – i.e., the conception of Man and of what is considered to be valuable – which, they think, is, and they wish to be, their own.

Meanwhile, the peoples of a third category of countries, of countries "in the process of modernization", who had opted themselves for "modernization", joined the discussion. What these, usually, conceive as "cultural development" is the resurrection or the revival – though their claim is that they wish to "restore" and "conserve" it – of the culture (i.e., of the conception of Man and of what is considered to be valuable) prevailing among them, before they came into touch with the West.

What we experience now in various countries "in the process of modernization" is a reaction to "Western culture", a reaction which leads each group toward the search of its "cultural identity" or of its o w n "values"; and since it is not possible to identify what it wishes to identify in the present state of affairs, it looks backwards and tries to find, in order to resurrect it, what it feels, or thinks, to be its own, i.e., the conception of Man and the conception of what is valuable (the value judgements) prevailing in this group before its industrialization efforts began or before its encounter with "Western culture" to which it reacts. Such a resurrection started even occurring, as the gradual spread of fundamentalism in some of such countries in different parts of the world shows.

In order to gain more and more ground fundamentalists defend their activities on the basis of the freedoms of thought, conscience and expression, as well as on the basis of the so-called "respect to cultural identities", or of "the right to be different". In other words, they defend their activities by using the mottos floating around, still mottos d e v e l o p e d i n i n d u s t r i a l i z e d c o u n t r i e s in order to tackle the problems t h e y face and which are problems of quite a different origin from the problems of the developing countries.

This is where the promotion of cultural development in the sense of cultural identity has led in the last decade of our century: it has created its own irreversible facts, the most striking one being the spread of antagonistic radicalism and fundamentalism, which gain ground in various parts of the world.

We are not sufficiently aware that we have made out of a fact, concerning a special kind of process, an idea (in the sense of the German word *Vorstellung*), a vague idea concerning a desirable state of affairs, that of the already "developed", affluent West in the second half of our century, yet interpreted in a very problematic way, i.e., reduced to only a couple of its ingredients; that we made out of a fact an ideal, which we put as a goal to be attained by the other, "not yet developed" countries.

Development has become an *idée fixe* of ours. Thus we keep on changing and multiplying the epithets of development – we speak of economic, social, cultural, indigenous, self-reliant, sustainable development, p l u s of equal respect to all cultures – but we don't even think of c h a n g i n g our goals and the objectives of our national and international policies.

As a testimony of this, let us lend an ear to the following words – under the heading of Principles and Goals – of the Heads of State and Government of the Copenhagen Summit: "We Heads of State and Government are committed to a political, economic, ethical and spiritual vision for social d e v e l o p m e n t based on human dignity, human rights, equality, respect, peace, democracy, mutual responsibility and co-operation, and full r e s p e c t for the various religious and ethical values and cultural backgrounds of the people".[6] I am afraid that those Heads of State and Government are not sufficiently aware that they have committed themselves to things, which, if looked at in their reality and singularity, may be, and often are, incompatible (e.g., respect to polygamy and respect to human dignity).

Thus I am afraid that the ways out from the stalemate of poverty promoted at present, when followed, will not only share the fate of "development", but also they will create their own predictable and unpredictable facts, i.e., new global problems.

Among these promoted ways out of the current stalemate of poverty, which are expected to lead to social development, we see the free market economy ("the new economic order", "globalization", "privatization", etc.) and the "right to be different", as it is called.

These are the two, very little noticed t r a p s, on which I wish to focus now.

[6] Par. 25 (emphasis added).

FREE MARKET AND HUMAN RIGHTS

After the dissolution of the Soviet Union the new trend in this respect is the fashionable linking of human rights, democracy and the free market. This triadic motto has become very popular all over the world.

Their linking nevertheless appears rather to be a result of linking value judgements than to express a factual or conceptual (necessary) connection among them – a linking which, if taken for granted, as it is done now, might, among other things, intensify even more social and global injustice and the already existing sharp economic disparities within and among countries, as well as create new disparities and disillusions in the countries "on the way to demarxization" as they are called.

If we are sufficiently aware of what the state of affairs at present is and how it emerged, it is not very difficult to foresee it. Let me give you the reasons for this claim of mine: social injustice is a problem related to the connection of social and economic rights with basic (human) rights. It is a state of affairs in which the possibilities of protection of one kind of basic rights, of the "indirectly protected basic rights" of the individual, as I call them, such as the right to education, the right to physical and mental health, the right to a minimum standard of living, etc., are not *equally* secured for all citizens in a country, i.e., the possibilities of fulfilling these rights are not afforded them in *the same degree*, whatever this degree might be.

It is a state of affairs which appears when social and economic rights are given – i.e., laws delineating *the limits* of social and economic rights are enacted (and often quite "democratically", through parliamentary decision) – without taking into consideration the implications they bear, *at that moment*, for the indirectly protected rights of the individual (for the right to health, education, etc.), in the existing conditions of a given country. In other words, it is a state of affairs emerging when determinants *other than* the demands that the basic (human) rights express, determine the delineation of the limits of social and economic rights in a country.

Thus economic disparities within non-affluent countries are the outcome of enacting laws, or of not abrogating laws, giving certain "rights", i.e., possibilities, used only by a few citizens, which have implications hindering the fulfilment of the basic rights of the majority of the citizens in the existing conditions of the given country. As a result, a few citizens may secure for themselves certain privileges while protecting their personal or group interests at the expense of the basic rights of the majority of the citizens, or sometimes even while protecting their basic rights to an extent surpassing the measure that the country's conditions allow. These are cases in which governments cannot or do not keep a part of the citizens from exploiting other citizens and the State as well.

It is usually claimed that social injustice is the result of unequal distribution of what "exists". Yet in many developing countries, either the State cannot dispose of what exists, or, what is at its disposal is not enough for the fulfilment, *even to a minimum degree*, of certain of the basic rights of all citizens at that moment. Social injustice appears not only because of the unequal distribution of what exists, but also because of the unequal distribution of deprivations. Thus I dare say that social injustice has little to do with the degree of protection of the indirectly protected basic rights; it has rather to do with the failure to afford the *possibilities of equal protection* of these rights for all citizens, whatever the degree of this equal protection may be.

In a country where, by the equal distribution of deprivations, these rights of all citizens would be protected equally, even though to a low degree, there would be no question of social injustice at the national level; there, we are faced with the question of global injustice.

*

Global injustice and mainly economic disparities among countries have also to do with the way of putting in order economic relations among countries.

A global fact of the present time is that in a few countries of the world, the indirectly protected rights of the majority of the citizens are "protected" much more than human dignity requires, while in most countries of the world these rights of the majority of the citizens are protected very little or not at all.

A way to help developing countries to develop was economic aid, which developed-affluent countries extended to poor ones as an "aid" in the form of technical assistance and loans.

Still it appeared that most of the affluent countries, which extended this "aid", usually were not willing to make the least sacrifice in "protecting" to the maximum their economic interests, and that their "aid" consisted in loans with high rates of interest, given usually in view of their economic *and* political interests. Some economic projects elaborated with a more humane concern – like that of the North-South dialogue – did not reach their aim, and even deepened the already existing social and economic disparities, because they were probably elaborated without evaluating the social and intellectual conditions in these countries. As a result, domestic economic arrangements were made, without keeping an eye on human rights.

Paul Trappe (the Swiss sociologist) in his evaluation of the Brandt-reports concerning "urgent" aid to developing countries, after a comprehensive analysis based on statistical data, has shown in the middle of the eighties how foreign "aid", *as it has been extended* to such countries for thirty years, has created conflicting classes which did not exist before (something which was to be expected, I would say); and he concluded that every aid extended to them without taking into consideration their social conditions would make the already existing situation – the Gordian knot – totally impossible to unravel; consequently "the plea of the many" should not be presented so as to evoke the feeling of obligation to give to these countries aid, which, since it does not reach the many, could not but make the situation more chaotic.[7]

I am afraid that an unconditional promotion of the "free market" in poor and non-affluent countries, as well as in ex-socialist countries, if considered to be t h e solution to the economic problems they face, would lead to similar results for human rights in these countries; and on the top of it, the free market coupled with the (well-minded, but not sufficiently scrutinized) demand to "respect all cultures" (*ergo* fundamentalisms included), i.e., with a demand implying the "respect" also of cultures possessing basic elements contradicting human rights, could lead step by step to a new communalism and a new Middle Ages.

Thus it appears that any solution deemed to be a way out of the current stalemate of poverty, which is not put in connection with, and is not evaluated at least from the viewpoint of its predictable implications for the protection of the different kinds of basic rights in the existing conditions of a country at t h i s moment, and at the global level, would probably make the existing situation more and more chaotic in non-affluent countries.

*

Let me put it quite sharply: not only do I not see any (necessary) conceptual or factual connection among human rights, democracy and the free market, but I also see a potential new impasse in the expectation that the free market (based on privatization, etc.) will lead to a better protection of human rights in most non-affluent countries.

Let me give you again m y reasons for saying so, i.e., let me say a few words on the philosophical problem I see behind this misconnection of the free market with human rights:

The demand of the free market, in principle, amounts, simply put, to the demand that governments do not interfere in the economic activities of individuals, that governments leave them alone in this respect. In this case – it is claimed – the order of socio-economic relations, i.e., their establishment and change, will follow a spontaneous open process. In this process individuals would not only better protect their interests but they would also have to protect the interests of other individuals.

This linkage of the free market with human rights betrays an intention to protect economic "freedom" as a basic right and to protect it in the way that o n l y o n e k i n d o f b a s i c r i g h t s, which I call directly protected rights (e.g., the so-called freedom of thought, freedom of opinion, etc.) can be protected.

This seems to be due a) t o a l a c k o f d i s t i n c t i o n b e t w e e n d i f f e r e n t k i n d s o f r i g h t s o f t h e i n d i v i d u a l, between an

[7] See Paul Trappe, *Entwicklungssoziologie*, herausgegeben und eingeleitet von Hans Werner Debrunner; Paul Trappe (ed.), *Social Strategies-Monographs on Sociology and Social Policy*, vol. 12. Basel 1984, pp. 3-16.

individual's basic (human) rights and his non-basic (social and economic) rights, and b) *to a confusion of the ways of protecting these two different kinds of basic rights of the individual*. The way to protect, for example, the so-called "right to freedom of thought" is assumed to be also the way to protect what is assumed to be an individual's "economic freedom" in the broad sense.

Let me now explain what I mean: when we read the basic international documents on human rights, in connection with the question "what are human rights?", i.e., when we read documents on human rights written before the start of inflation in human rights, *from the viewpoint of their intentions*, it is possible to distinguish between two kinds of demands, or between two kinds of basic rights in which all human beings are or are supposed to be equal: between a) demands requiring that "nobody" should hinder an individual to live and, more specifically, that nobody should hinder an individual from actualizing a special human potentiality, e.g., "the right to life, liberty and security of the person", "the right to freedom of thought, of opinion and expression", "the right to privacy", and b) demands related to the preconditions considered to afford each individual *the possibilities* to actualize special human potentialities, e.g., "the right to education", "the right to a minimum standard of living", etc.

Put in this way, it becomes obvious that the implementation of these two kinds of demands, or the protection of the two kinds of basic rights, means different things.

To protect the first kind of rights would mean to put them under the guarantee of Law: to put under the guarantee of Law that "nobody" (state organs included) will hinder an individual *while* this individual is exercising a given human potentiality, i.e., "nobody" will give damage to his other rights, and if there are any attempts to do it, this individual would be protected by the appropriate State organs.

Yet the protection of the second kind of basic rights (of the rights to health, education, etc.) depends on public institutions and on other given rights, the social and economic rights, which are *limits drawn* by Law, *within* which any concerned citizen is free to move. It depends on *how* the limits of social and economic rights are drawn, by taking or not taking into consideration their predictable implications for human rights in the existing conditions of the given country. And all such social and economic rights – both protecting and not protecting basic rights – are given by laws, i.e., by parliamentary "democratic" decisions.

Thus "freedom" with regard to economic rights (or economic freedom) would mean *the absence of limits in the economic activities of the individual*, which would be in contradiction with the very nature of such rights: *their being limits* set thereto – be they in accordance or not with human rights. It would mean the absence of limits in the economic activities of the individual, whatever their products, or their results, might be.

In connection with the question of social freedom, it would amount to demanding that "nobody" interfere with individuals, not only while they are engaged in actualizing special human potentialities, but also while they act to protect their own interests, which not only clash inevitably with the interests of other individuals, but in many cases also with their human rights.

Consequently, the demand that the "free" market now brings in the case of non-affluent countries would amount not only to discarding governments, which mostly delineate the limits of economic rights according to private or group interests; but also to discarding the possibility of making basic rights determinants in the establishment and changing of economic relations within and among countries.

Thus, a misconception of freedoms seems to be at the root of considering the free market as a way out from the current stalemate of poverty, since the free market may function in the economic relations among countries which are, more or less, on the same level of economic development, but constitutes a trap in the economic relations between developed and developing countries.

A misconception of freedoms seems to be also among the main causes of the spread of fundamentalism, which takes advantage of the so-called freedoms of thought, conscience, opinion and expression, as well as of the so much promoted "respect to the ethical and religious 'values' and cultural backgrounds of people" (i.e., the second trap that I mentioned) and propagates certain world views and norms, which are essentially contradictory to certain human rights.

HUMAN RIGHTS AS GLOBAL GOAL

This analysis leads us to anticipate a different possible way out of the present stalemate. This way out, if you allow me to summarize it in one sentence, would be to put as the main objective of national and international policies, in the place of 'development' – whatever its epithets might be – the protection of clearly conceived and differentiated basic human rights, which express demands for the treatment of human beings and are a special kind of practical principles or norms for the establishment of social relations and the deduction of Law.

To what would such a change of objectives or goals amount?

At the national level it would amount to abolishing social injustice immediately, that is to securing, by appropriate legislation, the possibility that the indirectly protected basic rights of all the citizens of a country (their rights to a minimum standard of living, to health, to education, etc.) be protected in the same degree, whatever this degree might be. This in turn would amount to enforcing laws concerning social and economic issues, i.e., laws delineating the limits of economic and social rights, by taking into consideration their predictable implications for the basic rights of all the citizens in the existing conditions of the given country.

I am well aware of the difficulties involved in such legislation, to be made through "democratic" parliamentary decisions: for example, the difficulty to formulate such laws and, if formulated, to pass them through parliaments, where the interplay of small interests plays a decisive role. Though this is difficult, it is not impossible, on the condition that those who possess sufficient knowledge for this a n d the sincere will to do so, are also able to find the appropriate strategy in each country.

*

The abolishment of social injustice, in order to be followed by an increased protection of the basic rights of all citizens in non-affluent countries, makes necessary the support of the affluent ones, still n o t in the way it has been done up to now and is done at present.

At present, to use Katarina Tomaševski's formulation, "free trade, which even in theory conflicts with human rights obligations of governments, is combined with free elections to form human rights conditionality".

> The recent spread of aid conditionalities to 'democracy' and 'human rights' at the level of rhetoric is in practice often reduced to the former, and 'democracy' is further reduced to multi-party elections. Contrary to what the public in donor countries may believe, this is not necessarily good for human rights. The reasons can be summarized as follows:
>
> * At the level of rhetoric donors are using 'democracy' and 'human rights' interchangeably, while in practice concentrating on support for multi-party elections. This may well result in the replacement of human rights by 'democracy' and the loss of donor interest in human rights once elected governments are in place.
>
> * 'Democracy' (both in rhetoric and in practice) has been confined to electoralism where countries are labelled 'democratic' as soon as elections have taken place. The fact that democracy takes centuries to develop (to which donors can testify themselves) is forgotten.
>
> * It is assumed that such instant 'democracies' can and will guarantee human rights and fundamental freedoms. Both history and the multitude of current examples prove this assumption to be erroneous.[8]

Tomaševski quotes from Nigel Barley's *The Innocent Anthropologist* (1983), the following striking example concerning the elections in Cameroon in 1979:

> At the polling booths democracy was in full swing. One man was being upbraided for not bringing all his wives. 'They would not come.' – 'You should have beaten them.' I asked several Dowayos what issue they

---

[8] Katarina Tomaševski, *Development Aid and Human Rights Revisited.* Pinter Publishers, London/New York, 1993, p. 13.

> were voting for. They stared at me blankly. You took your identity card, they explained, and gave it to the official over there who stamped it and your vote was marked. Yes, but what were they voting for? More blank stares. They had already explained, you took your card [...] Not one of them knew what the election was for.[9]

The protest of certain groups in my country, against the silence of the Western World in the face of the *coup d'état* in Algeria after the "democratic" elections there, can be also mentioned here, as another example of the problems involved in using interchangeably "democracy" (reduced to electoralism) and human rights.

The conditions for extending aid to non-affluent countries are at present "progress in democratization" and privatization, the latter which of which is a direct implication of free market economy. "The two main trends in the current aid policy concerning the social sector" observes Tomaševski, "are the decrease in investment into social services and the advocacy of privatization".[10] Still, privatization is based on the criterion of efficiency, as exemplified by the World Bank: "The administrative capabilities of all governments, not least those in developing countries, are severely strained by the weight of their numerous activities. The question I wish to pose [says G. Roth, in *The Private Provision of Public Services in Developing Countries*, Oxford, 1988, p. 5] is whether economic development could be accelerated by moving to the private sector those responsibilities, that would be handled more efficiently there".[11]

Thus development aid, i.e., the loans given according to these criteria to many developing countries, suffices only to pay the interests on their debts to developed countries.

This being the case, a way out of the current stalemate of poverty would be to efface (or forgive) most of the debts of poor countries and set different criteria for aid, to be made to poor countries not as loans but as donations.

This is the reason why I was glad to read in the speech that the Minister of Foreign Affairs of Denmark delivered at the Copenhagen Summit, the following:

> Development co-operation is not only a question of resource transfers, but also of trade and debt. In the Summit process the debt question has had a prominent position and commitments have been made to make further progress on this issue. I am proud to announce that the Government of Denmark this week has taken steps to implement debt forgiveness – beyond what follows from the 1978 UNCTAD resolution on debt – for a significant proportion of outstanding development loans, the amount being in the order of one billion Danish Kroner.

---

[9] *Ibid.*, p. 18.
[10] *Ibid.*, p. 18.
[11] *Ibid.*, p. 18.

> But we must also collectively address the problem of multilateral debt. One bold step would be to cancel outstanding IDA and similar regional development fund debt and in the future to give such assistance as grants instead of soft loans. That would require donors to compensate for lack of reflows in future fund replenishments. Denmark strongly recommends such a collective effort and would be prepared to participate fully in it.
>
> In view of the situation of the poorest and most indebted countries something must be done – now!

Thus to put as the main global goal the protection of basic human rights would amount to becoming aware of the traps hidden in the current promotion of the "free market" and of the full "respect to the ethical and religious values and cultural backgrounds of people" and to transform "development aid" to grants, given in view *to increase the degree* of protection of certain basic rights (of nutrition, health, education, etc.) to countries which take *the necessary steps to abolish social injustice and which remain truthful to the universality of human rights*, e.g., countries which increase the number of schools in which children are given the possibility to develop each his or her own human capacities, and do not increase the number of schools in which any cultural or other brainwashing is made.

Once acknowledged, these traps necessitate a change in our "official" approach to the old and to the emerging new global problems, a change to be based on a clear and cognitively justifiable conceptualisation of human rights.

Development and the arms race have marked our century. Let us try to do more than we think we can, so that the coming century be marked by a "race" *in* the protection and *for* the protection of our *few* basic human rights.

"HUMAN RIGHTS EDUCATION AND EDUCATION FOR SOLIDARITY. THE TRAINING OF THE TRAINERS"[*1]

The question of the training in human rights has been given special emphasis during the past fifteen or twenty years. Yet we are still in the period of experimentation.

In the variety of approaches we come across while reading the reports on what has been done and on what has to be done, I see, among other things, that two points – to my mind essential points – of this teaching are usually missing: one concerning the objective, the other the method(s) of this teaching. On these two points I wish to focus now.

The objective of the training in human rights appears to be, as worded in the Proceedings of the Vienna Congress, "raising consciousness", i.e., "increasing awareness of the necessity to act to put an end to violations perpetrated in all parts of the world". This objective is also worded as "awakening the consciousness of the need for solidarity with those, whose human rights are violated". The formulation of our topic, i.e., "l'éducation aux droits de l'homme et la solidarité", mirrors, probably, this conception.

The awakening of such a consciousness – I would rather call it 'a will' – in those trained, i.e., the will to do "something" against a l r e a d y p e r p e t r a t e d violations, is, no doubt, very important; still, to my mind, not enough for a training, the ultimate goal of which is an ever broadening protection of human rights in the world. For, as the objective of such a training, it does not embrace a more essential will: the will to act in such a manner that violations of human rights are not perpetrated, before being perpetrated; i.e., it does not aim at leading the trainee to acquire the will to act, not only for remedying violations, but also to act, in given situations, h i m s e l f o r h e r s e l f, as determined by the demands that human rights (as principles of action) express; so that in these given situations, he himself does not become, directly or indirectly, the cause of such violations, or he himself may contribute to the fulfilment of these rights.

The possibility of acquiring such a will, presupposes, I think, a consciousness: the consciousness of being a h u m a n being, or the consciousness of sharing the so-called 'human dignity'. This is a consciousness which can be

---

[*] This paper was published in Ioanna Kuçuradi (ed.), *Human Rights in Turkey and the World in the Light of Fifty-Year Experience*, joint publication of Hacettepe University Centre for Research and Application of the Philosophy of Human Rights, UNESCO Chair and Heinrich Böll Foundation. Ankara 2002, pp. 265-271.

[1] This was one of the subthemes of the meeting on human rights, held in UNESCO, on 5-7 December 1988, to which these few points of my relection on the training of human rights were presented.

awakened in some of those trained, a) by the transmission – the visual transmission of the knowledge of the value of certain human potentialities (potentialities which made, for example, Edison discover the uses of electricity, Albert Camus write *The Plague,* Albert Schweitzer go to Africa, as well as Mother Theresa go to India, and thousand others, known or unknown, to achieve what they have achieved, blessings all of us – those trained included – enjoy) and b) by the transmission of the knowledge of human rights, since this knowledge is nothing else but the knowledge of the conditions which in general make possible – but only possible – the actualization of such potentialities, as research shows us.

Thus the awakening, in those trained, of the consciousness of their human identity – i.e., not of their cultural, national or any other collective identity – and knowledge of human rights, seems to be a way more promising to lead some trainees to acquire the will to act, i.e., to deduce for themselves the necessity to act, in every situation so as human rights may be protected – to act against already perpetrated violations included.

*

Yet the will to protect human rights does not make also possible to be able to act in such a way in a given situation.

For a person to be able to act in a given situation so as to protect human rights, presupposes his being able to evaluate correctly this situation. The ways followed or anticipated in the training in human rights – so far as we can see in studying the relevant documents – do not appear to be paying any attention to this point.

The problem of correct or right evaluation – of an action, situation, event, etc. – as the first component of every action, is a quite complicated philosophical question. I shall not dwell on it here.[2] I shall confine myself a) to saying that it is a mode of evaluation which has to be distinguished from evaluation by means of prevailing value-judgements (from what I call 'value-imputation'[3]), and from evaluation according to a special relation between the evaluating person and the evaluated object (from what I call 'value-ascription'[4]); and b) to saying that such a right evaluation is indispensable for every action we perform, provided that we wish to protect value or human rights in a given – unique – situation.

This is why the philosophical knowledge of the activity of right evaluation is indispensable in the training of the teachers; since these teachers *(les formateurs)* will train others to do so, i.e., to find out what they have to do

---

[2] See my "From Revolt to Philosophy", in *Philosophers On Their Own Work*, vol. 11. Bern/Frankfurt-am-Main/New York, 1984, pp. 109-114; or my *Etik-Ethics*. Ankara, 1988, pp. 16-19 and 82-93.

[3] See *ibid.*

[4] *Ibid.*

in a given situation, provided that they possess the will to protect human rights.

*

Human rights have to be taught – directly or indirectly – in all levels of education. The programme of the teachers' training has to be developed according to the level of education they will teach, i.e., according to the aims put to each level.

For the primary school, awakening in the pupil the consciousness of his or her human identity seems to be sufficient. A special programme of ethics which selects the examples to be used in view of this aim from everyday life, children's literature and especially mythology, is a framework in which training in human rights could be done at this level. Thus the training of teachers for this level should focus around this aim; a series of courses in philosophical ethics should be the main area that they have to be trained in.

This consciousness of one's own human identity has to be given a special emphasis in the secondary school and be transformed into knowledge. A series of courses aiming to transmit to the trainee a) the knowledge of human dignity (by means of examples illustrating the components of human dignity, i.e., all kinds of human achievements through history up to the present, ethical achievements included); aiming to transmit b) knowledge of basic (human) rights and of their significance for the life of the individual, for the development of societies, as well as for the present and the future of mankind and c) aiming at training the pupils to evaluate correctly actions, events, situations, etc., and without neglecting to relate them to human rights, could be appropriate for this purpose.[5]

For these two levels of education the only differentiation we need is in the selection of the material to be used, i.e., the examples and the cases to be used during this teaching. Even the method can be the same – the Socratic method – adapted only to the level of the trained pupils. To be able to use the Socratic method is a point that teachers of human rights have to be especially trained in.

*

University education at the undergraduate level, as well as vocational education, is the only educational level where, to my mind, differentiation of curricula is

[5] I have elaborated a curriculum framework for secondary education in a report prepared for a Joint-Study on "International Education", published by the Finnish National Commission of UNESCO in 1986. I have also shown there its implications for teachers' training. *International Education in Twelve Countries*, Publication of the Finnish National Commission for UNESCO, N° 37, 1986, pp. 349-376.

needed. Even for the postgraduate level, I don't think that a differentiation of the framework of teaching human rights – i.e., a differentiation in the training of researchers and of future university teachers – is necessary.

Humanity today, in spite of the widespread "cult of cultures", is in search of common norms for action; it is in search of a "global morality".[6] I think, human rights are such norms, but their concepts are not, still, sufficiently clarified for such use. An effective training in human rights presupposes such clarity, as much as other applications of human rights – i.e., law making, etc. – presuppose it. This is why research in human rights has to be promoted, which also means that the teaching of human rights at the postgraduate level has to be promoted.

In the chain of goals – the ultimate one being broadening the protection of human rights in the world – philosophical research and then legal research (but based on the former), aiming at providing clear conceptual knowledge on human rights and on their ethical and legal implications, appears to be – just now – a prerequisite for the training of the teachers in human rights.

This amounts to the need of starting postgraduate university programmes for graduates from different disciplines, aiming at training researchers and teachers of the teachers of those who will train students and pupils at the other educational levels (who will train *les formateurs des formateurs).* These should be interdisciplinary programmes, but which give a special emphasis – a special place – to the philosophical teaching of human rights.

We need researchers able to clarify concepts, able to develop criteria for human rights and justify them, i.e., researchers who possess the epistemological tools necessary for treating this kind of objects of knowledge – the kind that human rights are; we need researchers able to evaluate correctly[7] situations, cases, etc., in order to deduce, and consequently justify, their theoretical and practical implications in existing conditions. The teachers of the teachers of human rights have to be able, for example, to show whether a claimed right is in fact a basic right or not; to be able to formulate new rights which will eventually be codified, able to evaluate each proposed law in view to show its direct or indirect effects on human rights in a particular country, etc. All these teachers are also expected to be able to evaluate events, situations and cases in different areas of life, since they will train teachers, each of whom will train, in turn, students in different areas and professions.

Though there is no profession indifferent to human rights, some professions are directly connected with their protection: all public officers, administrators, judges, prosecutors, politicians, policemen, soldiers; but also natural scien-

---

[6] See my "'Cultural' Morals and 'Global' Morality in the Light of Ethics", in the Proceedings of the World Academic Conference of the Seoul Olympiad 88 – *The World Community in Post-Industrial Society 4*. Seoul, 1989, pp. 176-185.

[7] See my "Speech" at the opening session of the Seminar on *Philosophy Facing World Problems*. Ankara, 1988, pp. 7-13; in the present volume pp. 171-176.

tists: biologists, biophysicists, etc., have to be trained in taking into account the demands that human rights express and in knowing how to do that.

Thus, what is expected especially from the teachers' training at the undergraduate level (and especially right now) is to train students in developing special programmes, 'special' with respect to the profession, as well as with respect to the conditions of the countries and those of the trained.

Introducing curricula of human rights at different levels and professions is, right now, a difficulty we have to face. UNESCO could be helpful in this respect, i.e., helpful in our endeavour to persuade ministries, Senates, etc., and other responsible people concerning the need to introduce such courses.

Another difficulty we have also to face in the beginning is to awake awaken the consciousness of being a human being (as I mentioned before) also in students at the University level and in vocational education, i.e., in people whose personality is already shaped. This is also a point to be taken into consideration in teachers' training.[8]

In concluding I would like to say that the training of the teachers of human rights appears to be mainly a special application of philosophical education: a training in value questions or ethical training based on philosophical knowledge. Teachers' training in human rights amounts to a sharpening of the eye, so as it can become able to catch, in every given theoretical or practical case, where human dignity is really at stake: for, this is what a teacher of human rights has to train the others in. And our own human dignity is also at stake in everything we, ourselves, do.

---

[8] For a couple of years, I was trying to persuade a high officer of the police of the need to train policemen in human rights. He used to listen to me silently, kindly smiling only, because he wished to be friendly, until the day I called his attention to a case which he himself had also witnessed: one evening in Ankara, the air was terribly polluted and thick snow was falling. To get a transport I had to wait, and a lot of people had to wait, for more than half an hour at a point of the city where it was difficult even to breathe. At this same point a traffic policeman had to stay there for eight hours, without a mask. "Basic rights are also rights of the policemen", I commented. "Yes, you are right", he said for the first time. I don't know whether he was persuaded of the need to teach human rights to policemen, but at least the way to persuade him was opened.

The Ethical Education of Human Rights as a Way to Combat Discrimination and Other Intolerables*

Most of you, I assume, have read Antoine de Saint-Exupéry's *The Little Prince*. Those who have read it, will, probably, remember the story about the discovery of the planet where the Little Prince came from, 'the asteroid 612' discovered in 1909 by a Turkish astronomer. This astronomer had reported, in detail, this discovery of his at the International Congress of Astronomy, but nobody gave an ear to him, because he was dressed in a strange fashion. "So do grown up people usually", comments the narrator. Fortunately a good statesman came to power in Turkey, who made his people wear European garments. Thus the fame of the asteroid 612 was saved. When in 1920 the same astronomer, in modern dress, made the same communication, everybody in the congress affirmed the truth of his discovery.

Though discrimination has received new faces in the second half of the 20th Century in Europe, we can learn something from Saint-Exupéry's criticism and especially to put our finger on the comment of the narrator.

At present among the main causes of discrimination we see racism and xenophobia.

Racism, i.e., the claim that a human "race" is superior to all other human "races", in itself constitutes a violation of human rights. It is curious that racism, though empirically falsified, has shown an increase in the past few decades. In Europe many acts of violence find their origin in racism. Racism is an intellectual cause of discrimination, while xenophobia a psychological one.

Besides racial discrimination, different interrelated discriminations against ethnic, linguistic, and religious groups have increased as well. Why?

Here I shall confine myself to saying only a few words on the c o m m o n intellectual causes, or on the intellectual background of this increase, and though interrelated I shall leave aside its social, demographic, economic and other causes, because everything starts in our minds. We have to combat racism, and all ideas that cause discrimination, in our minds first of all.

The Intellectual Background

Two main but discrepant tendencies characterize the intellectual climate of our world at the turn of the century. We promote, on the one hand, "respect to human rights", i.e., to certain u n i v e r s a l n o r m s, but on the other hand, we

* This paper was presented in a meeting of OSCE on Human Rights Education, held in September 2004, in Vienna, and published in *Seminar on Combating Discrimination in European Union and Reflections in Turkey*. Ankara, 2004, pp. 13-17.

equally promote "respect to all cultures", which are differentiated among themselves by their different world views and p a r o c h i a l n o r m s. Not rarely we see that the demands that such parochial norms bring are contradictory to those of human rights.

We are not sufficiently aware of this discrepancy. Still our simultaneous promotion of these two discrepant tendencies appears to be one of the main causes – and perhaps the main intellectual factor – behind the spread of religious fundamentalism, nationalism, racism, and ethnic prejudices, whose "embers of hatred" were "rekindled by the winds of freedom", as the former Director-General of UNESCO, Federico Mayor, observes in one of his papers connected with the proclamation of the year 1995 as the "Year of Tolerance". We have to put our finger on these "winds of freedom" as well.

In order to combat these intolerable facts, all of which are direct or indirect violations of human rights, we have to be well aware of h o w this "rekindling" occurred.

So far as I can see, this rekindling can be traced back to the nineteen seventies, when the promotion of cultural identities and of the equal respect to all cultures was brought on the agenda of the international community, after it was realized that "development" put as the main objective of national policies in almost all the countries of the world and understood only as "economic development" – and in fact in two different senses: as unlimited quantitative increase of industrial production and the development of technologies in the so-called developed countries, and as increase of *per capita* income, industrialization and the import of technologies in so-called developing ones – had created results contrary to the expectations of its introducers. Certain global problems we are faced with are the result of these policies – e.g., pollution, to mention only the most obvious one. Migration of large groups of people from countries with cultures quite different from "European culture" is directly related to this developmental policy in Europe.

To face these unforeseen results the idea of "cultural development" was introduced, yet also understood in two different senses: in developed countries as "access to and participation in culture", i.e., activities which help people to develop themselves as human beings, such as artistic, philosophical activities; while in developing countries as identification and resurrection of their cultures, i.e., of the world views and norms, prevailing in them before their encounter with the "developed West". The demand concerning the equal respect to all cultures, which was subsequently brought on the agenda of the international community, is a well-minded, but proved to be a very problematic, attempt to compensate historical injustice done to the "strangely dressed". This is an attempt to correct an error by committing another error, because it loses sight of a very simple point: that the object of (ethical) respect are human beings, independently of the culture they belong to, and n o t cultures – i.e., world views and norms which sometimes hinder individuals who adopt them and believe in their "truth", from actualizing their human capacities and from developing as human beings.

The emergence of what is called at present multicultural (multiethnic and multireligious) society in Western Europe is a result of these historical developments, as the promotion of "multiculturalism" in Europe is a result of the intellectual developments underlying them.

A rekindling of the embers of racism and of ethnic and religious prejudices in the multicultural societies of Europe seems to be one chain result of this well-minded promotion of equal respect to all cultures – i.e., equal respect to discrepant world views and to conflicting norms – simultaneously with the promotion of certain fundamental freedoms, i.e., freedom of expression, freedom of religion and belief, etc.

Instead of trying sincerely to find out the implications of clearly conceived human rights for the various cultural minorities – in fact, their different implications for ethnic and for religious minorities[1] – postmodernism was adopted, which, in its incapacity to evaluate philosophically world views and norms, claims the equal value of all world views, *ergo* also of those which prevent individuals from thinking for themselves, and the equal value of all norms, *ergo* also of polygamy and blood feud.

Thus, if we leave aside anti-Semitism which is an old calamity in Europe, cultural differences of non-European groups living now in Europe were ascribed – erroneously – to their ethnic origin, and racism, lurking in the thick forests of Europe, has invaded towns and cities, and gained ground not only because of xenophobia, but also because governments, though they are against racism, have not prevented its propagation, fearing to be accused of violating the freedom of expression of the citizens. This is why the introduction in some European states of legislation aimed at combating hate speech and incitement to racial and religious hatred is an important step in fighting against racism and ethnic or religious discrimination, though not a way that could eradicate them.

HOW TO COMBAT THEM?

A way to combat racism, xenophobia and discrimination was, and is still, considered to be "intercultural education" and "education for tolerance". "Intercultural education" is indeed a promising way to combat xenophobia which is a psychological cause of discrimination of the "stranger", but it is not, I think, a way to combat racism which is an intellectual, or ideological, cause of discrimination and violence. We need another kind of education to combat it.

---

[1] For this difference, see Ioanna Kuçuradi, "Universal Human Rights and Their Different Implications for Multiethnic and Multireligious Societies", in *World, Islam and Democracy*. Konrad-Adenauer Foundation, Ankara, 1999, pp. 42-52; and in the present volume pp. 139-147.

The idea of human rights originates from the knowledge of the identity – of the sameness – of human beings as h u m a n beings, not of their differences which are obvious facts, while to get an insight into the sameness of all human beings, which is not obvious, training is necessary.

This aim makes necessary to equip the trainees with the c o n c e p t u a l k n o w l e d g e o f h u m a n r i g h t s: the knowledge of what they are, because this knowledge includes also the reasons why they should be protected.

But in order that we become able to decide and act in given situations in accordance with the demands of human rights, something more and indeed crucial is necessary. And this is t r a i n i n g i n e v a l u a t i o n, which is the most difficult part in the education of human rights – a training that helps us to become able, as much as each of us can, to find in most situations that we have to act the implications of the relevant human right in t h a t given, singular situation, i.e., to find what we must do so that human dignity – our dignity – can be protected. Tolerance, in the sense I mentioned a few minutes ago, can be one result of such a training.

We need to train young people in order to become able to protect human rights while exercising their professions and not only in order to defend their o w n rights, which people easily confuse with their interests.

This is – put very briefly – the conception of human rights education underlying the programme and activities of the National Committee on the Decade for Human Rights Education of Turkey, established in 1998, and also of the MA and Ph.D. Programmes of Human Rights conducted in Hacettepe University (Ankara)[5] – i.e., the conception of human rights as ethical principles for the treatment of individuals in public life and as ethical premises for the deduction of law at all levels.

[5] And since 2007 also in Maltepe University, Istanbul.

Human Rights Fifty-Five Years after the Establishment of the United Nations*

Fifty-five years ago, after the Second World War, when a small group of nations decided to combine their efforts in order "to save succeeding generations from the scourge of war, to reaffirm faith in the fundamental human rights, in the dignity and worth of the human person, in the equal rights of men and women and of nations large and small, and to establish conditions under which justice [...] and respect for the obligations arising from treaties and other sources of international law can be maintained, and to promote social progress and better standards of life in larger freedom",[1] the first thing they decided to do was to prepare the *Universal Declaration of Human Rights.*

After two years of work, a committee chaired by Mrs. Eleanor Roosevelt prepared the text adopted on December 10, 1948 – a text which is still the best general international document we possess on human rights.

What happened during the past fifty-five years? Many things – foreseeable and unforeseeable. The states or nations which declared that they decided to work for the aims of the UN have become now 191 – large and small states, officially equal but not in fact so.

No World War has happened, yet small wars have burst out in different parts of the world, leaving behind them millions of dead.

Increasing efforts are shown to protect human rights in many countries – at the national level and by means of international machinery – yet flagrant violations even of the rights to life and to personal security are perpetrated by state officers and terrorists all over the world. Over one billion people live under unacceptable conditions of poverty[2] (in Kofi Annan's words: nearly half of the world's population still has to make do on less than 2 dollars per day. Approximately 1.2 billion people... struggle on less than 1 dollar) – the poverty which the Heads of State and Government who came together in the World Summit for Social Development held in March 1995 in Copenhagen, stated that they have committed themselves "to eradicate in the world through decisive national action and international co-operation, as an ethical, social, political and economic imperative of human kind"[3] – a commitment which they repeated *mot à mot* at

* A version of this paper was presented in a meeting organized by the UN office in Ankara, on the occasion of the Millenium Declaration. The Turkish version of this paper was published in *İnsan Hakları: Kavramları ve Sorunları*, Türkiye Felsefe Kurumu Yayınları. Ankara, 2011(second edition), pp. 231-244.

[1] Charter of the United Nations.

[2] *We the Peoples: The Role of the United Nations in the 21st Century*, p. 19.

[3] Draft Declaration of the Copenhagen Summit, commitment 2.

the World Summit held in Geneva a few months ago[4] and in the *Millennium Declaration*, though in the latter not *mot à mot*.

What happened of the efforts of all these years? What did we achieve and what are our shortcomings?

So far as I can judge, the most significant intellectual achievement in this respect, is the world-wide consciousness and acceptance that human rights should be protected. This is an achievement of a few people who all these years have sincerely fought for human rights and whose number is increasing all over the world. Still, in practice, often other determinants (interests for example) play the decisive role.

Due to this acceptance and the needs we are faced with, international human rights instruments go on increasing, still in most cases without any scrutiny of the concepts and conceptions they are based on. International meetings – World Conferences, Summits, etc. – are held, which often put the finger on the problems we are faced with, but without questioning how these global problems came about, i.e., without questioning the way anticipated and followed as solutions of problems faced earlier – ways, which often, instead of solving the existing ones, have created new problems.

In the document prepared by the Secretary-General of the United Nations, entitled "We the Peoples", concerning the role of the United Nations in the 21st Century, we find an excellent diagnosis of the concrete problems we are faced with at present. Also many of the concrete changes suggested and the solutions proposed in this document (for example, the need to revise the composition of the Security Council and debt relief of the poor countries), as well as many of the commitments of Heads of State and Government expressed in the *Millennium Declaration* are very important.

Still, so far as I can see, there is something missing. And this is: taking sufficiently into consideration the intellectual developments – or ideas – underlying these problems, i.e., taking sufficiently into consideration how these problem came about, by which decisions of ours.

Here I shall try to do what the Secretary-General of the United Nations advises us to do: "to step back [still fifty-five years back] from today's headlines and take a broader long-term view of the state of the world and the challenges it poses for the United Nations". In other words: I shall try to take a bird's eye view and summarize, very briefly indeed, the main intellectual developments underlying our decisions and practice during the past fifty-five years, i.e., the ways anticipated and followed in order "to promote social progress and better standards of life in larger freedom" – ways which, in spite of the problems they have created and continue to create, are taken for granted in our decisions and practices at this moment.

[4] Unedited final outcome document of the Geneva Summit, commitment 2.

*

After the proclamation of the *Universal Declaration of Human Rights* one of the first things that those who established the UN did, was to put forward the ideal expressed by the word 'development', as t h e way to fight poverty and secure social progress – an ideal which was put as the main objective of national policies of almost all the countries of the world and which the division of the countries of the world into developed and developing countries is based on.

Since the criteria used in this dichotomy were "high" national income and industrialization, in the countries falling into the category of "developing countries", increase of national income and industrialization became the main objectives of their national policies; while in most of the industrialized countries the efforts for "further development" or "progress" turned into a deadly competition, or race, in increasing industrial production – a race to which they had subordinated everything else.

The experience of the past fifty-five years – i.e., certain facts or "global problems" which are the outcome of these developmental policies followed in both the "developed" and "developing" countries – makes us see how the idea of development, as t h e main objective of national and international policies – not alone no doubt – has led us step by step to the present situation.

In most of the so-called developed countries the competition for more and more industrial production and technological progress has led to an uncontrolled use of natural resources which got nearly exhausted in various parts of the earth, to pollution, to the threat of nuclear energy, etc., and besides, to various unforeseen social problems.

In many developing – or Third World – countries, on the other hand, developmental policies, while they caused the slight increase of national income we see if we look only at figures, also deepened social injustice, i.e., broadened the unequal distribution o f d e p r i v a t i o n s in those countries and intensified various political disturbances in most of them.

These developmental policies have not only deepened social injustice, but global injustice as well. These policies carried out, i.e., financed, to a considerable extent, by "foreign aid" or as it was later called "development aid", i.e., loans from developed countries with political expectations, have not only broadened the gap between the rich and the poor within these countries, but (with the exception of a few countries) also broadened the gap between the few rich and the majority of the poor countries.

The debts of these latter countries have reached such a point that it seems improbable, if not impossible, that these countries will be able to pay them back at all. A cold-blood – rational, in the sense used in the science of economics – calculation, shows that most of the developing countries, if no "miracle" interferes, are condemned to remain for ever developing in the sense assumed.

In a UNESCO document written in 1982, i.e., after 36 years of the establishment of the UN, we read: "In the Third World, vast populations frequently enjoy none of the benefits of the progress and towns and cities – in many cases and at least as regards certain categories – are like islands of modernity cut off from the hinterland".[5] In the document of the Copenhagen Summit, i.e., 50 years after the establishment of the UN we read: "a) within many societies, both in developed and developing countries, the gap between rich and poor has increased. Further, and despite the fact that some developing countries are growing rapidly, the gap between developed and many developing countries, particularly the least developed countries, has widened; b) more than one billion people in the world live in abject poverty, most of whom go hungry every day." "In the Third World, vast populations frequently enjoy none of the benefits of the progress and towns and cities – in many cases and at least as regards certain categories – are like islands of modernity cut off from the hinterland".[6] This is a *mot à mot* repetition of the same words. And in the unedited final document of the Geneva Summit, i.e., five years after the Copenhagen Summit and 55 years after the establishment of the United Nation we also read: "Despite some advances, there has been little progress in some key areas, and r e g r e s s is evident in others. As noted in one of the key issues of the analytical report of the Secretary-General, one major development since the [Copenhagen] Summit is that inequality within and among states continues to grow".[7] This is a statement made a few months ago.

Thus "development", which was introduced and adopted as the most appropriate and promising way, i.e., as the way a n t i c i p a t e d and followed up, in order to abolish social and global injustice and to get rid of poverty; in other words, development as the main objective of national policies based on "foreign aid" or "development aid" made by rich countries to the poor ones, has created results contradicting the expectations of its introducers. While it afforded a few people the possibility of living on "islands of modernity", together with the increase of population in these countries, it did increase the number of those who are deprived of the means to answer even their most basic needs.

The impasse to which developmental policies had led throughout the world noticed in the nineteen-seventies, b u t m a i n l y the global problems faced in the industrialized countries (pollution for example), i.e., the consequences of the ever increasing technological development in the developed countries, made people in those countries start speaking of the need for "a new conception of development", or of the necessity "to bring a cultural dimension to development". Thus they introduced the idea of "cultural development".

What people in the Western-industrialized countries have mainly understood by 'cultural development' was the broadening for the masses of the possibility to have "access to and participation in culture", i.e., to activities consid-

---

[5] Draft Medium-Term Plan 1984-89, par. 19.

[6] Draft Declaration of the Copenhagen Summit, par. 16a and b.

[7] Unedited final outcome document of the Geneva Summit, par. 1 (emphasis added).

ered to afford individuals the possibility to develop their potentialities as human beings – e.g., to artistic, scientific, philosophical activities.

We have to keep in mind that t h i s demand for "access to and participation in culture" was a demand s t e m m i n g f r o m a n e e d f e l t b y t h e p e o p l e o f t h e i n d u s t r i a l i z e d c o u n t r i e s, considered to be a way out of the impasse to which industrialization has led them.

Yet another important reason which brought 'culture' to the foreground at the global level was that numerous developing (or Third World) countries, which do not belong to the so-called Western or European culture and which have obtained their independence a few decades ago, i.e., the people and especially the intellectuals of the decolonized countries, started revolting against the "colonization of the minds", as a result of which they brought to the agenda the question of "cultural identity". Thus they seconded the motion of "cultural development", still understanding it, mainly, as being allowed to develop – i.e., to identify and reconstruct – "their own" culture which, they think, was suppressed or forgotten under the influence of Western culture during the colonization era. They started trying to identify the culture – i.e., the world view, the conception of Man and of what is considered to be valuable – which, they think, is, and they wish to be, their own.

Meanwhile, the people of a third category of countries, of countries "in the process of modernization", which had opted themselves for "modernization", joined the discussion. What these conceived, and still mostly conceive, as "cultural development", was the resurrection or the revival of the culture (i.e., of the world view, of the conception of Man and of what is considered to be valuable) prevailing among them, before they came into touch with the West.

What we experienced in the past few decades in various countries "in the process of modernization" is a reaction to "Western culture", a reaction which has led each group toward the search of its "cultural identity" or of its o w n "values"; and since it was not possible to identify what they wished to identify in the existing state of affairs, they looked backwards and tried to find, in order to resurrect it, what they felt, or assumed, to be their own, i.e., the world view, the conception of man and the conception of what is valuable (the value judgements) prevailing in each of these groups before their industrialization efforts began or before their encounter with "Western culture" to which they reacted. Such a resurrection has already occurred, as the gradual spread of fundamentalism in some of such countries in different parts of the world shows.

In order to gain more and more ground fundamentalists are defending their activities on the basis of the freedoms of thought, conscience and religion, as well as on the basis of the so-called "respect to cultural identities", or of "the right to be different". In other words, they are defending their activities by using mottos floating around, e.g., the "right to culture" or "cultural rights" which are a demand brought i n t h e i n d u s t r i a l i z e d c o u n t r i e s in order to tackle the problems t h e y faced and which are problems of quite a different origin from the problems of the developing countries. Postmodernism has helped in this advance.

This is where the promotion of "cultural development" understood in the sense of promoting cultural identities has led in the last decade of the 20th Century: it has created its own facts, the most striking one being the spread of fundamentalism, which has gained ground in various parts of the world.

We are not sufficiently aware that we have made out of a fact, concerning a special kind of process, an idea, a vague idea concerning a desirable state of affairs, that of the already "developed", affluent West in the second half of the Twentieth Century, yet interpreted in a very problematic way, i.e., reduced to only a couple of its ingredients; that we made out of a fact an ideal, which we put as a goal to be attained by the other, "not yet developed" countries.

Development has become an *idée fixe* of ours. Thus we keep on changing and multiplying the epithets of development – we speak of economic, social, cultural, indigenous, self-reliant, sustainable, people-centred development, plus of equal respect to all cultures – but we don't even think of changing this main objective of our national and international policies.

As a testimony of this, let us lend an ear to the following words – under the heading of Principles and Goals – of the Heads of State and Government of the Copenhagen Summit: "We Heads of State and Government are committed to a political, economic, ethical and spiritual vision for social development based on human dignity, human rights, equality, peace, democracy, mutual responsibility and co-operation, and full respect for the various religious and ethical values and cultural backgrounds of the people".[8] I am afraid that those Heads of State and Government are not sufficiently aware that they have committed themselves to things, which, if looked at in their reality and singularity, may be, and often are, incompatible (e.g., respect to polygamy and respect to human dignity; respect to blood feud and the right to life).

*

Besides the well-minded but very problematic promotion of cultural identities (multi-culturalism), democratization and privatization-free market and its globalization are also considered just now to be among the ways to tackle the global problems we are faced with and to protect human rights. They have become the mottos of the world community in the last decade of the 20th Century, as well as the conditions for extending "development aid" to developing countries.

Here I shall leave aside the human rights problems created by the promotion of so-called democratization, and I shall confine myself to saying only a few words on the free market based on privatization and its consequences for the protection of human rights. We can perhaps learn something from the adven-

---

[8] Draft Declaration of the Copenhagen Summit., par. 25 (emphasis added).

ture of the idea of development as main objective of national and international policies after the Second World War.

This is why – in the face of the repeated statements concerning the failure of developmental policies to bridge the gap between the rich and the poor within and among countries, and the most recent observation that there is an "evident regress" in coping with this gap – I allow myself to repeat what I often said during the past fifteen years,[9] concerning privatization-free market and its globalization in relation to their consequences for the protection of human rights and to put it in connection with statements we find in the document of the Geneva Summit.

Let me put it quite sharply: not only do I not see any conceptual or factual connection between human rights and the free market, but I also see a potential new impasse in the expectation that the free market based on privatization will lead to a better protection of human rights in non-affluent countries.

The demand of the free market, in principle, amounts, very simply put, to the demand that governments do not interfere in the economic activities of individuals, that governments leave them alone in this respect. In this case – people assume – the order of socio-economic relations, i.e., their establishment and change, will follow a spontaneous open process. In this process individuals would not only better protect their interests, but they would also have to protect the interests of other individuals.

A kind of basic rights of the individual – the so-called fundamental freedoms – also demand such a non-interference. I am afraid that the linkage of the free market with human rights has been done through the unscrutinized concept of "fundamental freedoms". It is basically due to the lack of distinction between kinds of rights of the individual. It betrays an intention to protect economic "freedom" as a basic right and to protect it in the way that o n l y o n e k i n d o f b a s i c r i g h t s can be protected: The way to protect, for example, the so-called "right to freedom of thought" is assumed to be also the way to protect what is assumed to be an individual's "economic freedom".[10]

Thus considered, this "freedom" amounts to demanding that the State does not interfere with individuals, not only while they are engaged in actualizing special human potentialities, as one kind of human rights demands; but also

---

[9] In "'Cultural' Morals and 'Global' Morality in the Light of Ethics", in *WASCO'88. The World Community in Post-Industrial Society*. Seoul, 1989, pp. 176-185; "The Idea of Development. Its Past and Present", in *The Idea of Development Between Its Past and Its Future*. Ankara, 1993, pp. 13-17; "Goals and Traps in the Ways out of the Current Stalemate", in *Future Beyond Poverty-Ways and Means out of the Current Stalemate*. Turku-Finland, 1997, pp. 88-99, etc.

[10] For my classification of rights and human rights, see my "Philosophy and Human Rights", in *Philosophical Foundation of Human Rights*. Ankara, 1982, pp. 47-52; and in the present volume pp. 19-24.

while they act to protect their own interests which not only clash inevitably with the interests of other individuals, but in many cases also with their human rights.

Consequently, the demand that the "free" market now brings in the case of non-affluent countries amounts not only to discarding governments, which mostly delineate the limits of economic rights according to private or group interests; but also to discarding t h e p o s s i b i l i t y of making basic rights determinants in the establishment and changing of economic relations within and among countries. This is the point where things tend at present and this is what people who promote privatization and economic globalization call the "minimization of the State".

Promotion of the free market coupled with external debts not only in poor countries, but also in so-called middle income developing countries – i.e., loans which these countries have received in order to "develop" and which they are able to pay only the interest sometimes by taking new loans – "have crippled their social efforts".[11] "Increased constrains, including fiscal and political ones on Governments, have resulted in a reduction of the programmes and activities of the State".[12] "In some countries, the principle of universal free provision of services such as health care, education and water supply has been replaced by user fees and privatization and more targeted social service provision".[13] "National environments have been increasingly affected by global influences and forces beyond the control of individual Governments. Serious impediments to social development, many of which were identified by the Summit, still persist. These include: chronic hunger; malnutrition; illicit drug problems; organized crime; corruption, foreign occupation; armed conflicts; ethnic, religious and other hatred; xenophobia; endemic, communicable and chronic diseases".[14] These are statements we find in the Geneva document. Some of them are old and some are new problems.

This is the point where the idea of development, introduced fifty-five years ago in order "to promote social progress and better standards of life", a n d a misconception of freedom and freedoms have led us at the end of the 20th Century. We have to revise both of them, i.e., we have to revise the intellectual background of our decisions and practice, in general.

Let me give you an additional reason of this latter claim of mine: the same m i s c o n c e p t i o n o f f r e e d o m s, which we see at the root of considering the free market as a way out from the current stalemate of poverty, appears to be also among the main causes of the spread of fundamentalism which takes advantage of the so-called freedoms of thought, religion, opinion and expression, as well as of the so much promoted "respect to the ethical and religious 'values' and cultural backgrounds of people" and propagates certain

---

[11] Unedited final outcome document of the Geneva Summit, par. 41.

[12] *Ibid.*

[13] *Ibid.*, par. 36.

[14] *Ibid.*

world views and norms, which are essentially contradictory to human rights – e.g., blood feud, killing the heretic, etc.

*

At present, promotion of respect to cultural identities and of the free market and its globalization, which find their origin in the adventure of the idea of development as main objective of national and international policies, appear to constitute two traps – and if we leave aside certain ideological approaches, until now very little noticed traps – to human rights.

I say "until now", because in the Geneva document we read that "it is now recognized that an effective and accountable public sector is vital to ensuring the provision of social services",[15] and that "the growing interdependence of nations, which has caused economic shocks to be transmitted across national boarders, as well as increased inequality, highlights weaknesses in current international and national institutional arrangements and economic and social policies and reinforces the importance of strengthening them through appropriate reforms".[16]

A careful tracing of the intellectual developments of the past fifty-five years makes us see that what we need now is n o t appropriate reforms w i t h - i n t h e s a m e f r a m e w o r k in which we have moved until now, but a revolution.

And this revolution would be, as I repeatedly said since the late eighties, to replace "development" – whatever its epithets might be – as the main objective of national and international policies by the protection of carefully conceptualized and clearly conceived human rights; and to try sincerely our best to find and carry out courageously, step by step, their implications for action in the existing conditions of our countries and on global level – some of which we find in the *Millennium Declaration*[17] – well aware of the fact that most of the reversible and irreversible global problems we are faced with are the result of o u r decisions and actions.

---

[15] *Ibid.*, par. 43.

[16] *Ibid.*, Proposals for further initiatives for social development, 2.

[17] One of these implications is forgiveness of debts, as it is discussed at present and as I say in my "Goals and Traps in the Ways out of the Current Stalemate of Poverty", in *op.cit.*, note 9.